Richard Purden grew up in Edinburgh, but with family roots in Limerick and the west of Scotland he always felt a strong connection to Irish literature, culture and of course, Celtic FC.

While studying at the University of Stirling he began to write arts reviews for the student magazine *Brig* and on graduating he was first published in the *Celtic View, Scotland on Sunday, The Scotsman*, the *Irish Examiner* and *The Irish Post*.

More recently, he has contributed to *Four Four Two*, the *Sunday Mail* and *The Herald Saturday* magazine.

WE ARE CELTIC SUPPORTERS

Richard Purden

Foreword by Rod Stewart

First published in 2011 by
HACHETTE SCOTLAND, an imprint of Hachette UK

First published in paperback in 2012
by HACHETTE SCOTLAND

1

Cataloguing in Publication Data is available from the British Library

ISBN: 978 07553 6097 0

Typeset in Bell MT by Avon DataSet Ltd,
Bidford-on-Avon, Warwickshire

Printed in the UK by CPI Group (UK) Ltd, Croydon, CR0 4YY

Hachette Scotland's policy is to use papers that are natural, renewable and
recyclable products and made from wood grown in sustainable forests. The
logging and manufacturing processes are expected to conform to the
environmental regulations of the country of origin.

HACHETTE SCOTLAND
An Hachette UK Company
338 Euston Road
London NW1 3BH

www.hachettescotland.co.uk
www.hachette.co.uk

For Ryan John Purden

ACKNOWLEDGEMENTS

I would sincerely like to thank all the Celtic supporters I've interviewed for this book and over the last decade.

Also the matriarchal trinity of my wife Louise, my gran Mary and my mother Doreen.

CONTENTS

FOREWORD
BY ROD STEWART

MY RELATIONSHIP WITH CELTIC began in 1974 after a gig with The Faces in Glasgow, which was during Jock Stein's time of nine-in-a-row. Jock turned football into poetry and when you think of Celtic during this time your mind goes straight to players like Jimmy Johnstone and Kenny Dalglish. King Kenny was a star player and he looked the part too; he could have been in The Faces. Before I became a Celtic fan Kenny and I were already friends, he came along to a Faces gig and invited Ronnie Wood and I to train with the team the next day and, of course, we said yes. At ten o'clock in the morning there was a knock on the door of the hotel room, it was Kenny with Jinky and Dixie Deans; they had come to pick us up to go training. Suffice to say we didn't make the training but we went to the park and watched a few players on the track and that's how I first met Jock Stein; I remember him laughing at my shoes. That first experience is what cemented me as a Celtic supporter. He was a giant physically and in presence; I only met Jock a few times but he left an everlasting impression on me as did Celtic.

People say to me 'what it is about being a Celtic fan' and I find it very hard to explain, something about this club just gets inside you, the history and a strong awareness of it, the stories, the Hoops, the style of play, the support, the ground, the songs — it all runs very deep and becomes a part of you. Something happens when you arrive at Parkhead, you feel just how important it is when you are in amongst it and it goes way beyond football. That's part of what makes Celtic unique. My passion in the last 20 years has been unbelievable, I get to as many games as I can and I'm on the website every day but I'm no more of a fan than anyone else.

There's so much talent that has played for Celtic, players with an enthusiasm and energy for the club. The ones I've met over the years have certainly had a lot of character and humour. Perhaps none more so than Jimmy Johnstone, just thinking of Jimmy and some of the things he got up to warms the heart. I went to see him a few times just before he sadly passed away. His spirit was amazing; when I arrived he had a big smile on his face, popped open a bottle of champagne and told me to bring in all the lads that were with me. We don't remember guys like Jimmy just for their tremendous talent but also the kind of people they were. The Lisbon team that Jinky was part of never fails to capture my imagination; 11 guys from Scotland taking on the mighty Inter Milan for the European Cup, it's still the stuff of legend. That team changed the way European football was played, Big Jock revolutionised Celtic and the game forever. Had Celtic not made history that day, it's hard to imagine how things would have turned out.

From the last decade, wasn't Seville just the most wonderful occasion? Henrik did us proud with those two goals. We were also proud to win the UEFA fan award and Celtic fans remain recognised throughout Europe as the best in the world. As well as getting to the UEFA Cup final, we achieved three league titles under Martin O'Neill who brought with him a real time of change and a new confidence in the modern game. Gordon Strachan became only the third manager to achieve three league titles in a row for us. He also brought Champions League football to Parkhead, leading us to the last 16 of the competition twice – quite an achievement when you think about it. I'll never forget some magical nights with the Celtic support and those wins against the likes of Manchester United, AC Milan and Benfica.

With Neil Lennon as manager we are now going in the right direction once again; people laughed when we went out of Europe against Braga but they went all the way to the final only to get beat by Porto. I called into talkSPORT at the end of the 2010/11 season when I heard them having a go at Neil. I watch Celtic every week and there has been a vast improvement; you only have to look at some of the victories against Rangers. The manager has made some great signings, built up a team almost from scratch and he's got them believing in him. Neil has formed an unbreakable bond with his players and I think that says a lot for him in the modern game. He's got them playing what I consider attractive football, which isn't always easy in the SPL. You have to keep it in perspective; we lost that league by just one point, we left a crack in the door and they hammered it down; once again, we gave it away. At the end of that season for the last league game at Parkhead against Motherwell 60,000 people showed up to give their support to Neil Lennon, had that been the year before the place would have been half empty. The fans knew we weren't going to win the SPL but it turned out to be one of the most memorable days at Parkhead in recent years. There was a real sense of unity in the ground and I really do think that says a lot for the fans. I've been right behind Neil from the beginning and I have a lot of admiration for him; he has got to calm down a bit but he knows that. At the same time there's nothing wrong with passion; he's very proud to be manager of Celtic and he was the same as a player. Tony Mowbray was like a statue, the players need to see the manager jumping up and down and getting into it.

Outside of the football that was a horrible season and I'm glad to get it over and done with. I was in LA when I saw the threats to the manager and others on CNN news. I don't know if Neil is a good actor but it doesn't seem to affect him, he just seems to go into the next game with the same stoic approach. What has the game come to when a football manager is dealing with this kind of thing?

On a more positive note we finished last season with a much deserved league victory. I was playing a gig in Las Vegas at the time and invited a few supporters onto the stage to celebrate. I'd like to congratulate Neil Lennon, the players, the directors and most importantly the fans; we are still the best in the world. I hope this time next year we will be celebrating another league win and everything else in the bag with a good run in Europe under our belts. You simply can't beat the atmosphere in Glasgow on the night of a big European game. I love the drive along the Celtic Mile through the East End, past the Barrowlands Ballroom and Bairds Bar next door. I love going to the supporters' clubs when I can and I try to go to as many Celtic bars as possible. Part of the Celtic character is about those roots in the East End, the club started as a charity to help the area's poor. The generous character and spirit of that is ingrained in the club today. This book captures the story of those fans, the most important aspect of this club. It's the fans who keep the history alive and that is something we are all continuing to build together. I do hope you enjoy these stories from Celtic supporters around the world; they are the tales, events and histories that we all share.

Hail Hail

Rod Stewart

INTRODUCTION

SINCE DECEMBER 2002 I've written about Celtic Football Club in a variety of publications including the *Celtic View* between 2002 and 2008, the *Herald*, the *Scotsman*, *Scotland on Sunday* and the *Irish Post*. My own area of interest in this distinctive club has been the fans. From my earliest memories Celtic has held a romantic connection for me that undoubtedly shaped my view of the world. For many the narrative of this great club runs parallel to the history of our very lives. Beyond football, Celtic is a cultural phenomenon central to Scotland's Irish Catholic working-class community; the history forms part of our very being. From life's beginnings with family, school days and further education to working life; when you see the Hoops or hear the utterance 'I'm a Celtic supporter' something stirs the soul and engages the senses. Jumping on a Celtic bus, travelling to European competitions or rooting out a supporter's club while on holiday abroad are just some of the ways in which we have all engaged with being part of the Celtic family. Celtic is part of our community, our political opinions and our spiritual lives. There's no escaping the charitable Christian beginnings and outlook of this club in the roots of Glasgow's East End and how it has infused the unique ideology among a great number of our supporters throughout Scotland and the rest of the world.

Back in 2002 I was initially fascinated by the connections between Celtic and the arts which led me to interview an eclectic bunch of rock 'n' rollers, film-makers and actors that all supported, identified and celebrated something positive in their lives and world views that related to being a Celtic supporter. For many of them, Celtic was an early engagement with the wider world, a passionate, attractive and thrilling association with what shaped them as creative people. My work has led me to interview Marist Brothers, war veterans, artists, classical musicians, novelists, football legends and politicians that have freely nailed their Celtic colours to the mast. Some of the most insightful interviews have been from the supporters clubs I've spoken to around the world, the Celtic fans I've known all my life and the associates and acquaintances that I've met walking the Green Mile.

Undoubtedly we are a fragmented support with many different opinions, as this book will testify. But once we are boxed up and shipped out on the next part of the trip, a rich legacy will prove that as Celtic supporters we've left our mark on society for the better. Tommy Burns, one of the carriers of the Celtic flame throughout his life once said, 'We are all just passing through this life'. While we're here we are doing it, among many other things, as Celtic supporters.

What does that mean in 2011? Holding on to those traditions in more recent years has been difficult. This book asks the Celtic support and cultural commentators from all walks of life around the world about the foundations that have shaped this unique football team. It reflects a vast following, spanning generations and a number of social, religious, political, economic and class boundaries. Celtic is a football club steeped in traditions and ethics; it's a club rooted in a religious, political and social history which a large number of us continue to hold dear because we know where we've come from and we know who we are.

We are Celtic supporters.

CHAPTER ONE DREAMS AND SONGS TO SING

JAMES MACMILLAN'S RADICAL 'Scotland's Shame' speech was engaging and empowering in its discussion of anti-Catholic prejudice. The speech cited modern urban tragedies in the form of Celtic fans murdered on the streets of Glasgow for simply wearing the green and white walking home after a game, a deplorable and relatively overlooked fact from our recent history. When travelling to watch Celtic outside of Scotland, there's liberation, an assured feeling that when you pull on the Hoops abroad, you're safe to do so. Rather than having to watch your back, you're more likely to encounter well-wishers or find a connection with one of the faithful. It's a view I hear aired countless times from expatriate supporters who admit that the only time they don't wear colours is in Scotland; undoubtedly a hangover from our all too recent history. MacMillan's speech was considerately delivered at a particularly optimistic point in time. Labour's landslide victory in 1997 symbolically smashed the Conservative Middle England establishment values defined by the Thatcher and Major governments. The new prime minister's wife was from an Irish Catholic family in the north-west of England heralding further Catholic visibility. When the

Scottish Parliament was reconvened in 1999 after a 292-year absence, MacMillan composed an accompaniment for the Queen's entrance into the chamber. A few weeks later he delivered his historic speech during the Edinburgh Festival.

More than a decade has passed since the speech and undoubtedly debate in Scotland has continued to flourish around the subjects that MacMillan brought to the fore. His BBC Proms premiere, *The Confession of Isobel Gowdie* with the Scottish Symphony Orchestra, set a flourishing career ablaze. After a Friday night broadcast, MacMillan was tapped on the shoulder the next day at Celtic Park during a match against Aberdeen and was asked: 'Was it your piece I saw on the telly last night?' Twenty years on the international composer reflects on the day his passions collided: 'You don't normally associate these two worlds because of a perceived class division and there is a little bit of that, of course. I was at the Celtic game and to my astonishment someone who had seen the piece recognised me from a bit of the documentary and congratulated me on the premiere. It was a lovely moment and very surprising.' Since then, of course, MacMillan has been commissioned by the world's leading orchestras and opera houses. His articles, speeches and essays on Catholic life as well as compositions, such as 'For Neil, 25th May 1967' and 'The Berserking', celebrate the wider culture around Celtic Football Club and have raised a number of issues that are undoubtedly connected to the affection he developed for Celtic growing up in Cumnock: 'I first became aware of a great support and fervour for the club at family level with relatives. Grandfather, father, uncles, and then it was especially at primary school where I became completely engrossed by it. It was around the time of the European Cup win; I was very young but I remember not being very interested to begin with and having to be cajoled. I was gradually won over, like many others, by the 1967 European Cup campaign. I was only in primary two or three but we got the day off school because Celtic won the cup. It made them famous the world over because of the romance of the story; people can relate to that and feel a genuine affection for the club.'

His first game was the Celtic v Hibs League Cup final at Hampden on 5 April 1969. From the age of nine MacMillan began the regular journey from Ayrshire to Glasgow. The community, culture and strong social dimensions associated with the club undoubtedly had some bearing on his early political awareness. 'I was prematurely interested in politics, not as a boy but when I was a teenager. I joined the Young Communist League when I was fourteen and by then I was obviously interested in Celtic. The whole Stein thing became part of my awareness retrospectively. It does make sense that if he hadn't been a football manager he probably would have been a trade unionist of some sort along with Mick McGahey and all the other firebrands of the time, he had that sort of feel about him. Cardinal Winning is another one, had he not been a cardinal, because he moved in a similar direction with the same mindset and values along the lines of "The working man can better himself; we can all pull together and make things better." I'm sure that did pervade the Stein mentality and ethos. Gradually, growing up as a teenager, I was aware that other Celtic supporters were of a similar background. If you can talk about a clutch of values at all, they were quite left wing. Talking now as someone who has lost all my youthful certainties about politics I can look back objectively about that. I never encountered reactionary views among Celtic supporters; they tended to take the side of the underdog. Of course, they were shaped by a kind of quasi republicanism, which they drew from their Irish roots, but there was something of a Scottish dimension that was anti-hierarchical. As a young communist/socialist, that kind of appealed to me.'

MacMillan's political views were shaped by his grandparents' generation. Mick McGahey, in particular, is an important example. His father was a miner and a founder of the Communist Party in Britain and his mother was a devout Catholic from Derry. The miners' leader, who died in 1999, was born in Shotts, in North Lanarkshire and emerged as something of a working-class champion with strong values and loyalties. As well as looking to protect the community he came from, McGahey was typical of Scotland's left-wing illuminate in that they looked beyond the confines of their own culture to offer support and solidarity. At the age of fourteen he was stabbed for his beliefs while campaigning for communism. Not long afterwards he was battered by British sailors when he sympathised with the Chinese over the 'Yangtze incident'. In a move that even alienated Western Marxists he supported the invasion of Hungary by the Soviet Union in 1956. In his own words he was a 'devout communist'. Undoubtedly, these values were twinned with a strong distaste for material and monetary values above people, in this he was undoubtedly influenced by his mother's strong

Catholic ideals. Even more tellingly, McGahey displayed a strong biblical knowledge throughout his life.

It's an ethos that MacMillan immediately recognised in the majority of the Celtic support. 'I could see similar values pervading other Celtic fans, certainly. What made me proud and still makes me so proud today are the values that are in the Christian beginnings of the club. I don't think fundamentally that they are political values; I think they are gospel values. They made people value human dignity and so you didn't get racist organisations campaigning outside Celtic Park as they did outside other Scottish and English grounds, which turned into marvellous recruitment areas for fascists. That was never going to happen at Celtic, some might say it was because of the left-wing bent but I would like to think it was for gospel-centred values, and for those reasons Celtic football club and the fans have huge reasons to feel proud in this country.'

These priorities and the club's relationship to this kind of social history were illustrated in 2005 when supporters decided to erect a statue of the club's founder Brother Walfrid. The statue was commissioned by the Brother Walfrid Committee and the cost of £30,000 was paid for with donations from Celtic supporters. The unveiling of the statue on 5 November 2005 was an emotionally charged and poignant occasion. Sligo-born Celtic hero Sean Fallon unveiled the work while Archbishop Mario Conti blessed the statue. Thousands of fans, including Billy McNeill and former Rangers captain John Greig, were in attendance at the event, for which MacMillan also composed the fitting 'Walfrid, On

His Arrival at the Gates of Paradise'. The majority of football clubs are most likely to choose to celebrate figures in living memory that have had some impact on the club's success. For MacMillan the statue of Walfrid cast in bronze was an immeasurably more interesting proposition: 'I think Celtic has a charism of things at the heart of the club. These are things that are embedded into the bricks of the Christian faith that shaped Celtic. It might be very unfashionable to say it today and a lot of people recoil from it, including Celtic fans, but at the core of Celtic's foundations is the love, faith, hope and charity of what it means to be a Christian. Brother Walfrid knew that and he imbued the whole club with these traditions and values. I think there's no going back from that; if anything Celtic fans should always be aware of those roots and give space for gospel values to pervade what the club is about; even in a secular age.'

In an era when politics are less polarised, in what MacMillan describes as a secular age, it's hard to know whether a left-wing outlook charged by Catholic theology still exists among the club's supporters. But MacMillan remains optimistic: 'We live in a very different time to 1888 when the club was founded, people talk about the twenty-first century being a secular time or even a post secular time, we've taken a lot on board in the last century and absorbed a great deal. If you are talking about the question of faith and the practice of faith, of course there are a lot of Celtic fans who have abandoned their faith and they are a mirror for the rest of society. It's not my place to explore the pros and cons of that, except to say that among football clubs generally, not just in Scotland but in the United Kingdom and abroad, there is still a very high percentage of believing fans at Celtic compared to other clubs and a high percentage of practising Catholics. This is a strange phenomenon in this day and age but a delightful one. It's not to say that this makes them better people than everyone else but what it does is maintain the club's roots with an active practising Christianity.'

The novelist William McIlvanney once described Celtic as 'the bleeding of two rich cultures joining together'. After the formation of Hibernian in 1875 and Dundee Harp in 1880, it was evident that Glasgow would need a strong counterpart. Undoubtedly it was Walfrid's vision that gave Celtic an extra dimension. In terms of Irish culture in Scotland, at different points in history Celtic supporters and indeed the club itself have been the predominant keepers of the flame despite various attempts by establishment figures to remove all traces. While the Irish Catholic identity of some clubs in Britain has shifted, that component of Celtic's character has endured. The most memorable intimidation came from the Scottish football establishment. In 1952 there was a significant attempt to remove the tricolour from Celtic Park. This is largely attributed to long-term SFA secretary George Graham, along with its president Harry Swann, whose argument that the tricolour encouraged hooliganism was found wanting in a stand-off with Celtic's chairman Robert Kelly.

For MacMillan this is another of the club's core values: 'I think Celtic is and should be celebrated as both Scottish and Irish; that was the intention of both Brother Walfrid and the founders of the club. They wished to celebrate the Irish diaspora in Scotland and embrace that diaspora into another country. There was a great desire to encourage peace and reconciliation between people that were at logger-heads. That is the ethos of the Irish Republic's flag which symbolises a peace between the denominations of Ireland; that is at the heart of Celtic. It's a pointer to that open pluralism which Celtic is at its best and was always meant to be, it was never just another Irish Catholic club. It did have something of that but Walfrid and the club wanted to embrace others, he wanted to call the team Celtic to combine the two countries and probably embrace both Catholicism and Protestantism. That was his desire; to build openness in the roots and that has always been a feature of what I think the club is about.'

Des Dillon's anti-sectarian play *Singin' I'm No a Billy, He's a Tim* dismantles the prejudiced ideal that your ethnic or religious background makes you a superior to others. When the characters enter a debate about their ethnicity, Rangers fan Billy flips the argument on its head by revealing his parents were both Catholics, his mother raising him a Rangers fan to spite his wayward father. Likewise, Celtic fan Tim admits his mother is a Protestant disowned by her family for marrying a Catholic, his father is also renounced by the family for the same reason.

Celtic's ecumenical roots have left room for a more inclusive and vibrant multicultural and multi-ethnic support in line with its founder's vision. It's significant that almost 125 years later Brother Walfrid and his values continue to hold reverence among so many Celtic supporters. Born Andrew

Kerins in County Sligo, Walfrid spent only five years in Glasgow before he was sent to London's East End to carry on his work in the poverty-stricken districts of Bethnal Green and Bow. Throughout the club's history many Celtic fans have shown a concern beyond themselves looking to help other cultures in need. These ideas have attracted Celtic to other clubs with a similar ethos. Athletic Bilbao supporters similarly identify with the idea of fans trying to preserve a people and a culture in the form of the Basque separatists.

The link to the anti-fascist movement is important among the majority of the thinking Celtic support. One issue that has encouraged a negative response from the media and the public towards Celtic supporters has been because a minority of fans refuse to acknowledge the one-minute's silence for Remembrance Day. It's a complex issue that has found German club St Pauli's left-wing fans sympathising with those Celtic supporters who would not take part in this act of respect. Undoubtedly the German club's supporters are among the most gregarious and popular in Europe, but surely it is churlish to actively disrespect a now passing generation that fought in the Second World War against the ultimate fascist in the name of anti-fascism. In the main Celtic supporters have acknowledged the minute's silence out of respect for the dead, which includes former Celtic players and supporters that lost their lives in two World Wars, many of whom were from the Irish diaspora. In 2009, a small group of fans, ironically gathered outside the ground at Walfrid's statue, disrupted the silence by singing pro-violent Irish

Republican songs, leaving the silent majority to front the abuse from the visiting Falkirk supporters who chanted: 'You're scum and you know you are' long after the perpetrators had left the area.

MacMillan's response suggests that when the club's values are stripped from their roots they lose their potency. 'To say Celtic's values are socialist is not good enough. If our socialist values are disconnected from their gospel roots then they are not values worth having. I sometimes worry about the militant drift that some Celtic fans have taken. Obviously the support for Irish Nationalism is a given and that has been a good and defining thing in many ways, but a tiny minority have held on to the support for violent Republicanism and that has done untold damage to Celtic's reputation and still does today. Those people are now drifting to support other extreme nationalists in the Catalan district, Basque country and, God forbid, the extremists of Hamas and Hezbollah. Brother Walfrid will be turning in his grave. Had Celtic allowed the Palestinian flags at the Hapoel Tel Aviv game, as they were encouraged to by the STUC, it would have been an embarrassing own goal for the club. Hapoel are a team associated with the left and the trade union and Labour movement in Israel. As a club they have traditions that are very close to our own in bringing different religious and ethical values together among Arabs and Jews. The militants saying they were supporting Hamas are a disgrace and Celtic was right to disassociate from that.'

MacMillan's point is a good one. In general Hapoel supporters come from Israel's Palestinian minority and they are as politically and socially aware as Celtic supporters. They also share close links with supporters of St Pauli FC. Flags and banners that translate as 'Say No To Racism' in Arabic and Hebrew are prominent at home games along with T-shirts that feature left-wing figureheads such as Che Guevara. They have a strong rivalry with Beitar Jerusalem whose fans have displayed a strong association with far-right politics for over seventy years. MacMillan said: 'It's up to our support to gain a bit of understanding and do research on this stuff before they get involved with certain issues. If Celtic values lead people to supporting violent extremists in other countries that have nothing to do with football or even Celtic, then I'm afraid they are way off direction.'

For the majority of Celtic supporters the ethnic and historical connection to Ireland is celebrated romantically through song. The most obvious example being 'The Fields of Athenry' written in 1979 by Pete St John and sung by Celtic supporters since the early 1990s. MacMillan found himself defending the folk song being sung at Celtic Park after accusations that it was sectarian: 'There's been a malicious attempt in getting us to dump our Irish past including the attack on "The Fields of Athenry"; a beautiful ballad which is not equivalent to some of the dreadful things that are being sung by other fans. That kind of song we should be proud of and nurture.'

While keen to see the supporters continuing to celebrate the club's Irish heritage MacMillan feels that it is time to look historically at what songs give Celtic supporters a fresh and modern context, those which suggest where the diaspora community is today: 'The whole Celtic experience has been shaped by Irish history and that is an inescapable and generally very good thing, but I think we have got to a stage where Celtic fans need to have a really good look at their repertoire of songs and if things are offensive for no good reason other than they are traditional songs, then we should ditch them. All the pro-violent stuff should go. The truth is that they are going, they are gradually being filtered out; all the Irish cultural stuff is fantastic but if there is any hint of songs giving succour to the more violent fringes of Irish Nationalism then we should lose them. There needs to be a careful scrutiny of the words and what they represent. Irish rebel songs aren't sectarian; there's nothing wrong with centuries of legitimate political engagement giving rise to that sense of rebellion but you absolutely must weigh up how things are affecting us now! That doesn't mean they are any less offensive to people; especially those today that have had relatives killed when they were in the British army, many of whom are Celtic fans and I know because I've met them. I've been in the company of Celtic fans that are ex-British army and they are just as committed to the club as the rest of us. Some of their friends and relatives have been killed by extreme militant Republicans. Terrible things happen in war but if we are staying close to Brother Walfrid's ideals, especially in the context of Ireland, we must distance ourselves from that kind of extremism. We are on the last legs of it now, the older crowd are more sensitive to it, it does seem to be a younger crowd with a hot headedness about them but that will work itself out.'

Undoubtedly part of our 'rebel' identity is shaped by our football. Being the underdog anti-establishment football team in Scotland has become an attractive label and a rite-of-passage for many young Celtic fans. The romantic associations with Lisbon and more recently Seville have kept that flame alive but MacMillan suggests shifts in money and success have undoubtedly changed Celtic's cultural position. 'There's a certain romantic fascination that positions Celtic as the outsider and the underdog but to claim that Celtic are anti-establishment with the amount of money they have doesn't really ring true anymore. Celtic is as much about business as anything else and that business sense needs people like Peter Lawwell to guide a steady ship. We don't need rebel hotheads leading the club; we need men of vision with business acumen and sense. There is an edge to being the eternal underdog but we can't live off that legacy forever.'

Tommy Burns often-quoted line: 'When you are playing for Celtic; you are playing for a cause and a people,' remains suggestive of a particular character fans could relate to, on and off the pitch. Tony Mowbray's appointment was undoubtedly a romantic one, a popular player who is a Celtic man at heart but his vision of attractive football disregarded the much needed toughness that Martin O'Neill had implemented almost a decade earlier bringing a new era of continuity and success. Mowbray's Celtic team also seemed to lack an understanding of the Celtic philosophy and the fans they were playing for. On taking over towards the end of the 2009–10 season Neil Lennon's evaluation of the players after the previous manager's sacking, which came on the back of a record 4–0 defeat at the hands of St Mirren, was perhaps the most telling: 'I'm not questioning their talent, nor their application at times either. I'm just questioning their mentality. Have they got the stomach? Have they got the character? If it gets hard, can they stand up to the abuse they'll get? And the fans have every right to do that after the St Mirren game.'

Undoubtedly Mowbray misunderstood or was aloof to the Celtic support's alarm at the continuity of disaster, insisting they couldn't see beyond the game they had just lost. In reference to Mowbray's final game in charge as Celtic manager, Lennon tapped into one of Celtic's most important ingredients, mentality, not just of the players but also of the supporters. MacMillan suggests the Celtic supporter's belief that you are playing for a community is a direct descendant of the Stein ethos: 'I think our fans are right to have that puritan edge about playing for the jersey and what they do reflecting well on the club. Stein was special, there was kind of frank Scottish Presbyterianism that was very good for Celtic and a lot of that came from him and translated through players like Billy McNeill and Jim Craig. If you take someone like John Clark, what a fantastic understated man. Today at Celtic you have a Lisbon Lion and a star from the past washing the men's boots, kit and socks with no sense of big headedness. He really is an example of a true and faithful servant of the club. I think that takes a very special man and the fact that we hardly know anything about him says a lot. Strangely I think something of that same attitude came through Henrik Larsson, someone who was not a Scot at all.

He was not just a great player; he also seemed to inspire the club, the fans and the people who played around him.'

Inspiration was at its lowest ebb at the club for over a decade towards the end of the 2009–10 season – a time that will be remembered as an era that broke records in the negative. Significantly Neil Lennon was a direct link to the success that followed Martin O'Neill's appointment in 2000. Lennon's interim appointment provided a beacon of hope that brought back a winning spirit and mentality in the SPL and challenged what he described as a 'malaise' hanging over Celtic Park. On losing the Scottish Cup semi-final against Ross County Lennon addressed supporters waiting outside Celtic Park later that evening after the dust had settled at Hampden. He answered questions with dignity and respect while looking as broken as the support in front of him. It was a pertinent moment that in some way seemed to bring down the barriers that had emerged between the club and the fans. He handled press conferences with the sincerity and depth of someone who has had a profound emotional connection to the club. Lennon has suffered sectarian abuse, death threats and physical attacks because of a passion for Celtic that goes way beyond his professional association. MacMillan sums up his feelings about the club's current manager: 'Neil is a strong example for sticking to his guns; he grew up around the club. He was a young daft boy at times but when he came to Celtic he had to grow up fast; he was attacked in the street, attacked by the press and that was all part of that growing up process. Having met Neil he is great company and nothing like how the tabloids have tried to paint him. He is very humorous and a self deprecating kind of guy. Apart from a few unwise words here and there, he has upheld his dignity and the dignity of Celtic in the face of the worst kind of racism and sectarianism. Neil Lennon has emerged as a great modern example for what it means to be associated with Celtic Football Club.'

CHAPTER TWO THE MANHATTAN TRANSFER

BETWEEN WEST 86TH STREET and Broadway is where you'll find The Parlour Bar, home of New York's largest Celtic supporters' club. It's a surreal experience exiting the flight and hailing a yellow cab via Manhattan's skyscrapers to watch a European Celtic game on a warm October afternoon; although I had my flight timed to perfection there was a nerve-racking delay which led to each minute passing after kick-off like an hour. Walking into the bar I was immediately struck by the mix of New York, Irish and Scottish accents all glued to the SV Hamburg game, which is in the dying minutes. At 1–0 down a last-gasp shimmy from Paddy McCourt is blocked by Rost to deny Celtic a share of the points. Along the bar financial analysts rub shoulders with construction workers, opera singers and software programmers in their adopted home of Manhattan. Despite the obvious (Celtic are about to make yet another tortured competition exit during the 2009–10 campaign under Tony Mowbray) the strength of spirit, energy and wit flows in synchronicity with the line of taps along the bar.

Founded in 1995 the New York club is renowned for its welcome; it's like arriving on the set of a Celtic-inspired version of the popular US comedy *Cheers*. Star guests have entered the frame in the form of Rod Stewart, the Big Yin and Martin O'Neill's Celtic team, all of whom have moved among the throng of New York Celtic die hards. Sitting down after the game with a row of pints amid traditional wooden tables and beams I'm joined by financial expert Paul Hendry, his accent as New York as the Liberty Statue or coffee and bagels. Alongside him are English opera singer Barry Banks and two Scots: Steve O'Brien, who works for a financial software company, and occupational management consultant Ken Miller. Born in 1960, Hendry, the club's treasurer, grew up in Glasgow before his family moved to New York at the end of the decade: 'I come from a typical Glasgow family: one side is Catholic and the other Protestant. After we moved to New York I'd go back every summer, my uncle was a big-time Rangers supporter and he took me to some games at Ibrox; but I didn't get into the vibe. I went to a few Celtic games after that and it felt like a better fit. I also found this other connection; my great uncle's family is from Cork and moved to New York. He was born in Brooklyn and moved back to Glasgow and played for Celtic, so technically he is the first American Celtic player. His name was John Donoghue, he played in the 1920s and lived in the Gorbals. After a spell in England he came back to Celtic before moving to France. He must have been quite a hustler because he got to know some of the Friars on Franciscan mission and through them he organised a move to Excelsior de Roubaix, I think he was a bit ahead of his time. He also worked as a translator on some tours with Celtic after that. After moving to New York in the late 1960s, my dad worked for an airline so I got to fly back for some of the bigger games in the 1970s, aside from that we were tuning into a shortwave wireless for the scores.'

The internet permitted a seismic shift in how Celtic fans such as Paul could link up anywhere around the globe, and that coupled with the advent of satellite television gave many supporters an impetus to gather together no matter how far from the old country. Undoubtedly New York's Celtic diaspora community successfully preserved their identity through supporting the club in an environment that lent itself to those ideals. Says Steve: 'After leaving Scotland I moved to London and then my company sent me to New York. I love this city; the connections to home are much stronger here, no doubt about it. It felt closer to home than London ever did.'

'Now that I'm living here I can agree with that,' adds Barry. 'I've been to some supporters' clubs looking for games and the atmosphere hasn't been good. Strangely one of the places I struggled to find an Old Firm game was in Dublin, I eventually had to hail a cab that would take me to a place that was showing the game and even then it was on a small screen in the corner, the pubs in Dublin seemed to have a larger focus on teams playing in the English Premiership.'

It was during the early 1990s when New York Celtic supporters began breaking new ground in trying to establish themselves as a club. Born in 1956 Ken Miller reflects on the embryonic foundations, pre-internet: 'My introduction to Celtic in New York was via the American Sports Network who used to show the games three days later. Then all of a sudden we found this place where we could see Celtic games live; that changed everything and set about creating what's here today.' Paul gave us his take on the matter: 'In the mid-1990s we used to watch games in the Lower West Side, in those days it would change from game to game depending on whoever owned the rights so we moved around Lower Manhattan, one of the places was The Triple Crown right next to Madison Square Garden. The *New York Times* even ran an article about another bar where we used to meet called Boomer's. At that point we were the only club in the New York City area; we ended up moving uptown to this area and eventually The Parlour here today. Other sports bars would just look at Celtic fans as additional revenue, the people that run the bar and this club are Celtic fans, we understand what the club is about and we want to make people welcome. When people started coming it was just to see the game but by the second or third time it was because of the buzz around the place, it might have been 7 o'clock in the morning but that didn't matter, it was jumping.'

The members soon developed a unique and vibrant community that flourished in New York, something that undoubtedly wouldn't have happened without the diaspora's connections to Celtic. 'You look around and there's a guy with a baby here today; it's that kind of place. There's a real mix of people. If you come from the west of Scotland and are an Irish Catholic it's a given that you'll be here, but we have a lot of Scottish guys without that background drinking in here. Some work in finance, we have Irish guys that are construction workers, to be honest no one gives a crap about what you do, we don't have those kind of class boundaries, what we have in common is Celtic. There's one guy from Baltimore, Jim Denny, who works in the movie industry. His American football team got sold down the river and he became a Celtic fan. He was making a movie in Belfast and walked into a bar that was showing an Old Firm game, thankfully it was a Celtic pub and they gave him the whole story. We also have Tom Tessaro, he was chief of police for a major city in New Jersey.'

As The Parlour's reputation grew and live matches were beamed in via satellite television the club's open policy brought in rival supporters and visiting fans from across the globe. Ken takes up the story: 'People were flocking in and they weren't all Celtic fans, we'd get Manchester United and Rangers boys coming in. But the best night we ever had in here was when we played Liverpool in the UEFA Cup in 2003. The Liverpool fans didn't really have anywhere else to go and asked if they could come here, so we made them welcome. It did get a bit heated after the 1–1 draw, so we split the fans up for the second leg and put the Liverpool boys down the stair. At the end of the 2–0 victory at Anfield the Liverpool supporters were magnificent, they emerged congratulating us, and they were like: "Well done boys . . . we hope you win the competition," That was one of the best days yet.'

Such was the reputation of The Parlour that certain members of the Celtic board even began to pervade the welcoming atmosphere. Paul remembers how it came about: 'We've got some connections in here, Patsy Keane is the brother of John Keane who holds a share of Celtic and we've got acquainted with Michael McDonald who is a director. We got to know him because he checked in for an Old Firm game thinking there was going to be five old men and a dog in here, when he stepped into the bar there were 300 drunken hardcore Celtic fans chanting and singing songs with their fists in the air at 7.30 in the morning. I thought he was just a punter from Glasgow; we got talking and he asked me to film the fans in the bar, of course, just as I pointed the camera we stuck a goal in against Rangers. I had no idea who this guy was, later on I heard he was on the board and that he took this piece of film back to Glasgow and he showed it to the team. He even asked them: "Where do you think this was?" They thought somewhere in the west of Scotland, Belfast or even London but he was like: "That was New York at 7.30 a.m. last week."'

The Parlour Boys built up a cast-iron connection with the club, particularly during Martin O'Neill's time at Celtic, and members made regular pilgrimages to Paradise. One particular visit made quite an impression on Paul: 'I remember we had a pretty rough journey over to Glasgow where I had organised about twenty of us to go to the game and get something to eat at the ground. BA lost our luggage so we showed up looking pretty beat up, burnt out and bedraggled. We had our lunch and the club was like: "We've got your tickets, we tried to get you into the main stand and into the directors' box but we couldn't do it." There was this pregnant pause: "We've got you upgraded, we've got you the presidential box." At first I couldn't get in without a tie, I tried to order a beer and the waiter told me the meal comes with wine. I was like wait a minute I'm at a Celtic game with a tie on drinking wine; this isn't how it's supposed to be.'

Walfrid's vision for Celtic as a charity benefiting the community is also a strong arm of the New York club's identity, says Paul. 'The atmosphere around the club is amazing and that got a few of us thinking; we were determined not to be just another bunch of guys having a drink. That was when some of us decided that we wanted to include the charitable aspect in our own club. Part of what we are about is staying true to Brother Walfrid's ideals and we wanted to organise some charity events.' Ken Miller's opinion is that this ideal was best reflected when the community united in the aftermath of 9/11: 'The club has had some really interesting experiences over the years but probably one of the biggest things for us was after 9/11. We participated in a nationwide campaign with the Federation of New York Celtic Supporters Clubs to raise money for New York's firemen after the tragedy. We had official representatives of the city, the police and fire service and there was a presentation from the federation for about $67,000. A few weeks after that Paul, Tommy Donnelly (who is now back in Scotland) and myself were invited to Celtic Park on 23 November 2001 to receive the Bobby Murdoch award on the pitch before a game against Rangers. Our pictures were projected on the big screen and we got the opportunity to walk out of the tunnel in front of 60,000 fans. When we came out even the Rangers fans were flying US flags which was a great feeling.' At that point it seems that the ethos at the root of Celtic FC had brought shape to the New York supporters' club's identity, giving the fans a wider context in their adopted homeland.

The folklore surrounding Celtic's European triumph in 1967 continues to centre on the locality, camaraderie and community feeling that existed between the Lisbon Lions and their manager Jock Stein. Associated with that was a tangible respect, understanding and relationship with the Celtic support, which continues today with players from the era. The character that emerged during Stein's nine-in-a-row and Billy McNeill's double-winning centenary team of 1988 made an unbreakable connection to the support; the players of those eras were in many respects representatives of the Celtic community and often fans playing for the jersey, shaping the spirit and atmosphere around the club. Martin O'Neill was more than aware of that heritage and made a point of getting to know the Lisbon Lions personally, making his players aware of the history while cementing a team that would remain at the club during his five years as manager.

The Brian Clough man-management style that helped Nottingham Forest win back-to-back European Cups in 1979 and 1980 undoubtedly influenced the Irishman who played under Clough during the period when he dominated European football with what was previously a humdrum provincial English club. The former Celtic manager similarly made a point of getting to know his players, immediately winning respect while chopping away the dead wood. Fundamental to O'Neill was his understanding of the Celtic support and their expectations of what it means to play for Celtic; it's the ghost of Stein that haunts the club, continually fending off the twin beasts of self-interest and greed. Undoubtedly those same legacies remain with supporters at Liverpool and Manchester United due to the traditional socialist working-class values of Shankly and Busby. The arrival of Neil Lennon, Alan Thompson and Chris Sutton reflected O'Neill's determination to win games, each player displaying their own personal strength of character while making an effort to get to know and understand the support.

For many Neil Lennon has carried that tradition on, both as a player and latterly as the manager of Celtic. Paul is a long-term supporter of the current boss: 'The Celtic player that I have enjoyed meeting the most in the last ten years has to be Neil Lennon. The first time was in January 2001 in Florida when Celtic came over for a friendly; it was a few months after Lennon had signed for us. As I was checking-in this stocky, smiling guy in a baseball hat greeted me and asked if I had a good trip, it wasn't until he walked away that I realised who he was. The fact that a player had gone out of his way to talk to me and not the other way around was truly refreshing, I guess that he saw the New York CSC polo shirt and made the connection. A few years later he came to The Parlour with the whole team and I had a long talk with him. Again it was clear that he was not just some highly paid player but a supporter as well. Neil's always been the same at any of the functions I've attended back in Glasgow. O'Neill's players had a down-to-earth vibe about them. Petrov also approached me in Florida and started a conversation off his own back.'

'I don't see that from many players in our current squad, I

think some serious PR work is needed,' adds Ken: 'It was different under O'Neill, I'm not saying that players won't arrive that want to reach out to the fans, but I haven't seen examples of that recently. I remember getting the call saying the team is coming to The Parlour, I was like "aye", I thought he meant 'the team' as in the regulars here. Celtic were touring North America at the time, this was back in August 2004. The team doctor was friends with the owner and he told him: "One day I'll bring the boys here" and sure enough in walks the team, right away you could tell the guys that were really into it: Lennon, Sutton and Thompson all became one of the boys, Bobo was great too. Most of the foreign players were very polite but more reserved.'

'It depends on the player,' adds Paul. 'I remember Lubo came to our table on a trip abroad once and he was magnificent. That kind of thing really does make a difference, when you see members of the board and the players coming here it's good for relations and breaks down barriers. Dermot Desmond showed up once, the place was heaving and the doorman overcharged him. I looked up and saw this guy in a moustache and a pink vest clutching a bunch of dollar bills growling: "How do you get that?" It was then I clicked who he was. It was pretty cool, he was flying to the US for The Open and took a diversion to come here specially and watch the game with us.'

Born in Stoke-on-Trent in 1960, world famous English lyric tenor Barry Banks often watches Celtic games in the bar before performances at the Metropolitan Opera House and has been a regular at The Parlour since his work took him from his former home in Scotland to New York. He remembers a few incidents: 'I've got to say that one of my best times was when Billy McNeill, Tommy Gemmell, Bertie Auld and Dixie Deans turned up; they were so relaxed and had no qualms in telling you what they really thought. Billy was the coolest, he enjoys talking to supporters and everyone really respects him because he's a proper gent. Scott McDonald scored with a header and quick as flash Ken turned to him and said: "Did you teach him how to do that?" Steve was going nuts and Billy was just watching him saying: "This place is something else." He found out I was an opera singer while we were getting some pictures taken outside. This woman was watching us in the colours, singing; then she came over and asked what was going on. Immediately Billy announced: "This guy is an opera singer, c'mon Barry sing her a song." So I sang a little something but what was great about it was that I got a fantastic photo of Billy watching me, it's my proudest moment.

'I wear the Hoops all the time in New York, and you often get stopped but there was one time I was in Queens which is a big Greek area; I did come close to getting my head kicked in when this guy, who looked a bit handy, thought I was wearing a Panathinaikos jersey. He must have been Olympiakos, who are their big rivals, so I had to slowly explain: "No! Celtic, Glasgow Celtic, Scotland."'

'The exchanges you get with other football fans in New York is very different from Glasgow,' adds Steve. 'I was stopped by a guy from Romania, a Unirea Urziceni supporter, the other day, his team were playing Rangers. He shouted:

"Celtic, Celtic" and was stood there giving me the thumbs up. He then shouts: "Rangers" and the thumbs go right down. There was another occasion in Miami where this cab driver looked at me in the wing mirror and said: "I saw your team Glasgow Celtic in 1967." He was from Uruguay and had been at the World Club Championship game against Racing Club. My girlfriend just rolled her eyes; a few of our wives and girlfriends think Celtic is like a weird cult.'

After organising regular trips home to Glasgow, Steve suggested the New York club should make a European pilgrimage after Celtic knocked Spanish club Celta Vigo out of the UEFA Cup in December 2002. A fever of anticipation and speculation was set up for a fourth round tie in Germany: 'That Stuttgart game was a turning point in my career as a Celtic supporter. It had been 23 years since we'd gone into a European competition beyond Christmas; I remember saying to everyone that we might never see this in our lifetime again. I'd been to the quarter-final of the European Cup where we scored two cracking goals against Real Madrid in 1980. I'd been to the Rapid Vienna game in 1984 and suffered all the heartbreak associated with that. Celtic hadn't succeeded at that level for a very long stretch and not in my lifetime, I was born in 1968 so I hadn't experienced seeing Celtic in a European final. Eventually we talked the whole pub into going to Stuttgart.' 'I remember walking into this bar over in Germany,' adds Paul. 'We're all in Hoops and the bar was stacked out with Stuttgart fans. I started thinking: "Is it okay to be in amongst the inner sanctum of another support?" The next thing they welcome us with hugs and kisses; the beer starts flowing, then the schnapps and we all end up singing "You'll Never Walk Alone". The barmaid even turned out to be Martin O'Neill's translator for the day.' 'That game remains with me because it was an example of what I believe the Celtic family to be,' says Steve considering his words carefully. 'It's a way of life; people came from all over Germany to support Celtic that day. They proved just how passionate the support is over there, we made friends for life in Stuttgart.'

The 2003 UEFA Cup campaign and subsequent European jaunts have strengthened relations between the Celtic support and fans of other European teams. Between the supporters of both Celtic and Barcelona, as with a number of other Spanish clubs, there is a shared sense of taking pride in each club's unique history and celebrating much valued and irreplaceable community traditions in the face of globalisation. It's the instinctive nature of the Celtic support to reach out the hand of friendship and build strong relations abroad. The travelling support has built a formidable reputation around Europe's football clubs and cities that have made the Hoops welcome around the globe. The stirring words: 'We don't care if we win, lose or draw' from 'The Celtic Song' are some essential ingredients of the support's mentality. The representation in Seville imported sentiment and romance along with a sense of sheer joy and responsibility wholesale. Although the game ended in defeat, Celtic supporters delivered an unforgettable victory in securing fair play awards from both FIFA and UEFA: 'The thing is with Celtic, even if we lose, we lose together; we don't start fighting, or a riot. It was the same thing in Barcelona we went to the Michael Collins pub and the supporters there understood the history. We were applauded by the Villarreal fans when we left the stadium and welcomed by the people of Seville. When I arrived at the stadium that day I cried; when we finally took our seats I just wept with pride. I never thought I'd see a Celtic game like that in my lifetime. I wept for the people at home that couldn't be there; it was emotion beyond belief. At the end I shook hands and swapped scarves with a Porto fan, not only did they beat us but he gave me the scabbiest scarf you've ever seen.'

The boys have come a long way since tuning into the wireless, yet even without the technological advances these supporters would still have found a way to support Celtic. The club has remained an essential ingredient of their context in New York as well as being a fundamental reminder of who they are and where they come from. I'll leave the last words to Paul Hendry: 'I had a shortwave radio and that's how I stayed connected, at least that way you are getting the result and you are tuning into what's happening in some way. When I first got married we were looking at this house, the problem was I couldn't get a shortwave signal so I couldn't take the house. I even used to take that old radio to work; you could only get the score at certain times in the mid-1980s. I remember working in Wall Street and trying to get the Scotland results from the World Cup. I can clearly remember standing on the southern tip of Manhattan trying to get a signal, finally it clicked in; I'm looking out to the Statue of Liberty and I hear the news that Jock Stein is dead. I know that sounds dramatic but that's exactly how it happened and you don't forget a moment like that. It was the same with Seville, when we got there I met guys I went to college with, I was running into old friends that I hadn't seen in years, if I'd met them on 59th Street it would have been a bigger deal but it was like "Of course you are here, we are all here because these are the threads that hold us all together . . . that's why this club exists."'

CHAPTER THREE
GLITTERING PRIZE

The idea of transubstantiation can seem remote, mysterious and irrelevant mumbo jumbo until one analyses a symphony by Beethoven or Maxwell Davies. There before your eyes and ears one can see and hear musical material transforming itself into something other than its original apparent substance. **JAMES MACMILLAN**

JIM KERR RETURNED home in the summer of 2010, exchanging the exotic climate of Sicily for a dingy Glasgow basement in time for the live debut of his solo project *Lostboy!* After more than thirty years fronting Simple Minds the singer was motivated to return to the roots that shaped and inspired him while on a sabbatical away from his regular post. Critically rehabilitated, Simple Minds received some of their best reviews in twenty years for their sixteenth long player *Graffiti Soul* released in 2009. The live shows and optimistic evaluations that trailed the release built up a new awareness of the band's back catalogue, and their influence on a new generation of bands trading on the sound of yesteryear's punk and new wave scene had also emerged.

Kerr was delighted with the reaction: 'Bands are using sounds from the past, so in fact sounds from the past have become current again. When I hear The Killers, Editors or Franz Ferdinand I wonder if Charlie Burchill has joined the band.' Around the time of this interview one enthusiastic local greets Kerr in a Glasgow restaurant, while congratulating him on his *Lostboy!* solo effort: 'Haw, *Lost Bob* by ra way?'

giving Kerr the thumbs up, the humour and boldness of Glasgow life beautifully illustrated. The city undoubtedly gives Kerr perspective and momentum, the timeless socialist principles which he infused into the band's Street Fighting Years are undoubtedly what led to Simple Minds being deemed political by a London centric media; the critical kiss of death towards the end of the 1980s. A decade before, the DIY ethos of punk along with the theatrical authority of 1970s art rock, shaped their debut *Reel to Real Cacophony*. In 1980 *Empire and Dance* marked out a new modern, cool and experimental era for the band along with their desire to connect with Europe both musically and philosophically, leaning on David Bowie's 'Berlin' period.

From an Irish family and growing up on a Glasgow council estate, Kerr had no desire to hang about in his apprenticeship as a brickie's labourer. David Bowie, Lou Reed and Roxy Music had fired his imagination and nourished a sound and aesthetic for Simple Minds' acclaimed early work, but it was the mainstream successes of *New Gold Dream* and *Sparkle in the Rain* that set the Glasgow band up as one of the biggest international draws of the 1980s. Sonic blasts such as 'Speed Your Love to Me' were bombastic slices of pop with a primal power and energy that charged the soul. The artwork of both albums used striking Catholic imagery and symbolism that bolstered the themes of religious ecstasy captured in Kerr's lyrics and the abstract hymnal brushstrokes of guitar and synthesiser laid on by Charlie Burchill and Mick MacNeil on the likes of 'Glittering Prize'. With 'Waterfront' the band captured the spirit and energy of the Glasgow shipyards, the pounding bass emulating the tug of a ship built on the Clyde. The music tapped into a local pride, native philosophy and political ideal synonymous with Glasgow life.

The spirit of that culture became intensely alive for Kerr during boyhood when his family took him to watch Celtic for the first time. 'My first Celtic game was a pre-season friendly against Manchester United in 1966. I was with my dad and my uncles; it was just after England won the World Cup and nobody knew at that point that Celtic was going to be the first British team to win the European Cup. It was my first time at Celtic Park and you never forget it, it's the first time you see that crowd with everyone rammed in shoulder to shoulder and jam packed into the Jungle. We were playing against the great Manchester United team: Nobby Styles, Bobby Charlton, George Best, Denis Law, Paddy Crerand and we thrashed them 4–1. When I tell Man U fans they say it was only a friendly and I tell them "Damn right it was only a friendly or we would have gubbed you 7–1." That game was the beginning of a journey.'

What Kerr witnessed at age seven was the first glimpse of a football revolution that would cause a massive shift in the European game. After just over a year in the job Jock Stein had reinforced Celtic with a psychological strength. From his experience working among a squad of miners he channelled the same sense of dependence and dedication, stitching a heightened sense of solidarity and camaraderie into his players. He maximised individual ability in order to build a mental pride and indissoluble spirit into the character of the team as a whole. For Kerr this philosophical approach not only bolstered Celtic but the wider culture around the club: 'When Celtic won the European Cup that season it was an incredible feat. This was not only the team I supported but I'm also convinced that I adopted a mentality that was much, much needed at that time. Glasgow was arguably on its knees; it was the end of the industrial age, factories and the shipyards were shutting down. I was only a wee boy but I would hear my ma and da talking, they were worried and they didn't know what the future was going to be, coming from a place on its knees . . . but then something incredible happened. Celtic showed you that you could come from this place and be the absolute best and win, not only that but win in style. It certainly, in my case, became part of the psyche, you might have come from a one-scrape loser place but you could be as good as anybody and probably better.

'To put it into context with Simple Minds as a live band you've got to give the performance of your life every night and we are very competitive with ourselves and want to give it absolute hell because the audience don't care if you've been in Amsterdam the day before or if you are knackered at the end of the tour, there's an attitude of: "This is who we are and this is what we have done with our lives" and you can't give people second best when you've got something like that driving you.'

The success for Celtic in Portugal was also a realisation of Walfrid's vision for the club. Celtic had made visible a distinctive diaspora community that successfully bled into Scottish life and society. The mechanics of the club represented the best of both cultures merging together, anything that embraced violence or discrimination was a bastardisation of the vision, retarding the club of its true meaning, identity and heritage. An essential ingredient of the success and narrative was a Celtic manager coming from a fervent Protestant background and identifying himself with Scotland's foremost Irish Catholic club first as a player, then essentially, as manager. The move was a symbolic declaration against bigotry, one of the darkest and most negative aspects of Scottish life. While Stein didn't tolerate bigotry of an anti-Catholic/Irish nature from his own background, he publically ostracised anything in the Celtic support that besmirched the club's reputation. On several occasions he jumped into the crowd to confront supporters involved in sectarian chanting; it was an uncharacteristic attribute for a professional manager especially in the 1970s. Said Kerr: 'We know why it's been hard in the West Coast, because of politics, it wears out the sponsors, people take liberties and let us down.' Yet ultimately Stein exuded tremendous warmth when addressing the Celtic support; he gave the fans a new context and sense of ambition. 'The Celtic support had a tremendous respect for Stein,' says Kerr. 'He was a big intimidating guy and people listened to him. When you heard him talk he was like the headmaster, he always had decency. He would always say the Celtic people are great, great people and the fans are lovely people. Sean Fallon had the same integrity; it was running through them, he had a great pride in coming from Sligo and in Big Jock's case from mining stock. They told you that you could be working-class and still do something with your life, you didn't need to be a professor and study classical music in

Vienna because let's be honest, there is nothing better than being an underdog.'

The 12th European Cup final wasn't just the final of a competition between two sets of eleven players; it was two opposing philosophies, systems and styles of football. The same positive mentality that challenged the destructive and backward elements of Scottish society also squared up to the cynical force that was destroying the European game. On 25 May 1967 the restrictive catenaccio system deployed by Helenio Herrera and Inter Milan under the cold guise of professionalism was uncompromisingly toppled with a victory that personified flair, skill, imagination and vision. Says Kerr: 'Not only did Celtic win the competition they put the kybosh on that ugly type of football which was killing the game. It should have been 7–1 because when you look at it they absolutely tanked them with over forty shots at goal, a more one-sided game you have never seen in your life! They just kept coming at them again and again and again. The European Cup win wasn't a one-off either; aside from nine-in-a-row we got to two European finals, the second in 1970 and we reached the European Cup semi-finals in 1972 and 1974 – for a decade we ran riot in Europe.

'Looking onto the park there was just a feeling, you would think who else was better than Murdoch, Lennox, Johnstone, Gemmell, Auld and latterly Kenny Dalglish? The answer was nobody; Celtic were the best. The Dutch are credited with inventing Total Football – they didnae, Celtic invented it and a few of the Dutch players have even started to come out and say that now. Tommy Gemmell scored in two

European Cup finals: how many left backs score goals, never mind at the top level in Europe. The spaces that Celtic would create allowed him to run up the wing and batter the ball in. These guys were like Hollywood stars to us, and you could get close to them in those days. I used to watch Celtic's practice games with Charlie (Burchill) and my da. You'd see them in friendly matches with teams like Queen's Park. Jinky or Bobby Lennox would be playing from the Lions and that was kept going right through to the Quality Street boys, which I suppose was really my era. In the team you would see players like Victor Davidson, Paul Wilson, Lou Macari and Danny McGrain, I remember watching Kenny (Dalglish) score four or five one night; you were seeing these guys long before they broke through to the first team.

'When Celtic won the nine-in-a-row it's easy to assume that it was the Lisbon Lions that won it but, in fact, Jock Stein dismantled that team very quickly and within two years Celtic were a vastly different team. I saw some big European ties at Parkhead during those years. I was there the night Dixie (Deans) hit the moon in what was the first penalty shootout in the European Cup. It was a semi-final against Internazionale and the place was packed, the stadium fell silent, it was eerie.

'I never trust guys that say they've got two teams but that Ajax team in the 1970s was as close as I got. I saw Ajax play Celtic at Hampden in 1971, there was still a few of the Lions playing for Celtic. Even though they were getting on we still beat them at home but they won the leg overall. Cruyff was the best player in Europe at that point and Ajax had become the masters. You could tell there was a great respect between the teams, both had the same attacking philosophy; that is how football is meant to be played.' An opening round in Europe saw the two clubs meet again almost a decade later. 'Celtic were magnificent in those two games and the away leg is particularly memorable for that astounding Charlie Nicholas goal which he chipped over the keeper's head . . . it was amazing. That whole season Charlie was tearing defences apart; he was a team player as well as goal scorer. It was around that time that the game was going through changes and Charlie was our marquee player; he was our first rock 'n' roll star and we had a few of them over the years.'

Undoubtedly Charlie Nicholas was Celtic's first playboy, making the front and back pages of the redtops. Maurice Johnston and Frank McAvennie would respectively follow in his footsteps. Johnston, formerly known as 'Super Mo', and Paolo Di Canio are arguably the most controversial players to have pulled on the Hoops. Many supporters have written them out of the club's history for betraying values that are widely accepted as 'the Celtic way' of life.

Significantly Kerr has a more philosophical view of their relationship to Celtic: 'These guys are used for the marketing, they pull in the punters. They were worth the price of the ticket alone in their day. With Paolo Di Canio my attitude is this: if the guy made an arse of himself after his time with Celtic that's up to him but the thing to remember is he never made an arse of himself in a Celtic jersey, he was absolutely riveting and an unforgettable player in the Hoops. He was hilarious, he was gallus and he had Celtic pumping through his veins. I don't know a club where the fans haven't fell in love with him. He's definitely mental, he never got a game for Italy and yes the players grow on trees over there, but the real reason he didn't get a game is because he was seen as more trouble than he was worth but his worth to us was absolutely immense. If every guy that pulled on a Celtic jersey gave as much effort as Paolo did we'd have even more to talk about in the history of this great club. I feel the same way about Mo Johnston and I know that I'm in a small minority here but he was a great player for Celtic. When you look back at it now Celtic are as much to blame as Mo, imagine letting a player like that go. That was the start of an era where footballers became mercenaries; they went where the deal was and that was particularly true with players like Charlie, Mo and Frank. As Celtic fans we're all the same; I took the right hump when Kenny left, when Charlie left and when I saw Larsson in the Manchester United blue away strip I thought: "That's not the Larsson I know." As Celtic supporters we're all terrible like that, we get all jealous and judgemental about these guys and it goes well over the top but that's part of who we are and how we feel about this club, in saying that we usually get the ball back on the deck.'

When living a stone's throw from the national stadium Kerr was also a regular visitor to Hampden Park for Scotland international matches. The generation of Celtic fans that grew up watching the club's players get booed when turning out for their country persuaded many to take up support of the Republic of Ireland. Like a great number others Kerr has often felt split when it comes to supporting the country of his birth: 'I love supporting Ireland and Scotland, because I lived so close to Hampden I went to see Scotland all the time but there was a lot of things I struggled with. A big problem was the amount of caps Jinky got – which was twenty-three – that was miniscule in relation to his talent. I would go and watch Scotland on a Wednesday night and it was a very different experience from going to watch the Celtic. There were a lot of boys from the country, Stirling, the central belt and various other parts of Scotland; let's just say their second team would not have been Celtic. One night I clearly remember Jinky getting booed and you can't get away from that. It made me stop and think; as I'm sure it did for a great deal of others. The same thing happened with Kenny (Dalglish) but players from other clubs weren't getting booed so that changed your perspective on it.

'In those days though Scotland had a bit of flamboyance with Celtic players like Kenny and Danny McGrain or players like big Joe Jordan who would have a bit of a dig. There was something to support then. More recently I'm struggling with my enthusiasm; the energy is not pulsating through me in the same way. I was really scunnered by that dodgy decision in the France v Republic of Ireland World Cup qualifier. The goal that was scored after Thierry Henry's handball was a sickener. I think these things are starting to hurt the game.'

Notably in the age of the football superstar, Celtic have consistently managed to produce local heroes who display something of the club's character in their own personality and ambition. Perhaps tomorrow's biggest challenge is fielding at least a few players who understand Celtic's history while remaining contenders at the highest level. Kerr is aware of the pitfalls of this policy: 'In the last few years I just couldn't be bothered with the Champions League and I'd forgotten about the 2010 World Cup within months. It's a cliché but the game is losing its soul. The over commercialism is getting too much. We know far too much about how much the players are getting paid and about their wives; somewhere along the line something changed. In Scotland it becomes mundane when you meet the same team seven times in one season. For a lot of people it's just not the thing that it was. Once this last generation grows out it's hard to say how kids in the future will relate to Celtic Football Club. If you're a working-class kid from Glasgow trying to work your way up and you don't have a Charlie Nick or an Aiden McGeady that you know grew up in the same streets as you, then it becomes a very different thing. Even if you relate to one of the foreign players, the good ones are gone the following season. I know guys that have been Celtic mad all their lives and for the first time they are going less because they feel cut adrift from the team. I spoke to one guy recently and he said to me that he'd rather give the Celtic shirt to five guys from Castlemilk and I really know what he means. Someone might read this and say: "Wait a minute; you are in one of the biggest commercial industries going," but rock stars have always been like that, rock 'n' rollers are fly-by-night kind of guys, but the whole thing about a football team is that it belongs to you. Why would you go week in and week out otherwise? You are supposed to feel that it's your team and that you are somehow helping them and supporting them. How many nights have Celtic played magnificent and the players have said "It was the crowd that did it for us tonight." If that tradition goes then you are just another football team, and there are millions of them.'

It's not often a song can inspire a public gala but The Fields of Athenry Glasgow Celtic Festival in Galway was organised in 1999 to honour the song. The event gave Kerr an opportunity to join thousands of fellow supporters alongside his heroes, the Lisbon Lions, for a festival that united Celtic and the roots of the much-loved anthem. The singer explains: 'I got invited to this festival and I ended up taking my ma and da and my girlfriend with me. It was a double whammy because I knew the Lisbon Lions were going and so I thought we'll all have a right good time at this over in Ireland with all the Celtic supporters. Around this time the whole Donald Findlay controversy broke, somebody had got photos of Donald Findlay with him and a lot of guys singing "The Sash" and basically, to make it plain, he was nabbed. So looking at that before I went, I started to get right paranoid because this thing had been all over the papers and the news. I thought all I need is for a couple of Celtic boys to stand behind me with the wrong banner and I'm next. I got in touch with the organisers and I made it plain that I wanted to stay out the limelight and wouldn't be singing; they were like: "No bother; just come over and enjoy it."

'So I get to the airport and God bless them Jinky and Bertie Auld are steamin'. The first thing Jinky says to me is: "Jim this is going to be brilliant and when you get there we are going to get you up for a song." I'm like: "No way, I'm just going for the craic." Bertie and Jinky are having none of it; eventually Stevie Chalmers and Bobby Lennox cut in and they're like: "Listen it'll be fine; we'll make sure they don't get you up." So we get to the Athenry festival and it's in the car park of a supermarket, the stage is a truck and the band before the Lions are well hardcore; they're not kidding on so it's quite a scene. I'm having a good time but it's nothing to do with me and I've got a bunnet on so I'm just merging into the background.

'Bertie Auld walks on stage, this is after me saying to keep it stoom, he grabs the mike and says: "Great to be here and by the way we've got a special treat for you, Jim Kerr is in the crowd now and he's going to come up and give you all a song." I just started running and they never saw me all day. You can bet your life, as innocent as it all would have been, the next day I would have been in the *Daily Record*. Eventually I went back and all the Lions were doing a question and answer session with the fans. Jinky had sobered up and he said to me: "C'mon Jim, me and you, we'll get up and take questions; it'll be a laugh," so I went for it. People were asking various questions about the consortium with Kenny (Dalglish) and Bono because it had been in the air. It came to Jinky's turn and this guy asked him a great question about all the money in the modern game compared to his day and how it made him feel. He finished off his question asking how much his market value would be at that time, which was really the David Beckham era. So Jinky responded: "Son, I don't think money could have bought me. In truth, money didn't mean anything to us, we had a great life and money never came into it. I had my time and I don't regret any of it, money didn't register with me." So Jinky went on like that for a good five minutes. As soon as they passed the mike he turned round to me and said: "Big man, I was just thinking there, we should do this up and down the country, we'd make a fucking fortune."'

Undoubtedly a droll wit has continued to fuel the folklore of Celtic Football Club. Although too young to travel in the late 1960s and early 1970s, a Celtic daft neighbour would keep the young Kerr up to date with the Celtic fans' exploits abroad. The antics of 'George from the Clemmy' would entertain the whole stair, certainly one morning opening the paper to see the Glasgow Corporation worker standing alongside Elizabeth Taylor and Richard Burton in Celtic colours: 'That's a story you don't forget. George worked as a mechanic for the Cleansing Department. He used to go and see the Celtic everywhere and on this occasion he had gone to see them play in Hungary against Ujpest Dosza in the 1972 European Cup quarter-final; the only thing was he would go on the sick for these big games during the week. Burton was in Hungary making a picture, *Bluebeard* I think it was. Anyway the Celtic fans spot the pair of them in the hotel and there's nobody holding back, everyone goes right in, gallus as get out: "Any chance of a photae hen?" Of course, Burton and Taylor end up throwing a party for the Celtic fans, sing-song, photos in the Celtic colours, the lot. So after all the high jinx George, up the stair, gets back and he's telling us all about it, he then goes to his work and very nearly gets the boot. The boss has got a hold of the *Daily Record* with him standing next to Elizabeth Taylor and says: "I thought you were ill; you look that fucking well too standing there next to Liz Taylor."'

The famous pictures of Taylor and Burton in green and white have now become the stuff of legend but the surreal collision of these two worlds is by no means a solitary event in Scottish football. Comic actor Danny Kaye was introduced to an 80,000 strong crowd before Celtic beat Rangers 3–2 in the Glasgow Charity Cup final in 1950 and on 16 September 1981 Grace Kelly accompanied her husband Prince Rainier to watch AS Monaco play Dundee United at Tannadice. During an early visit to Celtic Park Jim Kerr spotted another Hollywood icon that would later become a particularly contentious figure among the Celtic support for his desertion to Rangers. 'I remember sitting in the wee stand and Sean Connery comes in. I was only a boy at the time so to me it was like James Bond sitting watching Celtic. The next week there's a picture of Connery in the *Celtic View* and I'm in the photo sitting with my da; somebody must have it.'

Today Celtic is owned and supported by some of the wealthiest and most famous people on the planet, those same fans become part of an authentic levelling process where worldly prestige and influences are left at the door to join their fellow supporters in cheering on the team. Certainly the world's most celebrated and recognised comedian Billy Connolly is famous for showing up at games and Celtic pubs where he can just be one of the boys. Kerr reflects on one such occasion: 'I'd flown to Australia and I arrived on the day of the Old Firm game. I was checking into the hotel and one of the bellboys said: "How you doing Jim? Are you going to watch the game tonight? I can recommend a fantastic Celtic supporters club not far from here; the place will be jumping and they'll look after you." I was knackered with jetlag so I said I'd see how I felt later. I woke up about midnight and you know what it's like; my first waking thought was "I've got to see the game." I got a taxi four blocks and right away I spotted this mad squad with one guy in particular holding court with his back to me. He had a profile you couldn't mistake with the long hair; it was like Jesus and the twelve apostles. So I tapped him on the back and the night started from there. Celtic won so you can imagine how it finished. After the game we switched the telly over and it's the All Blacks playing at Twickenham so Connolly starts leading all these Celtic supporters in the Haka. The best of it is he doesn't even drink and neither do I; we were the only two left standing.'

Significantly Jim shares a Celtic link with former Oasis front man, and now singer with Beady Eye, Liam Gallagher. Both men have previously been married to actress Patsy Kensit and made a connection through their sons James and Lennon. In 2000 Gallagher penned 'Little James' for Kerr's son and recently employed the teenager to work for his clothing company, Pretty Green. Likewise Kerr bonded with Liam's son Lennon through Celtic. Jim explains: 'Liam's wee boy and my son are half brothers. Wee Lennon wasn't really into football and one day he asked me for a Celtic top. I said: "Lennon, you don't like the Celtic." He wasn't having it so I said: "Okay Lennon I'll get you a Celtic top but here's the deal . . . when you go home and you're sitting with the boys, any time you hear Celtic mentioned I want you jump up on your feet, punch the air and shout 'C'mon the Celtic'. For every time you do it I'll give you a tenner." I later got a call from my son James, the boys had all been on holiday together. The first thing he said to me was: "Liam's cracking up laughing da, every time the Celtic are on the telly; young Lennon's punching the air and shouting for them." I must have put out a couple of grand through the years; it's still going on. He gets it all tallied up, I'll see him and he'll be like: "Jim that's forty quid you owe me."'

Celtic Football Club has always attracted big time movers and shakers from the worlds of entertainment, business, sport, religion and politics since its formation. Arguably it's the patter of the fans, the club's Irish roots and the enduring story of Lisbon that continues to bring a number of famous supporters to the club. The touch of genius in Stein's Celtic continues to spark the imagination and fire the soul, particularly for those working in the arts. Says Kerr: 'One of my best pals in Glasgow is a Rangers supporter and he said to me "What is it with Celtic; you have Celtic records, plays, books – what is it with you guys, you are always up to something?" If you look at the size of Scotland, we punch above our weight in proportion with the rest of the world. I think it has something to do with that mix of immigrant people because you know in that situation you have to punch hard. With what I've been working on recently and a lot of Simple Minds there is an atmosphere in the music. I try to capture that intangible feeling, that joyous optimistic fighting against the odds thing. There is also a searching for some place or somewhere. I'm not sure why these themes have come through but I like to think there is a genetic memory. When I talk to people in Europe about Scotland they have often heard of Edinburgh. Glasgow still seems to still have this "No Mean City" tag but at the same time I think a lot of people are aware of the contrast and enjoy the difference. Glasgow is like Ireland inside of Scotland, it's kind of schizophrenic because we have the Irish in our background but we're not Irish, and we're governed by London. We're not sure who we are but at the same time we are sure of ourselves; all of that stuff reverberates in me.

'With Simple Minds we never played the Scottish card, running around with tartan and that kind of thing, we looked to something bigger. We always used the Claddagh, which was fantastic for us as people really embraced it. When you think of poetry, you think of Robert Burns, he's the most famous and renowned poet in the world. When you think of literature, you think of Ireland; the most poetic and lyrical people are the Celts and wrapped up within all of that there is a mix of races and countries. I love Glasgow and anything good that comes out of the city makes my heart soar. I played Dublin recently and a couple of generations ago, my people came from there and when I go on stage in Dublin my heart pounds that wee bit faster, the way it does in Glasgow because that's my blood. In Glasgow I can celebrate both.'

As Kerr suggests, Celtic supporters have always presented a different idea of what it means to be Scottish; there remains a stronger bond with Europe for many because of a connect-edness to Catholicism and a sense of always feeling displaced from home in relation to the diaspora history. Perhaps the reputation of Celtic's travelling support gives sway to Kerr's theory that we will always be on the move or in transition embracing other lifestyles and cultures either following Celtic or moving on and supporting the club from distant lands. Says Kerr: 'I think there are two types of Scots. There are those that stay at home and are proud of the hills and the heather and there are those that get out there and get on with everybody and get right into it. They don't try and take over but they can adapt wherever they go. I'm shaped now by living in Italy, my girlfriend is Japanese, I eat Japanese food every day, she is part of me, we have been together a number of years now but if you cut me open with a knife you would find rock and rain that was made in Glasgow. I think some of us are travellers, it's in our heart and we have always been on the move. The original Celtic tribes were travellers and they came from the middle of Europe, I guess I've always hung onto that idea.'

Throughout the 1980s both Simple Minds and U2 became used to filling stadiums in their own right but they also still found time to visit the odd one together and cheer on the Hoops. Significantly both bands shared a similar ethos; Kerr and Bono in particular embodied a certain type of front man and both became particularly notorious in the early 1980s for the infectious political and spiritual energy in their live sets. Bono described Simple Minds as a 'glorious sound, noise and feeling', which both he and The Edge would point to for inspiration when making *The Unforgettable Fire*. Their reach was designed to invigorate the senses and charge the soul with 'inspiration over intellect'. The glorious noise challenged the air of doom inspired by anxiety over the Thatcher government, the threat of nuclear weapons and the death throes of British industry: 'Before I even met the guys in U2 we had already worked with a lot of the same people. Ten minutes into meeting them I loved them and why would you no', you know? Like us, they were a school band, like brothers. It's true we shared socialist principles, boiling it down our attitude was if you can help, you help. If there's something wrong or if someone is being attacked you stop it, you tell them "That's out of order, wrap it" or you wire in to stop it yourself. It's the way we were all brought up. The whole anti-apartheid thing for me started when I was a kid in Glasgow. My granda was in the British army, he loved Africa and he would tell me these amazing stories of this lovely country which was South Africa and about the city of Cape Town. He would also tell me about how black people were being treated and what they had to put up with. Growing up you know that's out of order. It was the same thing writing about life here with Thatcher. Perhaps the end of the age was coming in terms of industry but forget the issues of that, it was the lack of compassion and the way she went about it. That way of life is absolutely alien to me and let's call it what it was – colonialism – that's wrong, never right, time to stop.

'You look outside of yourself, and we certainly did, there is a joy in the music, a positive language and if you want to boil it down it was a positive noise. I like the early Bono line: "I

can't change the world but I can change the world in me."
New Gold Dream was a very positive noise; it was joyous,
optimistic and about looking beyond you, not self-centred. A
lot of music at the time was very self-centred; with Morrissey
outside of *Meat Is Murder* we are very much listening to his
trials and tribulations, we wanted to look a bit more to the
world outside ourselves.'

While both U2 and Simple Minds shared a sense of political
and socialist purpose both had the generational connection of
growing out of the punk and new wave movements while
sharing a similar set of ideas, traditions and beliefs. Naturally
it was down to Kerr to lead the Dublin-born Celtic supporter
to his first Old Firm derby. Two rock stars making their way
to Ibrox in full Celtic regalia would probably create a media
frenzy today but in the pre-satellite/internet era the pair
were just another two lads dressed in green white and gold
enjoying a day out cheering on the Celtic. For Kerr it's an
enduring image of the time: 'I took Bono to an Old Firm
game at Ibrox, he had never been before that. We didn't go
through the club we had tickets among ourselves; it was a
punters day. I told Bono we needed to hide him a bit and get
the tammy and the scarf on. I don't think he was ready for
that kind of intensity, this was before the seats came in so it
was more of the old pack mentality and pretty mental. I
remember we were about to leave and Charlie (Nicholas)
popped in an amazing goal which he thoroughly enjoyed. He
said to me it was like ancient Rome and he wasn't far wrong.

'I remember the Barrowlands gig when Bono joined us on
stage for 'New Gold Dream', both him and his wife Ali were

in Scotland for a few days driving up to the north of Scotland. I told them we were playing that night to come down to the gig, they didn't have a hotel so I told him they could stay at my folks. When he arrived my ma was like: "You look knackered son; away up the stair to your bed for an hour" and off he went. The motor he was driving at the time was an old Jag, I nearly died because after the gig he drove across George Square and I mean the actual square, I was like: "What are you doing man; you are going to get us arrested!" There's a few quotes from around that time, they loved *New Gold Dream* and they wanted the same kind of shades and colours, it was a very European sound we were both going for. I haven't seen Bono for a while; I think Larry put the kybosh on the Celtic thing. He was a football man but not a Celtic fan and he was worried about certain connotations with the band but Bono was certainly into Celtic.'

The optimistic spirit encased in Simple Minds has even been used to inspire the Celtic team on occasion, as Kerr explains: 'The 1980s was a period we loved through and through, some of the players would come to the gigs, like Tommy Burns and Paul McStay. I know Charlie was into the band. Pat Nevin wasn't a Celtic player but he played at junior level and he came very early on. The thing was football players were a bit more military, even in those days, we were a rock 'n' roll band, it didn't matter if we were out all night but the manager was like a big daddy keeping them in check and they had to be in their rooms by ten o'clock; we were free agents. I could really relate to the boys in those Celtic teams, they were just like the guys I grew up with, they were just working in a more athletic hard-nosed world and they happened to play for the best team on the planet. It was quite an optimistic time in general and there was a great spirit in the team right up until the centenary year. They became famous for the "last minute Celtic" thing and we loved all that; it fed the mythology. I loved the players from that team like Joe Miller, Mark McGee and Macca.

'When we went to Hampden under Fergus when the stadium was being rebuilt, that was really tough and it felt like a bleak and brutal time. Under Tommy Burns there were cracks of light with players like Paolo Di Canio, Jorge Cadete and Pierre Van Hooijdonk. Fergus McCann labelled them "The Three Amigos" but nothing was ever settled with those players and it was the same with big Mark Viduka. I could understand these guys wanted to sort out the business side because for a large part of it they were bringing the punters through the gate. It wasn't until Martin O'Neill came in that things changed. I could never understand Celtic fans that complained about O'Neill's style because we were getting battered every game against Rangers. It got dark in the 1990s; we had some fantastic and stylish players but they weren't able to perform to the best of their ability. We had to bring in the big boys like Chris Sutton, John Hartson, Alan Thompson and Joos Valgaeren; it wasn't rocket science that's for sure but it stopped our players getting thumped every week. Suddenly Larsson was a different player, he got rid of Regi Blinker and brought in some decent wingers like Agathe. O'Neill knew what was going on and he knew what had to be done; his teams were absolutely electrifying.'

Undoubtedly Kerr's is not a view all Celtic supporters are in agreement with and Pat Nevin will give a different perspective on O'Neill's Celtic tenure in Chapter 5. Following O'Neill in 2005, Gordon Strachan remained an unpopular figure among many Celtic fans during his four years at the club despite building on the success of his predecessor. For Kerr the appointment of Tony Mowbray after Strachan was one of the most disastrously backward steps in living memory calling to mind Celtic's rootless run in the 1990s. 'I think Gordon Strachan did a great job in handling a very difficult challenge; the budget was a fraction of what O'Neill had to spend. I think Rangers were also in a difficult financial position at the same time, I'm not taking anything away from him but he benefited from Rangers having a weak team. Strachan's Celtic was able to win leagues with comparative ease but his team weren't a patch on O'Neill's. People argue that Strachan got further in the European Cup, but we are psychotic, we win the league and we're still not happy. I just wasn't really a fan of his players; we didn't have the money for a Hartson or a Sutton.

'I still don't understand the appointment of Tony Mowbray – that decision was away out there and a lot of people said it at the time. It was really bad business on Celtic's part because what scalps had he claimed as manager of Hibs or West Brom? You would imagine the conversation should have gone something like: "How did you get on in your last job . . . Relegated? Well, maybe not the day son." But instead the response was: "Here's the job." I think there's a lot to be said for body language and how you handle the media when you are Celtic manager, I know a lot of people didn't like Gordon Strachan's jokey patter but I thought the man was a class act in that department especially after Martin O'Neill, who behind Stein is Celtic's most loved manager. Outside of Jock Stein there was never a man that the whole club was beholden to, he had practically everybody on his side. Mowbray came across as a mumbling nonentity. People say he was a lovely big man, well good on him, but as for a manager of Celtic . . . absolutely garbage.

'Of course, the situation has changed and you won't find anyone as passionate as Neil Lennon and, looking at his CV, so far his appointment is a great thing for Celtic. I recently got the chance to meet Martin O'Neill; it was great just to see the energy that runs through him. Martin is a Celtic man, it's not just the fact that he's been the manager for us, he loves Celtic with a passion and misses them desperately, with a real sense of conviction.'

Perhaps one of the most talked about Celtic stories of the late 1990s was the consortium – including Kerr, Kenny Dalglish and Bono – who were rumoured to be putting a bid together to buy the club after a period of financial turmoil had settled. Myth continues to surround what might have been. What's clear is that Kerr was afraid the club was about to be sold to the highest bidder, possibly someone with no understanding of the club's history. Kerr's relationship with Fergus McCann was famously terse. In 1999 he said: 'McCann built a stadium, oh what a great, great thing. Ceausescu built a stadium, so did Mussolini.'

Speaking today Kerr reflects on the previous quote: 'I did

not like the man; I thought he had a horrible manner about him. People used to say to me, "You've got to know him; he was only kidding," but I've always felt there was a decency about Celtic. For my generation it was as much about the way you talk to and treat people . . . whether it's the club, the team or the support. With Fergus it was purely business. Celtic had nearly gone bankrupt, the business was rotten and McCann knew where football was going. He was the only one who would or could help the club at that point and he was due his pay packet. There was a pettiness to the man. When Celtic won the league, beating St Johnstone to stop Rangers winning ten-in-a-row, Bertie Ahern was in Glasgow and he let it be known that he wanted to go to the game. No formal invite came forward so Brian Dempsey invited him to his box and it was quite a box; I was in there with George Galloway. So you can imagine the sense of occasion, it was one of the biggest games in recent history. The prime minister of any country attending Celtic Park, I would have thought would have been brought on to meet the Celtic support but can you imagine the roar that would have went up if the Prime Minister of Ireland was brought onto the ground on a day like that? Celtic would have scored seven.

'I think there was an ambiguity for Fergus around the Irish identity of the club and what he thought the club should be. Let's just say he was worried about the hardcore element and when it came to selling Celtic that kind of association would affect shareholdings and stock prices; it wouldn't be so good for his price when it came to punting the club. It was a time when big sponsors were coming into the game and he was worried. You have to remember though, there's a lot more to it; is it not Irish turf laid down at Celtic Park, what about Brother Walfrid? You start taking Ireland out of Celtic; what are you left with? A team in green; well there's loads of them, another Clyde, we've got one of them. The Irish history is Celtic's biggest calling card and it's in the name of the club – Scotland and Ireland together – you can't do away with any one part of that.

'There's no doubt it was business, what he erected and what he brought was a colossal change for the positive but the deal was that Fergus knew what he was doing from day one – build it up and punt it. Celtic is a hard thing to market: to one person Celtic is a glorious pure and innocent club but for others the club has severe connotations. He didn't get it right because he was involved in a blanding; he was trying to clean out the Irishness completely. At the time Fergus was clear the club was up for sale but you never really knew where you stood. A few of us gave him an option which he didn't want to go for.' Was Bono part of that deal? 'There were conversations but whether he would have or not in the end I don't know,' concludes Kerr. 'I'm glad it didn't happen for a number of reasons; I think ultimately the club has been in good hands with Dermot Desmond, but I'm as curious as anyone to see where we go from here.'

As our interview draws to a close, Jim reflects on the controversy surrounding Celtic's recent spat with the SFA, undoubtedly a divisive topic among the support. In Europe Celtic have certainly suffered from some horrendous evaluations, but what do you do when the man responsible for some rotten decisions against your team is a major fan of your band and is desperate for an autograph? 'I was listening to a Glasgow phone-in the other day and there was a Celtic fan reading a catalogue of refereeing disasters against Celtic, he got to the end of the report and it dated back to 1891, so this is nothing new. The worst one for me was the last Manchester United v Celtic game at Old Trafford where we got beat 3–0. Simple Minds were playing a few shows in Belgium and there was this particularly big show in Antwerp with an orchestra the day after the game. The promoter said to me: "Listen, there's a few dignitaries: politicians and some sports people would like to meet you after the gig and get a photograph, is that okay?" Of course, we said, "No bother". So the game is played and the referee is garbage – Celtic had two clear goals chopped off and Berbatov hits two clearly offside and they're counted. My pal comes on the phone and he's doing his nut, then my da phones and he's cracking up. Charlie and I then pick up the paper and there was the referee, Frank De Bleeckere, admitting he and his assistants had called it completely wrong and that he was absolutely disgusted with himself. Charlie and I are sitting there bewildered, having our breakfast and calling this guy every name under the sun saying what we'd do if we got a hold of him kind of thing. That night this guy comes in, big tall man with an attractive wife. I heard there was a Belgian cyclist coming so I thought this must be him. The only thing was the guy kept saying he was really worried before meeting me and he kept this up. I thought did someone tell him I wasn't a nice guy or something? So he starts talking about Glasgow and I said: "How do you know Glasgow?" He said: "I worked there as a referee; I was the referee at the last Celtic game." So I'm like, "Get him out the fucking door." There was a bit of kidding on, he was a big fan of the band and he knew we were Celtic boys obviously, so I said to him, "Autographs and photos are no problem but listen, next time you referee a big Celtic game, remember me and Charlie because you owe the Celtic one . . . right?" He was having none of it.'

While the future remains unclear, Kerr insists that a new generation of fans must be willing to engage with the reasons for Celtic's formation and the mechanics of what has made the club what it is. 'Listen to me,' he says, 'Celtic are nothing without that history, without it, who cares, it's the same with Barcelona, that's what makes them more than a club. If you take that away Celtic are just another team. I can't stand it when Celtic don't play in the green and white: firstly because it's beautiful, and secondly it's just not Celtic without that, it tells you where we are from. You can't vary the Celtic strip; it's in the name. We are not an Arsenal or Tottenham Hotspur, what are they? We are Celtic. My son is London born and bred, when he was young he asked me if he could support Arsenal, I said: "It's a big, big choice son and you'll no get any pocket money from me." He's eighteen now, he phoned me recently and I asked what he had been up to. He told me: "I've been in the pub watching Celtic, the fans are brilliant and this is a fantastic thing to be part of." He found his own way rather than me forcing him.

'I think it's important to remember that this is a great, great story, one that should never be forgotten. Immigrants come to Glasgow and to reinforce the community they decide to start this football club; so far so good. They make it a charity; even better. You take that away then you are just another club and then who cares? Every time the ball goes in the net I cheer for my da, my granda, my great granda and all my relatives that go right back to when the club was formed. There are not a lot of things in the world like that for me anymore where I feel that same sense of connection, and I think I speak for a lot of people in this. You might feel distance from the political party you grew up with, maybe the religion you were brought up in, even your ex-wife but your team is your team. It's like the old school tie; Celtic is our version of that. I'm a Celtic man and I have no problem with you if you are not; I just feel sorry for you if you are going to play against us.'

CHAPTER FOUR ROAMING CATHOLICS

CELTIC HAS UNDOUBTEDLY one of the most unique histories in European football and perhaps the most captivating aspect of that history is that the ethics and ideology, on which the club are founded, remain visibly important. The tension and pull between the temporal and spiritual are essential ingredients that have shaped the culture around Celtic since its formation. It's undoubtedly an anomaly to walk into a modern football arena and see banners displaying a poignant and graphic passion for a historical narrative, that doesn't necessarily always relate to the success of the club:

One million dead

Three million dispersed

The descendants remember

Next to it is another banner that features an image of Brother Walfrid with the quote 'a football club will be formed for the maintenance of dinner tables for the children and unemployed.' Also featured at games is the same representation of Walfrid in his religious attire, with a large cross around his neck holding a Bible with the words: 'Culture Heritage Identity History' emblazoned across it. Significantly Walfrid's mission as a Marist Brother, the French order whose name derives from a particular devotion to Christ's mother Mary, would have wanted to implement his order's instruction to educate and he would undoubtedly have approved of such banners today that lead to a deeper understanding of what Celtic represent.

Arguably Celtic's religious identity remains something of an anomaly in the modern game but the concept was common-place in the Victorian period. Many football clubs around Britain and Europe were formed as leisure clubs for working men to have an outlet away from the daily grind of industrial life. Others, such as Hibernian, Everton, Manchester City and Tottenham Hotspur, were founded by religious organisations to bolster people's faith. The mainstream understanding with Celtic, however, is not always a positive one. Type the words 'religion and football' into any search engine on the internet and you'll likely find a number of articles tying Celtic to Rangers in relation to sectarian violence. The negative perception is a cross Celtic supporters have had to bear, just for preserving their identity.

The original vision that Brother Walfrid discussed with board member John McLaughlin, when he was an organist at St Mary's in Abercrombie Street, was about mobilising the community through a sport that was popular with the host culture. In a time where global, consumer or secular principles are the standard ideals in modern society, Celtic and its supporters celebrate a founder that gifted them an inclusive, non-violent philosophy that did not involve the ideals of achieving power or wealth. As a Christian, Catholic and

Marist Brother, Walfrid held aloft the anti-establishment character of Christ along with gifting Celtic an egalitarian philosophy and value system that bled into the very lives of the support. It's these principles that have preserved Celtic's identity for a vast number of its supporters around the world who refuse to be fashioned by the mainstream. They reject Celtic's original traditions being watered down or polluted. Social ills such as sectarianism and racism are at least two views out of kilter with the roots of why Celtic formed and the typical nature of the support.

Walfrid's vision and Celtic's story has found its way into the narrative of Catholic Europe among football supporters who have embraced Celtic as their first team. Travelling to Rome I arranged to meet secretary of the Italian Celts, Roberto Longobardi. I was eager to find out how the ideas and philosophy around the club had shaped the lives of its supporters in Italy. Coincidentally my hotel turned out to be in the Quadraro district of the city where Roberto and his girlfriend live. It's a highly politicised working-class quarter and synonymous with anti-fascism. During the Second World War it was an active resistance stronghold, which the Nazis referred to as 'the hornet's nest'. The contempt in which occupying forces held its citizens lead to a raid by the German army in April 1944. The area has since been recognised for its struggle, solidarity and courage in the face of fascism by the Italian authorities and was granted a gold medal for civil merit.

Entering the city, a Celtic top in a sports shop window heralds my arrival as I pass by priests smoking cigars, Mods in pastel colours riding mopeds and tourists struggling with backpacks. At my journey's end I meet Roberto, proudly sporting the green and white Hoops and a scarf with the diagonal cross of St Andrew and the Italian tricolour. The Italian Celtic fan greets me with a hug and orders a bizarrely popular bottle of Tennent's Super for us both while explaining his introduction to the club we support: 'Trying to describe my love for Celtic is not straightforward at all. I have to do it often here with my Italian friends when they say "Scottish football is nothing." I tell them Celtic is not a simple football team, for me Celtic is not about football; it's something other, something more. I support Celtic for religious, political and historical motives. In Italy it is different speaking about religion. I am a Catholic Christian but I have a free mind. I don't believe everything the church is doing but I believe in God, I just don't talk about it all the time like the Americans do! It's political because I am against fascism, racism and sectarianism and these are problems all over Europe. I know about the rage against Scottish Catholic people and in a similar way Italian culture has a problem with racism, it creeps into many areas of life in a very subtle way.

'I did not begin to support Celtic for political reasons because I was very young when I became aware of the team. Subbuteo is very popular here and the first team I played with was Celtic because I was so attracted to the Hoops, visually I think it was so important, it's a powerful and beautiful image because it symbolises more than just a football top. I also read an article about the Lisbon Lions in an Italian magazine and how these eleven Scottish players changed the game, the first British team to win the European Cup and beat this mighty Italian team Inter Milan. The story made my heart fly and I realised what an important team Celtic was; it was more than football, there was a Celtic spirit, which I began to feel. My brother and I would look for the Celtic result in the newspaper every Monday, the history of this club became very important to me and who I am, they reflected something that tied up the kind of person I hoped to be.'

As with the New York Celtic supporters, the internet became an essential tool in unifying the Italian supporters' club members scattered around the country. Forming in 2007 from the ashes of two previous clubs originally set up in the early 1990s, Italian Celts first gathered together in Finnegan's Irish Pub to watch Celtic v Rangers. The sense of passion and camaraderie at that first event led to more being arranged in Italy and an organised trip to Scotland. Significantly Roberto talks about a sense of responsibility when first becoming part of the travelling support: 'Pulling on the Hoops and being part of a group you feel the importance on your shoulders, conduct is very important. If you know Celtic's history, you understand that these are good motives to form a football club; you feel it in your spirit. It became a dream to travel to Scotland and visit Celtic Park. I wanted to see where Brother Walfrid walked and I wanted to see where this club was born, where Walfrid helped the poor and the unemployed Irish people going to Scotland to survive. This is what inspired my passion; this is the reason I am a Celtic supporter. When I wear the Hoops I hold my head up high. Win, lose or draw, it is not important to me because I am a Celtic supporter through and through, nothing can change that. The Celtic philosophy is the reason; and it runs very deep. To explain to some of my friends here, it is very difficult. I find even some Celtic fans have forgotten the spirit of solidarity and charity. For some it is just about the team winning but for me it is very different because the spirit of the club and the team run parallel, you cannot pull away from the philosophy, the charity and the way of life. Celtic is not just a football team and we shouldn't be just ordinary supporters.'

Roberto's relationship with Celtic was formed from a distance, pre-internet. He talks about the club, in spiritual, philosophical and cultural terms, making a significant impact on his formative years. Celtic reflected his politics and values. In Rome he became part of a Celtic community of supporters. The experience of going to see Celtic, meeting the home support and engaging with the culture in the East End of Glasgow has only added to the mystique and a sense of reverie: 'In September 2008 we travelled from Italy to Glasgow with twenty-seven members to watch Celtic v Aberdeen. I can't think of any experience I've had similar to this in Italy or in my life. We walked into the Gallowgate and the neon light began to spread along the front of the Barrowlands, it was a very atmospheric night. We decided to go to a concert by Charlie and the Bhoys in memory of Tommy Burns and the money raised was for a cancer charity. It was a journey into the Celtic spirit, something deep inside begins to stir. It was a very emotional experience with people of all ages, men, women and young people all singing Celtic songs in solidarity. People would just keep buying us drinks.

'The next morning we went back to visit Tim Land, Bar 67 and Bairds Bar, the locals understood that no other team would motivate us in this way. We walked to St Mary's, you can still see the reason why Celtic was formed, that intense poverty still exists, you see the poor, the needy and you understand why a victory for Celtic is a victory in the lives of the people living in the area. Celtic is about trying to make a change in that culture. We played football with some other CSCs, who are friends of ours, and some young children from the Gallowgate, we swapped scarves and flags, made friends and sang 'Willie Maley' together.'

Undoubtedly, part of what attracts Roberto to Celtic is the narrative; the history has become part of his own story in Italy. He recounts his experiences in Scotland or his local club to friends who fail to understand his passion for the club. What Celtic stands for gives Roberto context in his own community. His heroes are players that are widely celebrated for their skill but what is equally important is how they have conducted themselves as Celtic players and as people: 'Yes, you could say I am a romantic, my Celtic heroes are the players who don't use their talent to get rich. I pick the players who love the green and white: Tommy Burns, Jimmy Johnstone and Johnny Doyle. All of these players came from poor backgrounds; their dream was to play for Celtic. On film you can see the great desire and tremendous skill of Jimmy Johnstone but you can also feel how much the man loved to play for Celtic, he didn't want to play for anyone else, he would have played for Celtic free of charge.

'On the Sunday morning after the game a few of us travelled to the grave of Johnny Doyle in Kilmarnock; it is important to remember this kind of player, a man who was a fan like me and you. If we lose that then we lose what the club is really about and what made it great in the first place. I've interviewed and met a few Celtic players for our website and you get to know the guys who love Celtic. I talked with Massimo Donati and I would say he was not a good example of a Celtic player for two reasons. He doesn't understand the spirit or the history. There is a strain of Italian players who only think of the money and it drives their whole life; it's like an obsession, it robs them of the hunger for the game and the will to win. Donati asked me why I was a Celtic supporter. I told him, "because this history is fantastic, the atmosphere is the best in the world and the supporters are the best in the world." I told him Celtic supporters want to see players that want to play for our club and that understand our history. I asked him various questions about the Green Mile, Barrowlands, the supporters, Charlie and the Bhoys. He was vacant; he just shrugged it off and said: "I don't live in Glasgow." This was very difficult for me because, of course, I want to see Italian players at Celtic but I want them to know what this club is about or it's no good. Look at the situation with Paolo Di Canio, the only thing worse than a mercenary is a fascist. I have read the story about Di Canio also discovering Celtic through playing Subbuteo; that might be true. The problem with him was not his passion or ability, it was a political problem, he is a fascist, he soured his relationship with Celtic fans by giving the Nazi salute when he was a Lazio player. He has also in the past suggested a support of fascism. I think if you are a fascist, racist or sectarian person you would find it impossible to support Celtic. Di Canio destroyed his relationship; it is shameful. Enrico Annoni is a different story; he is a very good servant and popular player for Celtic. He was part of the team that stopped the ten-in-a-row, he brought character and he wasn't afraid to go out in Glasgow to meet up with other players; he had a good relationship with the city, which is how it should be.'

Italian maverick Paolo Di Canio left Celtic fans with some unforgettable memories. In many ways he was typically Celtic, in that he was a skilled, passionate, entertaining goal scorer – among his goals were the cool penalty against Rangers in the quarter-final of the Scottish Cup and a transcendent right-foot volley against Hearts at Parkhead. Though most of all, Celtic fans remember the sublime first touch with the left foot, the right foot over the keeper's head and the right foot finding the net against Aberdeen for the goal of the season at Pittodrie. Despite being temperamental, difficult and ultimately unable to break Rangers' dominance, memories of Di Canio's 1996–97 season remained ultimately positive until his political beliefs emerged. Roberto explains it well: 'Something like this might not matter to fans of other clubs but to Celtic fans it is very important for many reasons. If we don't care what someone represents it's very dangerous. Barcelona became the voice and expression of the Catalonian people when General Franco tried to suppress the culture and stop the language from existing. Real Madrid was

Franco's team, the team of the conformist. Barcelona is the team of liberty and of the free. You can understand why a player like Cruyff with his long hair, his attitude and style of play went to Barca. We shouldn't celebrate Di Canio's time at Celtic because the Nazis and the holocaust still hang over us; it is the worst memory in our recorded history. It makes sense for Celtic fans to wave Palestine flags because of the struggle over land in Ireland and because of Bloody Sunday. That political situation has changed over time but the issue is complex, there are many Jewish people who are not anti-Palestinian or sectarian, they feel no connection to what Israel's political powers are doing. The answer is never black and white, but neither is it terrorism and violence, these have no place in football or the world. Ninety-nine per cent of people in my country say they are Catholic Christian but they have no philosophy of helping their brothers, helping the poor, I hear racism against African people, against the Eastern Europeans. All I hear is, "it's not my problem, so what, I can't help." To be this cold is to be dead. They forget about the Italians, their own relatives that had to leave Italy to survive only a few generations ago for the Americas, Australia and other parts of Europe such as Scotland. The Barga Celtic supporters remember this and have a very strong bond to the west of Scotland, the singer Paolo Nutini's family come from Barga. Like the Irish, the Italian people left to find work and survive. Many have come back but they don't forget their history, it becomes part of them, the culture between them remains very strong.'

Undoubtedly the Italian Celts remain proud of the cultural

Scottish-Italian links and can also boast of Giovanni Moscardini, the only Scottish-born Italian to play for Italy at international level. They've also kept an eye on Italian Kilmarnock midfielder Manuel Pascali who agreed to exchange his kit with Shunsuke Nakamura in aid of the club's charitable work. As Roberto explains: 'Our supporters believe it is important to carry on the tradition of charity. We have a friend of the club in Switzerland, also a massive Celtic fan, who works in south east Thailand, trying to build a community while working with poor farmers and the children in the area. Manuel Pascali is a good man, he helped us by swapping his shirt with Naka and we auctioned it off. This kind of activity is very important: it is our reason for being, it's why Brother Walfrid started the club and we will carry it on, as Celtic fans we carry the torch; you do what you can to help others. There would be no Celtic without this idea and you are not Celtic if you are not helping those in need.'

Outside the Pacific Fish Bar on Edinburgh's Mayfield Road stands Michael Pacitti. The street – with its bank, baker's shop, chemist and newsagent – retains a typical suburban image reminiscent of The Beatles' 'Penny Lane'. Under a cool Edinburgh dusk Michael is sipping cappuccino in the nostalgic neon of his chip shop lights. He greets me behind a sharp black quiff with typical Latin enthusiasm. His presence and the shop itself inject a gallusness into the area. Wrapping the suppers, Michael is often found in hot debate with his customers usually about Celtic. 'I've had a few punters tell me where to stick my supper, I know I shouldn't but when it comes to Celtic I can't help it.' Behind the bar his wife is reading Barack Obama's *The Audacity of Hope*. For many Italians in Scotland the memories of immigration are still fresh. Like the Irish, leaving behind famine and poverty, many Italians suffered racist and derogatory indictment at the end of the nineteenth century. Often running chip shops and cafes the Italian immigrants suffered for the Sunday opening of ice cream parlours. One article that appeared in the *Herald* in 1907 entitled 'Ice Cream Hells', included the comments of a Mr D. Drummond who suggested the parlours were 'ten times worse than the evils of the public house.'

Significantly it was support of Celtic Football Club that offered many in the Italian community something that was 'Scottish' but at the same time represented something of their own culture. Irish Scots felt represented by Celtic because of the club's Irish history, while many Italians associated with the club's Catholic heritage. Says Michael: 'My father came over to Scotland in 1962 with one suitcase and a broken handle. It took him about a week to get here on boats and trains. He only had about a fiver but he borrowed some money and bought a dingy chip shop from a very old woman and built it up from scratch. I was born in Easter Road and as a small boy I would see all the Hibs fans passing my window on their way to the game, many people have said to me you should be a Hibs fan. I don't think Celtic fans buy into that way of thinking because support of this club is something very different from any other team in the world. If I had to explain it, what drew me to Celtic was the religious aspect. "Keep the faith" has become a Celtic saying and it's a powerful one, you can literally feel your spirit rise when you say it. I come from a family with a strong faith, we went to chapel every Sunday. When I looked at the charitable roots of Celtic, the founder Brother Walfrid and something as simple as seeing fans wearing the crucifix, this was the culture I came from, yet I was also engaging with the country I was born in. I wanted to be a part of life in Scotland too.'

Perhaps it's the charism of faith that James MacMillan described earlier, the Catholic gifts of faith and grace that attract supporters such as Roberto and Michael to Celtic. Undoubtedly, Celtic have a significant number of fans globally who are not born into supporting the club. Support of Celtic often means breaking away from traditions and accepted ways of thinking in the family. Michael explains the story of his family's football traditions: 'My dad was a Juventus fan, but he is from the Lazio region and like me he didn't support his local team. Some of my uncles and family in Italy are Lazio fans, there was an element of having to explain myself not just to my Italian family but also to my friends at school who were Celtic fans, they also felt that I should have been supporting an Italian team. As a boy I wanted my first football top to be Celtic, my father was reluctant. He said: "What . . . Celtic? It should be Juventus, why do you want to support Celtic?" I explained that Celtic was an immigrant story like ours, as an immigrant you have to make a go of it against the odds, you have to be better than the best and Celtic was that to me, it represented me. I was Italian but I was also half Scottish. Celtic is a story of doing the best you can with what you've got, that's why Stein is the best manager these islands have ever seen. He should be embraced by the whole of Scotland not just Celtic fans. Pulling on the Celtic top for the first time you are hit with a tremendous sense of pride, it's a very important thing for a young boy.'

While the west of Scotland's Italian immigrants largely hailed from the Tuscany region, many of the east's Italian families travelled from Lazio. From an early age Michael would travel to his ancestral home for long summers in the historic Monte Cassino region outside Rome where football was a way of life in his family. 'Most of the Italians in Edinburgh who run the many restaurants, chip shops and delicatessens are connected through family, but it was particularly back in the old country that my family began to become fascinated by Celtic. Of course they knew about the European Cup win in 1967, but what they were less familiar with was the Old Firm derby. This fascinated them because ninety-nine per cent of people in Italy are Catholic; the idea of having two religious cultures opposed to each other was both captivating and shocking to them. That two sides of a city would split, at least for ninety minutes, really pulled them in. You could see their eyes light up when I would tell them about the Celtic v Rangers games I was going to.'

The 1970s is often viewed as a dark decade of struggle, a time of strikes, power cuts, riots, bombs and the rise of the far right. Popular culture undoubtedly drew on the darkness and anger of the times with films such as *Clockwork Orange*, *Straw Dogs* and *Scum* along with the punk rock movement reflecting the restlessness and public agitation. Michael's memories of this era remain strong: 'It was at the end of nine-in-a-row that I started going to watch Celtic. Growing up in the 1970s and coming from an Italian background you would relate to Scorsese films or *The Godfather* or characters like Rocky and Tony Manero: tough, cool urban characters . . . but we also had that with Celtic and that was an experience that was much closer. You weren't sitting in a movie theatre, your heroes were right there in front of you and who was cooler than Lou Macari or Kenny Dalglish? Even better than that you had Danny McGrain and McGrain had character, he's still my hero now, I don't think there is anyone in the modern game you could compare him to.

'As a young lad there were other factions coming into play, a friend of mine started to paint a lot of political graffiti, life was hard for many people that came from a working-class Catholic background. Some of my friends who were Celtic fans started to identify with the IRA and the hardcore Republican politics in Northern Ireland. I knew it came from desperation and a need to blame or identify with something, but I had a problem with it. It felt very dark and I began to wonder, "Is this what Celtic is about?" It felt out of touch with the spirit that attracted me to Celtic as a boy and something about that side of the culture was getting into some nasty stuff whether it was songs or the graffiti, there was just a really bad feeling coming through it all because we were only young lads. I couldn't contemplate Celtic with violence and bloodshed, I felt disappointed that some of my friends had chosen to go down that road with it; it seemed to become a defining factor for some. If my father thought I was involved with guys that were into this stuff, believe you me I would have been black and blue, it didn't fit with my faith and my culture. Eventually I asked my dad what it was all about and he explained it to me, at that point I thought maybe I don't want to support Celtic any more . . . but that was wrong. I was very young trying to understand the culture and that experience shaped the guy I am today.'

Significantly it was in practising his faith that Pacitti worked out his social dilemma. 'Celtic to me is about family and religion and there is a strong community aspect. My first confession really put it all in perspective, I walked into the confession box not really knowing what I had to say or do with a very daunting feeling. I was no clean tatty and had been borrowing the odd penny from my father's till to pay for games. I thought of it as a kind of loan. I used to tell my father I was round the corner at a pal's house when really I'd be heading through to Parkhead whenever I got the chance to watch Celtic. After confessing I said to the priest, "Does this make me a bad person?" I told him that I planned to make the money up. He just turned round and said: "I'm a Celtic fan too" and he asked me what I thought about Kenny's goal against Hibs that weekend. That's Celtic, you wouldn't get that with Juventus or Motherwell; Celtic fans have that extra something, there's a sense of fun but there's also a com-passion and character, no other fans in the world have that.'

Significantly Pacitti often felt he had to prove his Celtic credentials to fellow fans, particularly the hardcore support that travelled home and away. 'I was the only Italian in the village if you like and I used to work in the chip shop at night. There was one lad who used to walk past shouting abuse while giving a certain hand gesture. I remember it got especially hot when Italy were in the World Cup. One day this guy walked past in a Celtic top. I thought I've got to reason with this boy, he's a Celtic supporter. The next time he passed the shop he shouted in with some derogatory comment, so I jumped over the counter, made a run for him and grabbed him. I said: "I just want to let you know I'm a Celtic supporter; we're on the same side." He came into the shop and apologised to my father, we sorted it out and he became a friend of mine and we ended up travelling to the games together on a minibus with a bunch of other lads in Edinburgh from mostly Irish backgrounds. The banter was good but usually involved me proving my Celtic credentials a bit more than the rest because I was Italian.

'The same thing would happen in the shop, the banter was good and if you dish it out you've got to learn to take it. The worst one was Mo Johnston signing for Rangers; everybody knew I was a big fan of his and so I took some stick over that. I think the worst thing about it was that he really hurt the fans; you don't say you only want to play for Celtic and then sign for their biggest rivals; you don't do that to people in life. He'll always be remembered for that which is a shame because he had been a very passionate and entertaining player for Celtic.'

As Michael pulls the shutter down on the Pacific and switches off the neon lights, he reflects on what feels like the end coda of classic comedy *Open All Hours.* 'There's been so many good memories in the chip shops over the years, I had to move down here from Tony's on Ratcliffe Terrace after my father passed away, too many memories. I remember us watching Celtic v Juventus together. He was supporting Juventus; I felt so proud of Celtic that night. There was also the time Charlie Nicholas came into the shop, a true Celtic great . . . but the UEFA Cup final still goes down as one of the big highs, although I have to admit I was so low on the night of the final that I had to shut the shop, the one and only time I've done that. It was one of the best seasons in living memory because we knocked out some class teams along the way and it was a turning point, we hadn't been that good since the 1970s. In the shop I was betting customers the odd bit of small money or a fish supper here and there. I was coming out on the winning side of course right up to the final. I was literally willing certain customers to come in so I could give them some stick. My father was in Italy at the time on family business so I was disappointed not to go to the match. I remember waking up in the morning thinking this is my day. I was frying in the shop and watching the game. After we lost the shutters came down. I was so frustrated and I knew I wouldn't be able to hide my emotions if someone came in and tried to wind me up. I just wanted to go home. A few did come in and twist the knife but some came back and said: "Hey Michael; you were the better team, the way you went about it." Rangers may have won the treble in Scotland but everybody knows, even the Rangers fans, that deep down that it was our season. We put Scotland back on the map in Europe. The thunder really was back, it was exactly what it was like when I was a boy, there was a confidence that hadn't been there since Stein was manager.

We put up with insults from other teams, dirty play and we handled it the Celtic way. We may have lost on the night but when I look back now all I feel is a sense of victory.'

CHAPTER FIVE I WAS A CELTIC SUPPORTER!

SUPPORTERS FIGHTING AMONG themselves can be as intense and uncompromising as sparring with their most bitter rival. This notion was referenced in Ken Loach's film *Looking For Eric*, in one scene that takes place in a local Manchester United bar during a Champions League encounter. Spleen, a character played by stand-up comic Justin Moorhouse, marshals the arguments for wearing an FC United shirt against a barrage of abuse from fellow supporters. The protesting Red suggests Manchester United should be fan-owned in a similar vein to Barcelona as opposed to 'corporate fat cats' earning from a club that was set up by working-class railway workers. 'Just look at the car park' the character hotly protests as his opponents become more aggressive. Their arguments sound like the fears of men who deep down are aware that their lifelong investment in a football club is being abused and milked for all its worth with very little coming back in return, or worse lukewarm supporters with very little feeling about anything in particular. The challenge mounts further until one supporter admits he simply can't afford to be at the game; Spleen's point is perfectly demonstrated.

As Jim Kerr suggests it's socially acceptable to change

most things in your life except your football club. But what happens when your club begins to employ people who are out of step with the values on which the club was founded? What happens when a history, shared beliefs and a group ethos is exploited for the profit of a few? What happens when you don't like the style of play the manager employs or find it hard to relate to the mercenaries and millionaires on the pitch that don't engage with the club's history or the fans? What happens when a divide appears on the terraces?

Until the mid-1960s Irish Catholics may have shared the family values associated with British conservatism but the open expression, language, linguistics and humour of that culture were vastly different from the routine repression prevalent in Scottish Presbyterianism and wider British life. In many ways the Irish made Scotland less British and more Scottish. Post-1950s Britain has ultimately become a more individualist, secular and middle-class society and those values continue to be resisted by the majority of the Celtic support. The club is built on the idea of a faith-based, working-class community serving others, something to which you can belong and, through it, can contribute in some way to wider Scottish society and the world. These identifiers have preserved the identity of Celtic fans in Scotland as the wider culture has shifted beyond recognition. Celtic fans in a variety of forms and experiences often struggle with obvious identifiers such as being described as British, Irish or even Scottish depending on the context. Being described as a Celtic supporter carries a clearer cultural definition that transcends the difficulties and possible negative associations with any of the above.

Born in 1963, Pat Nevin grew up on the backstreets of the East End of Glasgow raised by a progressive, devoutly Catholic family of Irish descent. It was a pivotal time for the community who were living in some of the worst housing in Britain, in many cases homes purpose-built for Irish migration workers had remained beyond their function. The housing situation created the famous slums and subsequent clearances which led to the construction of high-rise tower blocks. The Catholic faith and the success of Celtic were an essential focus for this community of Irish Catholics. Nevin explains: 'My mum is gone now but she was a fanatical Catholic and my dad remains a strong and practising Catholic. I believe in the Christian attitude of helping others, where Christianity meets socialism and all that side of it, but I'm not a believer myself. The ethics remain and I like the idea of taking care of other people.

'My dad still lives in the East End of Glasgow, it was a rough place and there was a lot of gang fighting. My family were working class but were hugely proud, even in the most difficult of circumstances. On our street in Easterhouse not many families were as pushy as mine when it came to education and sport. My dad trained every day of his life; no one else was doing that. You were encouraged to speak as correctly as you could; it wasn't about being posh, my dad was from the Garngad – the idea was progression.'

Undoubtedly, the Nevins used sport and education as means to progress for reasons beyond basic self interest: 'I think there are other things deeply built in to it all such as, "Don't do anything unless you do the best you can." My dad would never get angry with anything but if he thought you weren't doing your best or trying in a game ... that was the end of the world. My daughter is a badminton player and I have the exact same attitude. I'm not a pestering dad but if I think she's not trying she just gets a look. I let her know that it's disrespectful to the opponent, to the coach and to me and her mum for having us travel the length of Scotland and Britain. You need respect for what you are doing, not just respect for yourself but everyone else involved in what you're doing.'

On joining Chelsea in 1983 Nevin quickly became part of a potent strike force that helped raise the club from a legacy of lacklustre football caused primarily by a catalogue of financial struggles. The winger's individual style and gifted ball control along with the jinking and foxing of opponents with a gallus drop of the shoulder or twist of the hips made him an enduring favourite at Stamford Bridge. Nevin believed in entertainment whether it was 'a big mazy dribble' in his own half or a sudden and dramatic change of pace. The crucial dichotomy was to win and entertain while doing it. This reliable team player who set up and scored goals with ease was shaped by watching Celtic's nine-in-a-row winning team, particularly Jimmy Johnstone, and Brazil in the 1970 World Cup. 'If you are going to learn through that, you are going to learn the purest of football skills and entertainment. The other important thing to remember is it's not showmanship for the pure effect of being a poser. That kind of football is there to entertain; it's not for you, it's for the viewing public. I got to see Jinky and Bertie Auld play for Celtic in the late

1960s and early 1970s. I watched Kenny Dalglish breaking through, Lou Macari and George Connolly. Danny McGrain had skills in a full back I've never seen since; you'd literally watch him dribble up the line. Watching a player like Brian McLaughlin, we thought he was as good as Kenny but he picked up an injury and was never the same. Davie Hay was world class, he was a left back, Stein moved him to the midfield and he would literally be everywhere. It was devastating when he got the injury that forced him out the game.

'Kenny (Dalglish) became a better player at Liverpool but he was never as exciting to watch as he was with Celtic. That's what happens, it happened to me. When you're young you'll do anything, it comes straight off the top of the head; it's absolute pure joy. As you develop you learn what works and what doesn't so you begin to do the right thing; you do the professional thing but what goes with that is a bit of the raw power and energy in the discovery of it. I used to have an agreement with my dad, he came to watch every game I ever played bar one, which is pretty impressive when you consider he lived in Glasgow and I was in London. For him coming to the game, I was to do something totally outrageous for his enjoyment and so it often ended up I did a big mazy dribble for no reason other than having a bit of fun and trying to entertain. If we were 2–0 up, I'd do it all the time. My manager at Chelsea John Neal would say, "We go three goals up; do what you like son."

'I've got to know Bertie Auld and we talk about this, he would be a bit arrogant but I couldn't do that; I don't mind beating someone in a really fancy way with an outrageous flick though. It's a bit of a tightrope but with Celtic there was always a point to what the team were doing, there was always a goal at the end of it. I hated Leeds United with a passion because they would do a number of passing moves just to embarrass the opposition. To the outsider it might look like the same thing but it's not; you need to have respect for the team you're playing.'

Nevin didn't just take the dichotomy of winning and entertaining the fans with him from the East End of Glasgow to west London, he also carried the Celtic ethos at a time when racism, violence and far-right politics were second nature on the terraces at Stamford Bridge. Coming from an Irish Catholic conclave in Scotland and moving into a hotbed of racism, Nevin was in a position to challenge: 'I had this concept of why I followed Celtic and it had nothing to do with religion or the historical stuff. My family feel Irish but I've always felt Scottish, so it's not that. One of the things was a political ideology that was firmly on the left. Certain clubs have a distinct philosophy and Celtic is clearly one of them. I was politically aware, I was a Celtic supporter and I had joined the Anti-Nazi League as a student in Glasgow, that was all there before I moved to London.' Nevin immediately struck up a rapport with the hardcore support at Stamford Bridge. Twice player of the year he became a Chelsea hero alongside team-mates Kerry Dixon and David Speedie for his knack of setting up as well as scoring exceptional and entertaining goals at the most crucial point in the game. Despite being told to keep his head down the then teenager revealed his public disgust on hearing an unrelenting swell of menacing and racist abuse directed towards Chelsea's first black player Paul Canoville. 'I remember I was called to do the press conference after listening to this from the fans, I was only a kid at about nineteen but I wasn't having our supporters boo a Chelsea player because he was black. I told the press that I wouldn't be talking about the game but I did tell them I was disgusted by the Chelsea fans for what they were doing, which I believe is the first time that anyone stood up to it. People might say today anyone would do that, but this was in the early 1980s and nobody else at the club was saying anything. I just did what any kid from my background in Glasgow would do in response to such blatant bigotry. The papers understandably went mental with the "Nevin slates Chelsea players" headlines. The chairmen and the manager said: "You're not a politician; you're a footballer." Their attitude was "We back our players quietly." For the next game I told the players he's not walking out on his own; they might boo us but I don't give a shit. So Kerry Dixon, David Speedie and myself walked out beside Paul . . . and the Chelsea fans sang his name first. I don't get that emotional but it was that moment I realised you can have an effect and there were a few tears in my eyes.'

Following Celtic home and away, growing up in Glasgow and relating to a club and a culture that expressed political optimism, undoubtedly Nevin must have felt a wave of insecurity about the far right frequency among the fans and, allegedly, some players at his new club? 'Chelsea do have that tag but it's a tiny minority, everywhere we went our fans would out-sing anyone whether it was Barcelona in Europe or Newcastle on a wet Monday night; there would always be 12,000 fans wherever we went and that only reminded me of one group of fans – Celtic's. They were noisier than everyone else. I understand there is a feeling between Rangers and Chelsea because of a certain day in 1985 and I was there but they should have gone for Celtic because I believe Celtic and Chelsea fans are much closer in the way they follow a team and they have the passion of a big travelling support. There were some nutters but they didn't care about football or support the team. I know that because I got to know the fans well, I met a couple of right-wing thugs and I told them what I thought about them. They didn't know anything about what was happening in terms of the football, which was being used as a vehicle for the fighting, in this case right-wing politics. There were one or two players I knew that were racist and one was in the team and I despised him for it. I'm not going to name him but read Paul Canoville's book and work it out.'

Aside from his skill and getting stuck in against opposition players, Nevin literally got in among the home support, travelling with them to games home and away. The experience led him to the centre of English working-class culture in the company of cockney wide boys, Second World War veterans, fathers and sons, thugs, pensioners and the unemployed. He became part of the community around the club exactly as he had done watching Celtic; inhaling grease, onions and petrol from burger vans while being herded onto freezing trains with the windows smashed in amid wild negotiations about the more dazzling moments of the game. 'I knew what it was like to travel and if I wasn't playing for Chelsea I'd be following Celtic across the country. I'd be in Aberdeen getting stuck on trains and getting treated crap by the police because I was a travelling fan. I hadn't lost the memory. I would travel with the fans to keep my dad company, so I wasn't getting the team coach. We would be on a journey from Huddersfield sitting on the worst train in the world. The conditions were terrible and the fans were treated like cattle. You'd be waiting on a train for hours at one in the morning but I felt comfortable with that. When you get into football, your heroes can lose their mystique but I never felt apart from the fans, that relationship has never changed because I've never left that world. My dad only ever missed one game in my career. He worked on the railway and would get the train on a Friday night or even get up at five on a Saturday morning and get the train home again the same night. If we were playing Plymouth or Portsmouth he would get an overnighter, he would be there. He would write a diary of the people he met on his journey; my dad's got a book in him so he has.'

The more Nevin reflects on his family the vowels get stronger and he occasionally reaffirms his sentences, the memories clearly shining up a Glasgow Irish dialect, particularly when reflecting on his early life and a burgeoning Celtic career that was never meant to be. In his youth Nevin crossed paths with a clutch of players who would come to define something essential in the character of Celtic during the 1980s. Unquestionably there were the understated pragmatists and journeymen who quietly knitted everything together but it was also an era when players, at least for a short spell, would blaze an incomparable trail on and off the pitch. An idiosyncratic example, Nevin was somewhere in-between, never pushing forward or believing it was possible to play for Celtic but displaying an outrageous skill on the pitch typical of the greats. True to character he steered clear of the champagne lifestyle often associated with flair players blessed with indisputable skill. It was while playing for Blue Star against Celtic that Nevin attracted the club's attention scoring a hat-trick in a 4–1 win in 1975. Significantly he didn't sign the S-form for another two years, Sean Fallon only securing his name after Dundee United's Jim McLean expressed an interest. 'When I signed for Celtic as a boy it was something to be proud of but I didn't tell anyone at school; it wasn't my personality to do that. After I signed the S-form I won player of the year, the winner the previous year had been Roy Aitken and after me it was Paul McStay. After that you expected to sign as a Celtic player but they said I was too small, that I would never make it and I said "fine". I wasn't upset because I never thought I would be a Celtic player; I didn't think they would sign me. I was studying for my A-levels then going for a degree; that's what I wanted to do. I told my dad and he was a bit disappointed. After about three or four months I chucked playing football completely and just continued to follow Celtic as a fan.'

Another of Nevin's contemporaries was Everton manager Davie Moyes who considered leaving Celtic for Arsenal, fully accepting it would be a step down after the north London club had articulated an interest in him. Those Celtic players eager to make football their career often reluctantly moved to lesser clubs, perceived or actual depending on the personality. In fact Moyes signed for Cambridge United after a stint in the Celtic first team that had secured him a Scottish league medal. The dream of regularly playing for the club, particularly for such a practical player, seemed outlandish. Despite his obvious skills Nevin fell into the same category: 'I played alongside guys like Roy Aitken and Davie Moyes when I signed for Celtic boys. Before I signed for Celtic I knew Mo (Johnston). We played in different school teams for Glasgow and later played together for Scottish schools; we hated each other.

'I'd obviously crossed paths with Charlie (Nicholas) a few times; I admired him as a player but he was the antithesis of everything I was. We went to London the same week he signed for Arsenal and nobody would know that because "Champagne Charlie" arrived in a blaze of glory and everybody knew about it. I would have been at a gig somewhere in east London. I remember playing Arsenal halfway through my second season down there. The Arsenal fans loved Charlie; they didn't need much encouragement. He scored to go 1–0 up; then I scored with a diving header and got brought down for a penalty and we won the game 2–1. The next day I got all the headlines and it felt very strange. The press were like "the new Charlie" and I told them "Don't bother calling me that"; nothing against Charlie but we are not the same style, even now when we do analysis, we're opposites. It's not that he's bad; we're just different.'

It doesn't take much to imagine Pat Nevin's halcyon days being played out at Parkhead in green and white. Celtic even strived to rectify their oversight by trying to sign the player three times during his playing days down south. On the third occasion, during his spell at Tranmere Rovers, Nevin rejected the bid believing it was from Bolton Wanderers. He remained a Celtic fan throughout his career and it was always his intention to return home. That feeling was accentuated by an emotional visit to Parkhead while playing for Everton. 'I never get nervous. Even if the game was on telly in front of millions, I really didn't care but I was nervous for one game in my life, a friendly with Everton at Celtic. My nerves kicked in big time because this was Celtic, it was the Jungle and it was my team. They gave me a great reception and it was fantastic, that was always my concept of the fans. That was the other reason I followed Celtic; the fans, the vibe around the club, Celtic was cool. It's well known my passion for music and the two things went together, musicians use instruments to bring out the beauty of the song, footballers do something similar with their skills. I've always wondered why so many bands and musicians are Celtic fans, going right back to the first indie bands in Glasgow in the early 1980s: Altered Images, The Bluebells, Simple Minds and the Postcard bands; there has been this strong connection between Celtic and indie or rock 'n' roll bands. Is it that the schooling is different? That the Irish spirit is more about song? I think then it becomes a really philosophical question.'

In the fifteen years that Nevin was away from Scotland the game changed beyond recognition. In 1989 a space rocket carrying the Astra 1A Satellite would beam Rupert Murdoch's Sky channels back to earth changing British football and social life unrecognisably. The Taylor report, published after the Hillsborough disaster, forced the government to examine infrastructure and safety after a series of tragedies in the British game including the Ibrox disaster in 1971 where sixty-six supporters lost their lives. The proposals in the report would change the relationship with the ordinary working-class supporter in a number of ways, the major shift being the recommendation that grounds become all-seated. During the 1990s football attracted a larger middle-class support, adopted aggressive marketing campaigns and embraced a stronger corporate identity. Nevin undoubtedly witnessed these changes playing in England where perhaps a shift was more pronounced but, aside from the culture, the actual game was changing. The idea of entertaining fans became more peripheral and certainly secondary to grinding out results.

'I came back up to Scotland around 1997 and signed for Kilmarnock,' explained Nevin. 'I was well into my thirties by this stage. In terms of Celtic it was at that point something in me began to waver. It was especially around the John Barnes season and then during Martin O'Neill's time. For me personally it all felt very different, after the Jungle had gone I sat for some games and it didn't feel right. Now that might not have been the fault of the fans but when the Jungle was removed parts of the ground began to feel a bit corporate, particularly the East Stand. I know I'm not the only one who felt discomfort with that. A lot of people I spoke to felt the same. The first major thing was Martin O'Neill's team, I was playing against them and I thought: "I don't like this style of football." I was convinced the fans would turn against it because while it might have been successful, it wasn't Celtic. I've had discussions with Martin O'Neill about this and he disagrees strongly as is his right, but I used to play against his teams and it was power-play football. It's not Wimbledon but it's a slightly more sophisticated version of that. Look at the defenders Balde, Ramon Vega, Valgaeren – all forceful well-built guys, the same with the forwards such as Hartson and Sutton. It was big beasts of men everywhere you looked with an advantage of height, power and physique. I remember thinking "These guys score from a lot of corners." I have to say that Henrik Larsson is not part of this discussion because he's special, he's different and fair enough. But, aside from Henrik, I had a specific view of what Celtic's style of play was and this wasn't it.

'It's nothing against Martin because I admire what he did and I admire his team, it was a successful time for the club. If you think about the money he had to spend a purist football team would never have got as far and would never have been as successful, they probably wouldn't have got to Seville or won those league championships. The thing is this: it just wasn't a style that I liked. I wondered why the Celtic fans were not complaining. Years later I discovered that a lot of fans that I spoke to were enjoying the success but not necessarily the football. There's something wrong when a talent like Moravcik can't get a game, he was a beautiful player and fabulous to watch but he couldn't fit into that team. I'm not saying build the team around him but I watch football to watch guys like that. Agathe had the pace and Thompson was a fantastic crosser of the ball but I thought, "Would I pay money to watch this?" '

Nevin spent the last two years of his playing career at Motherwell, retiring from the game in 2000. He was then appointed chief executive at Fir Park leaving the post in 2002 after the club went into administration. By his own admission he never struck a rapport with the North Lanarkshire club. At the same time Nevin felt a distance growing between himself and Celtic: 'When you're playing against Celtic and Rangers in Scotland you realise that the big clubs get the decisions. Celtic fans won't like me saying that but if you ask anyone else on the planet, they'll say it's true. When I was on the board at Motherwell I invited family and friends to sit beside me for a Motherwell v Celtic game, they watched the game through Motherwell's eyes and they all admitted the team got nothing. You don't look at it through anyone else's eyes when you're in the Celtic end, I had always looked at Celtic as the anti-establishment team and I related to that but when the team you are playing against gets all the decisions it starts to feel closer to establishment than is comfortable. Again that's not Celtic's fault, just like it wasn't Martin O'Neill's fault.'

In the face of globalisation Celtic Football Club and its support have affirmed their Irish roots in a variety of expressions. From the many supporters that travel from the north and south of the country to players such as Robbie Keane joining the club for a loan stint in 2010, these are undoubtedly commitments and affinities shaped by an affectionate, historical and romantic connection that suggest a shared sense of perspective and values that travel across the Irish sea. To an outsider the connection between Celtic and Ireland is often viewed as a spiteful expression that relates to glorifying the tragedy of the Troubles in the north of Ireland. This has been informed by a minority of supporters who sing songs or chant in relation to the Troubles for provocation or to assert a misguided association. To the majority of Celtic supporters this relationship would be an alien concept. Undoubtedly one of Brother Walfrid's reasons for creating the club was to assert the survival of the Irish after leaving a land of famine and political unrest. Though it wasn't his ambition to import songs that related to bloodshed and violence, sporadically these songs have appeared.

Nevin recalls: 'When I was in the directors' box at Motherwell I heard the IRA chanting. Maybe I'm naive or I hadn't been around for a while but I thought that had gone twenty years before. I was never into it. I'm not into the idea of killing people for a concept, I've never been that way inclined, so it came as a real punch in the face. Now that was purely travelling support, I couldn't imagine a scene like that at Celtic Park. People are allowed to have their views but I couldn't sit beside that. The Motherwell fans were singing some very dodgy stuff; I'm not backing them up. I've heard the Rangers fans sing some disgraceful things while I was there. A bit of me started to think: "I want to boo you down." There was still a bit of a Celtic fan inside of me saying . . . this isn't good enough; this isn't Celtic. I was really angry and I still think the vast majority of Celtic fans would boo those responsible for it down, if that expression was an Irish traditional song, that's fine. The problem is when it jumped from Irish traditional to sectarian and IRA chants . . . that's an embarrassment. This was just about the time my son got into football, I was living in the east coast of Scotland by this time and he wants to start going to games. He loves Chelsea but he wants a Scottish team . . . by that point I thought it's not going to be Celtic.'

In arranging this interview in the aftermath of the last Old Firm match of the 2009–10 season, Nevin is approached by a number of Celtic supporters spanning generations for an autograph or a quick word. Even though there are a number of former Celtic players in the media section they all flow towards Nevin. While his switch to Hibs is widely acknowledged, it's not something he's fully explained until now. 'The thing that is vitally important to understand is I have not suddenly started to despise Celtic Football Club and everything that Celtic stands for I now hate, that's not what this is about. Hibs were always my second team and after watching a few other clubs I decided to take my son to the East Stand at Easter Road. The game hadn't even started and I thought, "This is it, hundred per cent." The strange thing was how much it felt like home, everybody around started talking about Iggy Pop and David Bowie. I thought; this is what I remember. The feeling in there was precisely what the Jungle felt like in the 1970s; it was grotty, the toilets were prehistoric and it was back to the wee benches. It was just a bunch of working-class guys that I would hang about with who immediately accepted me and my lad. I just looked about thinking, I love this.'

Home is rarely a fixed position for Celtic supporters. It's a fluid idea and displacement is common. Ireland often represents home in the spirit and the mind, there is a sense of belonging to a place as opposed to feeling ownership over where you live or were born. This is a phenomenon common in diaspora communities. In Catholic life a sense of home is also an other-worldly concept giving many a multi-dimensional outlook on their sense of belonging. Home in Scotland for the Celtic support may also mean that the generations born, living and contributing to that land have a feeling for that country and culture also. Like an expat returning home from a period of exile, Nevin found his home among the Celtic support had changed beyond recognition. The changes in Celtic had not been subtle and the shift in ideology on a number of levels was too vast for him to reconcile.

While Celtic and Hibs are the only two British clubs with an obvious Irish identity, examples of solidarity would be few especially for two clubs that play against each other competitively in the same league and cup competitions. Had there not been a miraculous twist of fate in which Nevin accepted a bet over an LP to play for Gartcosh against Clyde, resulting in him being picked up by Craig Brown, it's probable he would have remained a Celtic supporter, living through the changes. For Nevin something of what Celtic represented, the nostalgia and feeling around the supporters has remained at Hibernian. 'What takes you to where you sit? I've not moved for six or seven years and we're halfway up the back of the East Stand and in synch with the eighteen-yard line down at the south side . . . precisely where I stood in the

Jungle. There's got to be something in that because I was looking for that feeling I had before, I wanted to find it again and oddly enough I found it at Easter Road. I couldn't find it at Celtic Park. The ideology of the play was another pull for me, looking back these last few years they go the other way and they over-play. If they go 6–2 ahead then a bit of sense is needed in the central midfield. It's a battle of dichotomy but that's why I support them. Even if you leave Easter Road after getting beat 3–2 you see people walking out happy, they turn to their pals and say "Did you see that flick?" or this goal or some silky bit of skill. That's why I got into Celtic. It relates to why I love football because it's about the sheer entertainment. You wouldn't get that at Celtic Park now and I understand why.'

As a Celtic fan Nevin witnessed 'Turnbull's Tornadoes', the Hibs team that challenged Celtic for the Scottish league in 1974 and were runners-up again to Rangers the following year. It was a particularly intense period of competition between two clubs who shared a reputation for all-out attack. Celtic lost the Drybrough Cup to the Easter Road club both in 1972 and 1973, Hibs challenged Celtic a further three times between 1969 and 1974 in the Scottish League Cup, with the Hoops winning twice. The games produced some memorable score-lines with Celtic beating the Leith team 6–1 in the 1972 Scottish Cup final and 6–3 in the 1974 League Cup final. Like a number of Celtic supporters around the time Nevin developed a soft spot for the Edinburgh squad's style of play. 'Both teams were very similar, if Celtic hadn't had the Quality Street Gang at that point in the 1970s Hibs would have been a very successful club because they were challenging Celtic for everything. They had a powerful squad that featured the likes of Pat Stanton, Alan Gordon, Joe Harper . . . the list goes on. The third strip I owned was actually Hibs but even weirder than that my first strip was Chelsea, especially because it was blue; my second strip, of course, was Celtic. One of my favourite memories from roughly around that time was sitting on the back of a coal lorry with my dad on the way home just after we had won the league title at Easter Road in 1977.'

There's undoubtedly a romantic connection with the time for Nevin and while that Celtic strip may have ultimately taken third spot in Nevin's affections his essential memories connected to family, lifelong friends and the world he grew up in are undeniably Celtic. The positive values around the club from the mid-1960s until late in the last century are partly what define Nevin today. 'The 5–1 win against Kilmarnock in the League Cup is a moment every Hibs fan has savoured. It was one of those happenings that transcended the game in the last few years. It was one of the most moving moments I've witnessed at a football match. I knew how much it meant to John Collins because his dad had just passed away. When Dougie Donnelly said, "Let's go outside and enjoy this with the Hibs fans", it was a brilliant moment of television because it was just as the supporters began to sing along to 'Sunshine on Leith'. The cameras caught the passion and the connection that the Hibs fans have to this beautiful song. You also see John Collins with the tears streaming down his face.

'Brilliant as that was it doesn't beat ten men winning the league.' In the throes of what became known as Britain's 'winter of discontent' Nevin made his way to Parkhead for one of the most mythical evenings in Celtic's history on 21 May 1979. Earlier on in the month Margaret Thatcher had risen to power as piles of rubbish and dead bodies mounted during refuse and gravedigger strikes, factories closed and hospitals were picketed. Bad weather had interfered with a number of fixtures in the Scottish league and Celtic had to win this rescheduled Monday night match against Rangers. Although some grainy black and white footage exists, the memories of this particular night were reserved for the fortunate 52,000 who had defied both a transport and a television strike to see the fixture. 'The build up to the game was particularly spectacular. It was Celtic's last match of the season. I was about fifteen years old and had bought my mate a ticket for his birthday. I remember all the tension of the time and that day very clearly. I remember feeling how important it was for Celtic to win as I took my usual seat dead on the eighteen-yard line. Everything happened: Rangers took the lead, Johnny Doyle was sent off and I had known Johnny a bit from my time at Celtic boys. I can still see Murdo (MacLeod) banging that fourth goal into the top corner to make it 4–2 and realising that we'd won the league. I was in a throng of Celtic fans going absolutely berserk, as you can imagine. After the game we couldn't get to Carntyne station after being corralled away from the Rangers support. I lived in the East End so we walked from the Jungle to Bellgrove, there was a squad of us walking together and singing all the way home.

That was the best day I've had at a football match. I'm not religious but that's the closest I've came to that kind of experience.'

CHAPTER SIX ITALIAN AMERICAN IRISH SCOT

The poets down here don't write nothing at all, they just stand back and let it all be.

BRUCE SPRINGSTEEN, 'Jungleland'

THE GLASGOW GALLOWGATE resembles something of a Catholic feast day prior to kick-off. There's a vital flow of energy released from the Celtic tribe on the road to Paradise that takes the form of conversational burrs in an array of Scottish brogues, chants and songs that revel in the glory of an ever-present past and an endless procession of vivid Irish colour. In the bursts and clusters outside landmark pubs such as Bairds, the green and white masses are smoking, debating, guzzling chips and wildly gesturing as rock 'n' roll blasts out onto the busy Glasgow thoroughfare. The steady concentrations of Celtic themed institutions, such as the infamous Tim Land to the notorious Bellgrove Hotel, have all become essential markers on the Green Mile. The vibrant street scene often features tour buses outside the famous Barrowlands Ballroom where acts of the day frequent the varied drinking establishments prior to showtime; alongside them some of Scotland's cinematic illuminators such as Peter Mullan have been known to drink in the Martin Scorsese Celtic Supporters' Club, better known as Hielan Jessie's. The famous Barras market fuses with match day patrons and a main drag that features an assortment of traders, antique hunters, bargain shoppers, prostitutes, tourists, drunks, feral adolescents and pensioners who all flow into the Celtic mass. There are scenes of random and abstract madness such as one local entering a pub in his 'goonie' and slippers looking for a wayward relative, while spouting varying degrees of psychobabble. A regenerated Glasgow hasn't neutered the visceral animation of Gallowgate life, which retains a distinct neighbourhood feel as well as serving up an unadulterated slice of inner-city living. The backstreets defy global trends, fashions and opinions, in these sandstone tenements and public houses.

Irish America has been an essential marker in Scottish life for generations. Inside Bairds the familiar JFK towelling is a symbolic image I've witnessed in countless Catholic homes, visions of Irishness in movies such as *The Quiet Man* and *Gone with the Wind* were romantic markers and projections of progression. My friend John Fitzgerald Kelly would refer to his Aunt Grace, the family all claimed Maureen O'Hara, Bing Crosby and Spencer Tracy among countless others as their own. For the generation that followed there was a massive shift between those shaped by the Irish aspirational values depicted in the Golden Age of Hollywood and a new vitality and urgency reflected by postmodern cinematic authors such as Scorsese and Coppola. The characters that dotted the urban sprawl of the Gallowgate were in many ways a mirror to the lives that were depicted by Italian-American cinema, particularly representations of urban working-class males in films such as *Mean Streets*. The strong Irish influence in Little Italy, a once Irish area, and the various representations of

Irish and Italian-Irish characters in Scorsese's work all displayed nuances of those Irish Scots, through body language, linguistics, views, beliefs, attitudes, estimations, behaviour and speech. This representation of a people grew stronger with Peter Mullan's *Orphans*. Watching the film's premiere was something of an epiphany that led me to write about representations of Catholic life in Scottish and American cinema, such was the impact of seeing character representations that truthfully reflected the culture. This experience was only usually reserved for going to Mass or a Celtic game.

For many Catholics, mainstream Scottish culture often represented rigid, grey standards; a well presented world of conservative values and ideas. When writing a series of articles for the *Celtic View* that sense of association with America became more significant. The painter and writer John Byrne told me: 'Some of the family went to America. I had cousins coming to visit from New Jersey. We'd get sent food parcels after the war wrapped with comics and newspapers. In Paisley there was a shop, Yankee Mags, where the owner used to travel to America to buy DC comics. There was such a great smell in that shop; it just smelled of America. My grandmother's house in Cardonald was the centre of it all. There would be lots of talking, playing cards, singing and regaling each other with stories tinged with a nostalgic yearning for Ireland.' Glasgow-born Hollywood actor Tony Curran also recounted: 'I went on a three-week holiday to New York and stayed, working for six months, the red hair, the accent, there's a whole Irish community that look after you. My friend Sean Conaghan's brother Tommy came over from New York to see Celtic stop Rangers winning ten-in-a-row, his mother grew up in Brooklyn and his father was born in the Gorbals. Tommy is like a 250-pound bear of a man, he's got a strong New York accent and he turns round and says to me: "Tony, I swear to you I gotta see the game today." I told him that I tried everything, there was just no danger, but his attitude was: "I'm coming in; I'm gonna be there." Tommy walks in and flings someone some money to get in on the fly but because he's a big boy he gets stuck on the turnstile. Apparently a cop just grabbed him and went "Up the stair you" . . . we were all in tears at the end of the game.'

The 'Scotch-Irish' is an American term used to describe Ulster Scots during the colonial era. Significantly they predominantly had little or no Scottish or Irish roots but were often a variety of other races: English, Welsh, Dutch or French, united under their Calvinist beliefs. Although originally describing themselves as Irish, the Scotch was introduced to separate them from Irish Catholic famine survivors in the nineteenth century. Undoubtedly it has taken generations to establish a confident Irish-Scot identity that has held the same clout as familiar terms such as Ulster Scot or Irish American. The Irish, who settled predominantly in Glasgow, Edinburgh, Dundee and Coatbridge, were a people trying to work their way out of poverty, the effects of famine and the related problems of self confidence, mental illness and heavy drinking. The common motivators in the culture were: industrial work, the Catholic Church, Celtic Football Club and Catholic representations from Hollywood cinema.

Irish American and Ulster Scot are easily understood and

popular terms for the concerned mixed-race cultures.

Coatbridge playwright Des Dillon effectively highlighted the use of 'Irish Scot' in an argument over Scottishness between a Celtic supporter and Rangers fan in his play *Singin' I'm No a Billy, He's a Tim*. Dillon, along with a new generation of confident world-class artists, musicians, writers and film-makers such as James MacMillan, Andrew O'Hagan, Richard Jobson and Peter Mullan, have all articulated the vitality in this blend-culture that is inextricably linked to Celtic. In doing so they challenged a sightless media and wider culture that struggled with manifestations of Irishness that weren't presented as first generation. All of them in one way or another shunned what James MacMillan described as the 'keep your head down' philosophy. Since the mid-1990s Irish Scots have begun to establish themselves globally through the arts and media, a new confidence has been fed that for many years was only nourished under the banner of being a Celtic supporter. Members of this fledgling movement have, for a number of reasons, often been forced to choose between Scotland and Ireland but undeniably our contrib-utions, struggles, ethnicity and very lives have been significantly tied to both cultures.

This ethnic survival has been tied up in stories, for many Irish Scots any reference to Catholicism, Celtic or Ireland in the context of Scotland is devoured. On 19 July 1993 *New York* magazine featured a cover story entitled 'Tuesday Night Fever'. The piece predominantly focused on a recently divorced Glasgow couple, drawing attention to New York's upcoming karaoke scene. The feature by Irish American journalist Suzanne O'Malley concentrated on John Manfredini whose life story reads something like a cross between *Mean Streets, Rocky* and *Saturday Night Fever* in its portrayal of an Irish-Italian American trying to make ends meet as a boxer and singer while working construction on the streets of Manhattan in the late 1980s and early 1990s. Manfredini was something of a local face, as well as a living embodiment of this transatlantic Catholic exchange between Glasgow and New York City. His story mainlined straight into Scotland's Irish diaspora culture and particularly around Celtic, which ultimately proved to be a stronger pull than New York.

John explains: 'I was born in New York City on 2 June 1967. My father was Sicilian, a good-looking typical Italian guy. He was a hairdresser working in the Astor salon off Broadway. Carlo Manfredini was one of the top hairdressers in New York; he would have the best clothes, eat in the best restaurants and drive brand new Cadillac cars. He had the absolute best of everything. My father owned racehorses and would travel to races all over the east coast of America. He never took me to games or to the park; it was always the track. He was what is known as a degenerate gambler and had some connections with the Mob in New York at that time. He was like a showbiz personality, living a millionaire's lifestyle; he had a lot of charisma. I remember on one occasion we met up with the actor Anthony Quinn, this kind of thing was normal for my father.

'My mother was born in Donegal and had to leave Ireland for Scotland after her mother passed away. She was brought up by my aunt at her home in Hill Street, Glasgow, which is where she stayed until she turned 17 and moved to New York City. My mother worked as a waitress at a cafe where Carlo was a regular customer and a big tipper, he kept asking my mother out but she wouldn't entertain him, eventually they went out on a date and they were soon married. I was born at Elmhurst Hospital in Queens, although we lived in Thompson Street in Greenwich Village for a long time.'

By the end of the 1970s John's mother was making plans to return to Scotland as her husband's mobster life: gambling, womanising, domestic violence and drug taking had all taken their toll on a strained relationship. Although completely absorbed in Sicilian culture and with a strong New York identity Manfredini was about to relocate to Scotland and absorb his Irish roots for the first time. 'My mother had enough of New York and my father's lifestyle, my dad had never hit me or my sister but on the last occasion when he returned home having run out of money, he decided to beat my mother, not for the first time, so I hit him over the head with a baseball bat. Although I went straight to the police, when I returned home my father had gone, at that point my mother had enough, for her it was time to go home.'

John, then aged twelve, was reluctant to go to Scotland having just been accepted into Julliard, one of the most prestigious performing arts schools in the world. 'At that point I was the lead singer in a glee club and was about to go to this great school with a world reputation but my parents split up and my mother wanted to go home, so we headed back to Scotland. I was then signed up for St Ninian's in Kirkintilloch and from that moment I was a "Yankee bastard".

Scotland didn't have a very high opinion of Americans, thinking we were full of ourselves. I just absorbed myself in the Irish culture, I travelled to Letterkenny to see the ancestral home with my uncle and I threw myself into Celtic. Home and away, week after week, I sang every song and went to every game. The best way of understanding that culture and life in Scotland was going to see Celtic and that's what happened. My uncle Chris, who today is a Labour MP, took me to see a Celtic v Hibs match in March 1980. It was a memorable game for all the right reasons, we won 4–0 and I got to see the last Lisbon Lion, Bobby Lennox. He scored as well as Johnny Doyle and Frank McGarvey.'

For Manfredini Scotland represented a seismic shift in lifestyle and culture. Italian and particularly Sicilian culture had been the dominant influence on his life in New York. Scotland and its Irish diaspora represented a new beginning; despite a reluctance to forgo his opportunity at Julliard, John decided to support his mother and embrace this new way of life. 'I'd been to American football and baseball games: Giants Stadium, Yankee Stadium and Shea Stadium. Soccer hadn't taken off in America at that point, I think I might have heard of the Cosmos but that was it. When I walked into the Jungle for the first time what hit me was that I had never seen people sing at a game with such passion. The energy was relentless. In this sea of green and white you'd hear Irish songs, rebel songs, there was a lot of drinking, guys pissing where they stood, shouting, swearing, laughing and carrying on; I couldn't wait to go back. After the first time I begged my uncle to take me again, I'd get lifted over the turnstile, he'd warn me to stay away from the railings so I wouldn't get crushed and that was it, I was now a Celtic supporter. This was a way of embracing the Irish side of my heritage. My uncle bought me my first scarf and introduced me to all the songs like 'Hail Hail', 'You'll Never Walk Alone' and 'Willie Maley'. I became friendly with a guy called Liam McPhail who was a relative of the former Celtic player Billy McPhail. I was getting into a lot of fights and Liam started to look out for me. When I started going to games on my own, away from the supervision of my uncle, I got a bit more rebellious leaning towards the Provo songs like 'Roaming in the Gloaming', 'Soldier's Song'. I'd sing anything travelling on the specials from Queen Street and Central and would always be draped in a tricolour. Towards the end of that period I went to prison after a night of stupidity that involved drinking and fighting. I hadn't even turned twenty.'

While John was in Scotland his father's fortunes exacerbated. Without his wife and family, his health deteriorated rapidly and he lost his job in the salon. For that and a number of reasons John and his girlfriend Jacqui decided it would be best to return to New York. 'My father was dabbling in drugs. In terms of the Mob I don't know how deep he was involved but it was deep enough. He had a stroke and had to have his leg amputated above the knee. After that he wasn't in any condition to cut hair and so he moved in with my grandparents at Gerritsen Beach in Brooklyn. My grandmother was a seamstress and she was the head of the family; it was very matriarchal like the Irish family in Scotland. I knew I'd find my father around the Kings Highway area of

Brooklyn. When I got there it was very sad; my father had long white hair like Father Christmas and was begging from a plastic coffee cup. His downward spiral had only got worse.'

John's time in Scotland had opened up a new Irish community and network of friends in New York, particularly in Irish bars, Celtic supporters' clubs, boxing gyms and construction sites: 'If you're Irish or a Celtic fan you could get yourself in work. It might be a bricklayer making $100 a day or a labourer; you'd find someone that could help you, not in the Mickey Mouse theme bars but in the old working men's pubs. It might often be illegal but you're still living the dream, making money that you could never make back home. I knew guys that would go to New York on holiday and end up staying. There was always a place to crash and work on offer; it was a ready-made community. Outside of that life New York can be a lonely place. People live for themselves and do it at one hundred miles an hour."

Manfredini worked on construction sites during the day, and once again New York fed his dreams of returning to a singing career, performing at the city's fledgling karaoke clubs in the evenings. His new connections also opened the door to another aspiration: 'I got to know a guy called Brendan Mitchell who worked at my dad's hair salon. Brendan was born in Paisley, his father died when he was very young and his mother brought him to New York. He'd never been back since he was a kid, so I'd tell him all about my experiences: the scenery, the life and, of course, the football. Brendan lived in a Puerto Rican area and had that whole look with the red bandana and a little goatee beard; he looked like he walked off the set of West Side Story. One day he took me to box in a place called Gleason's, which was once the axis of the Irish fight world in New York. It was there Brendan said: "C'mon let's lace up the gloves and try you out." He was shouting: "C'mon, hit it", "Again" and would make all these noises, he kept asking me to throw punches over and over again. He then turns round to me and says: "I think you could do something with this." Brendan became my trainer and I'd be at the gym every day. The place had an atmosphere, it had been at the core of boxing during the golden age of the sport and all the greats had trained there from Jake La Motta to Muhammad Ali. Around that time Mike Tyson was training at the gym and so was Buster Douglas who knocked Tyson out in 1990. One day a well-known boxer from Glasgow came into the gym. I went over to say hello and he told me to "fuck off", a real arrogant bastard of a man. I asked if I could spar with him and, not doing what you're supposed to, I hammered him; he didn't get one punch at me. I just turned round and told him I was the guy that said hello earlier and walked away.

'Another confrontation I remember was with the Puerto Rican boxer Hector "Macho" Camacho. He used to get called gay but he was just the flamboyant kind, dressing up like he was in the Village People. He was the most arrogant boxer you could have ever met but the Puerto Ricans loved him. He pulled up outside the gym in a red Ferrari one day and told me to get the fuck away from his car, so we squared up. At that point I had a flashback to street fighting in Glasgow and thought I could give this guy a Glasgow Kiss. You should never get too close to someone fighting in Glasgow because bang, the head comes down and it's all over. That was just how it was among the boxers; there was also a lot of division and bigotry over religion such as the fighters who were with the Nation of Islam, it would either be that or some kind of ethnic rivalry. Mike Tyson was on the rise but he wasn't like that, he wasn't rude to other boxers but in the ring he was an animal, his focus and fitness were incredible. Outside the ring he was very quiet. It was clear boxing was his life-blood. It went wrong for him because of the money, the hangers on; he went down the wrong path. He just had an incredible presence at that time; there was something different about him that other fighters respected. Now it's different, it's very sad, he's a wasted man. We all have that rebel inside of us, no matter who we are in the world.'

In seventeen amateur boxing bouts John was undefeated with fifteen knockouts appearing in the Empire State Games and Golden Gloves boxing competitions, building up a following in the Sicilian and Irish communities. His marriage to Jacqui, which he admits was something of a 'marriage of convenience', ended in divorce.

Throughout the changes John's community was built around the Irish bars, something that was only strengthened by the satellite broadcasts of Celtic games in the mid-1990s: 'Some of my best times in New York and as a Celtic fan were at Rocky O'Sullivan's on Lexington Avenue. Going to watch the game every nationality would stop you and ask about the top. We would go for a drink the night before and get a lock-in for the game in the morning. There was a guy there called

McCafferty, he would bolt the door, shut the blinds and we would all be transported back to Glasgow for those few hours, especially in the winter when it got dark outside. It was like being back in the Jungle because it was full of guys from Glasgow or Edinburgh and Ireland all after the same experience. When I left the pub it was like being in the twilight zone walking out the front door to steam rising from the gutter, sixty-storey skyscrapers, yellow taxis and hot dogs on the corner. In the summer you could walk out into ninety degrees of heat.

'One of the best days was wearing the Celtic top going to the Giants Stadium to support Ireland against Italy. My uncle travelled over from Australia and we left on a double-decker bus from the Bronx. We got on at a local Italian cafe, I knew all the old guys who would sit drinking coffee, gambling and playing dominoes. They were confused when they saw me in the green and white, the shoulders start shrugging and the Sicilian dialects become loud and clear. There was some swearing in Italian because I had pledged myself to Ireland that day. When we got back after the match none of them spoke to me for the rest of the evening.'

Towards the end of the decade John decided to return to Scotland, aside from meeting up regularly to watch Celtic with fellow supporters New York had left him feeling alienated and alone. An accident with his hand had put his boxing career on hold, friendships had turned sour and his father had passed away. 'Things seemed to change after the feature by Suzanne O'Malley. I started to get recognised on the streets and then offers started coming in from trainers and various clubs who wanted me to be the resident singer. I had been performing at a place called Flemings on 86th Street. Suzanne O'Malley had got right into my background in Scotland: the boxing, the singing, she researched a lot of people for the piece but ended up focusing on me and that seemed to cause resentment. It all became a bit too much to handle. People have this idea of the American dream but it's very deceitful because life can take over. I fell out with Brendan who was my trainer and my best friend, my marriage had failed and my girlfriend had a miscarriage. These were all very painful experiences. I was then leaning on drink and eventually got kicked out my apartment in New York, which at that point felt like the loneliest place on earth. My friend Brendan in the meantime had died of AIDS, a result of drug sharing when he was younger. It was something in his life that caught up with him, I never saw him at the end, he was so full of life and that's how I like to remember him.'

Today John lives a very different life from his rise and fall in Manhattan. Unlike the portrayal of Henry Hill at the end of Martin Scorsese's *Goodfellas* who is forced to swap the Mob for suburbia, Manfredini is grateful and contented to be living a more moderate lifestyle in North Lanarkshire. Getting off the train at his hometown of Croy I hear the muffled strains of Thin Lizzy's 'The Emerald' pumping out his motor as he arrives to pick me up in a black 4x4. Outside Holy Cross in the chapel garden is a monument of Christ on the cross, across the street is an array of Celtic tops blowing dry on washing lines on a crisp spring afternoon. John takes me to a local bar-restaurant and orders double espresso. 'In Croy you practically know everyone, it's a staunch Irish Catholic mining town and there are a lot of Celtic connections in the area. My wife is a relative of the Celtic player Jimmy Quinn; that's one I like to boast about on the forums. Today I'm just as passionate a Celtic fan as I ever was. I have two season books and I never miss a game. My young nephew uses my daughter's ticket; I take the family. My relationship with it is different. When I hear the IRA stuff now I just cringe, I don't sing those songs, not because I'm being told not to, I just don't think it's right anymore. You still see the young guys singing them today or sometimes its guys over from Ireland; the difference is people don't tolerate it the way they used to. People shout them down and tell them to wrap it. I don't think it's an easy thing to do especially when you are sitting with your family but parents don't want their kids growing up with that, things have changed. For me it was something I grew out of and moved on from. I have the scarf dangling out the car on the way to the game, you get some abuse but I just give it straight back, that's about as bad as I get these days. I'm married now and have three children.'

Sectarianism was something John hadn't experienced in New York, in many ways it put his faith in perspective and strengthened his character. For the former boxer his Catholic identity and support for Celtic were inextricably linked: 'I was free to make the choice but what I struggle with is when I see young kids indoctrinated into a way of thinking. I'll always sing the folk songs and the Celtic songs, but even when Rangers come to Parkhead I won't sing IRA songs. I think that's something we want to distance ourselves from, when I sang those songs it was my choice but it was also my choice to stop and I think youngsters are put under a lot of pressure by people that should know better. I see the Orange Walks in Scotland and it's something I disagree with strongly, but that's what they want to express. What I don't agree with is when I see young children on the march. In New York my Italian family didn't really take faith seriously, you only went to Mass to keep your mother happy. In Scotland it's different. The majority of Celtic fans I know are practising Catholics, those beliefs are tied up with the idea around why the club was set up. I see the same guys at Mass going to the game. I've found that it's very important in Scotland and it's something I'm grateful for in my life. I go to Mass on a Sunday because my faith is something I strongly believe in and I would hope my kids will grow up the same way, although they will make their own choice. It's my hope for them.'

Negative press around the Catholic Church, the rise of secularism in Scottish society and anti-Catholicism haven't affected John's personal faith, in many ways the threats to his beliefs have only strengthened his Catholic faith and Christian ideals: 'You hear the stories of what past generations went through here just to practise their faith. The perceptions of the Catholic Church are bad just now because of bad priests and the abusers in the Church. It's important to understand that Catholics are just as disgusted by this as anyone else; it's despicable and they should be severely punished. Unfortunately the media always focus on the negative; in the interests of fairness we need to look at the positive work the Catholic Church is doing across communities here in Scotland. I do believe the Catholic Church is changing, we have a fantastic priest in our parish who isn't afraid to address the big issues. He's quite outspoken and when things got really bad in the media he thanked everyone for being there, his Mass is heaving on a Sunday morning now. Brother Walfrid is part of that legacy; it's a way of life that helps those in poverty and in need. It's very easy in life to sit back and condemn but what about getting out there and doing something about it and changing things for the better, that's what Walfrid did. Celtic is ultimately tied to a truth and a wisdom that passes from one generation to another. My son Antonio is only two years old but I hope one day he might be the first Scottish-born Celtic player with Sicilian and Irish blood running in his veins.'

CHAPTER SEVEN
WELCOME TO THE JUNGLE

Gallus
1: To be ethnically or culturally Celtic
2: Self-confident, daring, cheeky, stylish

HISTORIANS ARE SPLIT OVER the existence of the ancient Celts, some believing them to be a fanciful idea and even a divisive one because of their separateness from British identity. In his book *The Celtic Revolution* author Simon Young undoubtedly felt compelled, challenged and inspired to bring this tribal, romantic and much debated people to life in a historical tour de force which revealed a clan of head-hunters, warrior poets and tribesmen that conquered northern Europe and even defeated the Romans in a pitch battle. Were these perhaps the same Celts that St Paul preached to in the New Testament text Galatians? In Europe today this tribe has been digested into other races and ethnicities aside from the British Isles and France. Young argues that these wild men shaped the frontiers of Western civilisation, trading primal violence for religious zeal, bringing Christianity to Britain as well as shaping the romantic imagination and literature through their language, ethnicity and culture.

Of late there seems to be a glut of books on the Celts and the Irish that shaped the West but what of the Irish that fled starvation, oppression, famine and political unrest to strengthen Scotland's Celtic stock in the mid-nineteenth century? Towards the end of that era the creation of Celtic Football Club allowed a spread of ideas that related to ethnicity, religion and politics in an emerging and progressive class of people. Unlike Hibernian, which was formed exclusively for Irish Catholics, Celtic's ecumenical root has been an attractive option for people with non-discriminatory and progressive beliefs. Among Celtic's most celebrated figures today are Jock Stein, a Mason from a staunch Protestant background, and Johnny Thomson, a member of the Protestant sect the Church of Christ. Kenny Dalglish was the first Celtic player to have the kudos of a pop star yet he was also a Protestant who grew up supporting Rangers. Despite sectarian tensions in Scottish society, Celtic as an institution has proved that Scotland and Ireland's polar opposites can be united under the banner of Walfrid's vision of sporting excellence and the naming of the club was essential in uniting the many contradictions in the culture which worked together to build the club's success.

Some of the most important figures in Irish history remain romantically connected to both Scottish football and the culture of the game. Edinburgh-born James Connolly, a well-known Hibs supporter who played an important part in the team's formation, was also a key figure in the Scottish and American socialist and trade union movements before taking a leading role in the 1916 Easter Rising. Michael Davitt, who founded the Irish National Land League to assist poor tenant farmers in Ireland against landlordism, was asked to lay the centre turf at Parkhead in March 1892. He is also said to have been active in suggesting the name of Celtic. Significantly Davitt encouraged Irish migrants in Scotland to become actively involved in the politics of their adopted home and was a prominent figure among the Highland community and campaigner for the rights of crofters. An essential figure in the fledging Labour movement, today he is commemorated with a monument in the Lancashire town of Haslingden where he lived and was educated.

The socialist philosophy laid down by these key Irish thinkers with strong connections to Scotland was significantly bolstered by the start of the Great War. With Scotland providing more men than any other part of Britain, many of them Irish Scots, there was the birth of a radical new political awareness among the working class in the west of Scotland, an area that would become known as Red Clydeside. Due to the greater need for munitions and industry Glasgow became known as the Second City of the Empire, generating arguably the largest industrial capital in the world through shipbuilding and steel production. The war boosted the Labour movement and charismatic anti-war militants such as John Maclean and James Maxton were among those arrested for organising protests against the war and imperial control.

Of course the war had other effects too. In 1915 money hungry landlords raised the payments on appalling housing conditions, in turn this led to rent strikes. The post-war economy suffered further and was particularly hard for those in industrial jobs. Unfair conditions were the cause of a mass protest in January 1919, when over 100,000 people took to the streets of Glasgow to protest. The huge crowd clashed with 12,000 British troops, armed with tanks and machine guns. Among those arrested in what became known as the Battle of George Square was a melting pot of figures associated with the politics of Red Clydeside, including Manny Shinwell, a London born Polish-Jewish immigrant, and Willie Gallagher, the son of a Highland mother and Irish father. Perhaps the most famous anti-war protestor and supporter of the rent strikes was John Wheatley, a devout Irish Catholic strongly associated with Glasgow life. Wheatley pushed through the landmark 1924 Housing Act which finally made affordable housing available to Britain's working class. Today the John Wheatley College in Easterhouse is part of an essential regeneration programme in the East End of Glasgow and specialises in teaching English to new immigrants as well as offering vocational and academic studies to people from the area.

Political life has been an essential part of the social life of Celtic supporters and the melting pot of working-class life in Scotland has been reflected through the club's vast following since its formation. Betty Devlin was born in the year of the rent strikes and has been following Celtic since the mid-1940s, living through the vast social and political changes. 'My first visit to Celtic Park was on honeymoon. My husband Tom Devlin was a Catholic, he was born in Glasgow but his family relocated to Edinburgh. His father had also served on the Celtic board in the early 1940s; the club was in his blood. He had a place on the board at Celtic Park from the late 1940s and was director before he died in 1986. I met Tom in the mid-1930s at our local tennis club in Edinburgh. At that stage we were just dating. I didn't know about the prejudice against Catholics but I was about to find out. In Leith, where I'm from, a key member of the Protestant Action party, John Cormack, nearly cost my father the election, he was a councillor and senior magistrate in Edinburgh. Sir Andrew Murray was also a great friend of the family and he also nearly lost his seat as a result of my dating Tom. I took abuse for being a Catholic at Ibrox and even at Easter Road, even though I wasn't, but I was married to a Catholic and a Celtic supporter. I still have a tremendous feeling for the club. I'm still a Celtic supporter, it's been part of my life for so many years.'

For a generation born in Glasgow after two world wars, the great depression and industrial decline, a violent, dark and smog-filled past simmers with glorious Technicolor memories of stained glass windows in 'wally closes', the city splitting into two on the day of the Old Firm derby and the arrival of Dali's *St John of the Cross.* Two fragments of Glasgow's contradictory nature, as a working-class football capital and a bohemian European art metropolis, suggest a city that shuns elitism but allows a flourish of ideas on all paths where articulation and expression are a way of life. Today the 'dear green place' is a melting pot of ethnicities where the sons and daughters of the city describe themselves as Glaswegian first and foremost; such is the strength of character and personality spliced with passion and anecdotal patter. It is an architecturally idiosyncratic city bursting with theatres, artists, writers, musicians and film-makers. Glasgow is a cineaste's dream, which perhaps explains why so many baby boomers from the city and indeed Scotland itself have migrated into the film industry.

Film producer Peter Broughan brought the lavish $30 million epic *Rob Roy* from dusty libraries to cinema screens in 1995 – the film remains Scotland's largest production. The Glaswegian also produced the story of record-breaking Ayrshire cyclist Graeme Obree in *The Flying Scotsman* as well as working on John Byrne's classic television series *Tutti Frutti* and *Your Cheatin' Heart*. Broughan remains one of Scotland's leading professionals in the film and media business, a subject he also lectures on and teaches at a number of colleges and universities throughout the UK. His journey getting there is an absorbing one and it's fundamentally and profoundly connected to Celtic Football Club.

Peter explains: 'I was born in 1952 at Stevenson Street and baptised at St Mary's in the Calton area where Celtic came into existence. My earliest memories would be where the Gallowgate and London Road connect at the Saltmarket. My aunt had a newsagent in the East End, which they opened after a win on the Irish sweepstake. It was there that Johnny Thomson and Jimmy McGrory would come in to get their fags. My granny and grandad lived on the corner of the Briggait and the Saltmarket above the Old Shipbank Inn. My da and granda would go for a couple of pints and then go upstairs where my granny would be cooking tripe, which they would wallop back after the game.

'If you were trying to capture an image of what it was like going to a game it would look quite dark, the only colour would be the green of the Celtic scarf or the green and yellow of the tricolour; everything else would be very black and white, very smoky and there wouldn't be many cars on the road.

'My father had been a quartermaster sergeant during the war, serving in the King's Own Scottish Borderers. When he came back he worked in Boots but had to chuck it because it meant missing the game on Saturday, so he became a postman. I can't remember a time when I wasn't going to Celtic Park, my father took me from an early age. For my first European game I was about fourteen and there were five of us crammed into a Ford Anglia for Celtic v Liverpool in the semi-final of the 1966 Cup-Winners' Cup at Anfield. It was terrifying and amazing because this was in the days of the old A-road motorway. There was a blizzard going through the Shap, which was a village that linked the North West with Scotland until about 1970. All the way down there was an endless procession of cars with Celtic scarves and tricolours flying out of windows; it was astonishing. The greatest regret of my life is that I wasn't at Lisbon the following year. My father couldn't get time off work but arranged for me to go in a car with a couple of his pals, unfortunately they didn't want to take me when they found out I was only fifteen.'

For Broughan political awareness was an essential ingredient in the mobilisation of the community and had been for generations, it was something that couldn't be separated from the plight and outlook of the Celtic supporter: 'My grandmother, who was a Kelly from Ireland, married a Thomson, he was a founding member of the Independent

Labour Party. He survived the trenches and lost his arm in a forge. My granda was the generation that came back from the war wanting to make the world a better place. He came from a background of Protestant radicalism so I was getting it from both sides. I never felt separate from the Protestant community because we'd play football together at Greenfield Park although I went to a different school. Today I'm a socialist, I don't like the separation, but looking back St Mungo's was great for me, the schooling there improved society in this part of the world. It gave me an advantage in my so-called career because the Mungos was determined to educate people that wouldn't have got an education otherwise. The drive was to educate the fuck out of you and I used that to forge my way forward. We were all fuelled by the same working-class hero juice and we were all out to prove ourselves.

'Celtic were never far from your thoughts and you'd see some of the teachers at games, we would head to the Jungle with our school blazers and pitch up right in the middle where the steam would be rising off the pish in the cold damp air. The singing would often start with the Mungo boys, we'd make up the songs at school and then deliver them at the ground. In the Jungle you'd also see the gangs like the Shamrock boys from the Garngad and the Cumbie from the Gorbals.

'Travelling to the away games was an important part of the experience; these were the days when Perth was an overnighter. I would get the bus with my da and uncle Jimmy. To me the men on the bus were automatic heroes, mature and knowledgeable. They had all fought in the war and were defined in many ways by who they fought, who they fought with and who they fought for. There was camaraderie, you felt involved and a part of something, part of a cause and a fight, not in the physical or violent sense but a cause nevertheless.'

Just what the cause has been is confusing for the wider media who often chose to associate the mainstream of Celtic supporters with political extremism of a violent nature. This has somewhat masked the more common views expressed by Celtic fans. In November 2009, after the Remembrance Day game against Falkirk, journalist Rod Liddle wrote in the *Spectator*: 'What an unspeakably foul club it is, bigoted and filled with sectarian hatred.' As always these views of Celtic stem from observing a minority of supporters behaving in a way that doesn't represent the majority. Undoubtedly there is a political ethos among the support and historically it's been one that sits somewhere between Catholic or Christian socialism and non-violent left-wing radicalism. As the game and wider culture has changed, so have the values and traditions associated with the support. Broughan explains the situation as he sees it: 'I would never take exception to anyone singing a political song, but I hate hearing people shouting about Orange bastards. My attitude to that is, can't you support Celtic in a more positive way? There is also a peace process going on in the north of Ireland and it's really important that it succeeds.

'Today you see a lot of "neds". I'm a fifty-nine-year-old man and I can't be bothered with neds. I'm sure they are very misunderstood young people but I don't want to hear them spit their bile, poison and stupidity all over the place. A lot of people now just support Celtic because they are from Glasgow, maybe learning about the club's history could change that, the point being that they get socialised and civilised. If they understand some of the values and the history they might be reminded about what the club stands for. Today the vast majority are not interested in politics; it's a depoliticised generation and I don't understand that because politics are what controls your life. If you are not interested, then you are not interested in life; it's the fabric of reality. In terms of Celtic, that's where we come from. Today there's a feral thing around the support, I look around and see an alarming lack of human standards about the way people deal with each other which I find really depressing.'

Undoubtedly the Celtic support is not immune from the problems in modern society but in saying that the political dimension for a new generation of thinking supporters remains strong. Flags and banners from historically aware groups of highly politicised fans are among the most visible and vocal at Celtic Park today. The supporters themselves are often split by the appearance of non-football related flags, often from other countries, that suggest a human, political or social solidarity that connect to a variety of causes. Says Broughan: 'I find even the Celtic websites contain some very socially conservative debate that just toes the party line. A lot of that comes from paranoia and that's justifiable historically, but it's tended to produce an uncritical approach in and around Celtic, people didn't know how to object. I resigned from one organisation that should have been in the vanguard of protest, you still have that conservative tendency today but mixed up with that is a radical left-leaning politics. They are both part of the DNA because of the connection to the Labour movement in Scotland, which is part of the history in this part of the world. Celtic is still a part of that manifestation today. I think the Green Brigade have made a very public and sustained expression. A lot of it looks like youthful idealism. There's nothing wrong with that and I like some of what they are doing, but I'm more interested in connecting Celtic with the Jacobite tradition. If you look at who was behind the massacre of Glencoe it was William of Orange, these ideas pre-date Celtic but they are also part of its history.'

Significantly Broughan once thought about giving his life to the priesthood, an idea that came from a time when the Catholic Church held a significant importance among family, friends and the local community. Today, the information age has created a generation who look less to authority figures in both educational and church spheres; cyber communities have typically replaced the role of traditional structures and lifestyles. Those in authority who have abused their power and position have led subsequent generations to question the authority and integrity of institutions which previously held an important sway in the structure of society and human behaviour. Since the mid-1990s ideas, opinions, expressions and experiences can be found at the touch of a button. Despite the rise of secularism, Catholic identity, spirituality and philosophy have remained an important aspect of the Celtic support. Although no longer a practising Catholic, Broughan believes the educational and social aspects of the culture have traditionally been essential vehicles for the community. 'I yield to no man in my admiration for someone like James MacMillan but I'm not Catholic anymore. I'm not religious; I'm a curious atheist but profoundly Catholic socially. I think the Catholic Church was a cohesive, unifying and protective force in Scottish society when the club was formed.

'I don't think you have to be Catholic to support Celtic but the traditions are yoked to the Catholic Church and I recognise the importance of that historically. Perhaps it's because Celtic fans have been excluded from more traditional industries but my own exotic take is that people of the Celtic persuasion are so heavily involved in the arts because of Catholicism. In celebrating the Mass there is a strong sense of theatre, colour and ceremony, which is directly related to the artistic. That experience is very different from Scottish Calvanism with its mistrust of ceremony and colour. It's a philosophical fact.'

Despite having a profoundly Catholic identity the club's history contradicts any ideas about it being exclusively Irish Catholic: 'We are all human beings and the story is profoundly complicated. If you look at the history: Willie Maley was an Empire loyalist, Jock Stein was a Mason, the back line he played in was known as 'the Brothers', Bertie Peacock was allegedly an Orangeman and Bobby Evans was also a non-Catholic. I obviously don't agree with the idea of being a Mason or an Orangeman, but I think that's what makes Celtic a far more interesting prospect and expression. These men were very human; we shouldn't turn them into gods. I also don't think Celtic have ever been about the "ourselves alone" mentality that sometimes crops up.'

Driving through the Cumbrian village of Shap to watch Celtic in Europe was one of Broughan's first journeys over the border, significantly it was also the location for cult film *Withnail and I* in which Richard E. Grant's character muttered the much-quoted line 'we're bona fide, we're not from London', comically suggesting the shift in cultural attitudes between the British capital and the north. Not coming from London would resonate much stronger in the 1980s when Broughan moved south in the throes of a burgeoning career: 'There was a period when my life took me away from Celtic. I was working for the BBC in London and this was in the days when it wasn't as easy to get up the road for games. There was no Ryanair or easyJet, if you wanted to see the game you had to get up the road because this was decades before internet or satellite broadcasts. I used to travel home a lot, getting the train at five in the morning on a Saturday or occasionally I'd have enough money to fly up for some midweek Old Firm games, using up most of my disposable income. I was still very connected to it, even though it was difficult. One of the reasons I moved back was because I was so pissed off with Thatcherism; I didn't feel like a full person not having access to Celtic Park. It sounds absurd but it's true. I came back because politically I was in a different place, it was a yuppie nightmare and I couldn't stand it anymore.'

Today Broughan has relocated to Gartocharn on the shores of Loch Lomond; the area was also home to the veteran

Scottish broadcaster Tom Weir. Looking around Broughan's office there's no mistaking he's something of an 'Uber Tim': Jimmy Johnstone's first Celtic contract signed by a 'Mr John Stein' is framed on the wall amid a number of fascinating Celtic articles and artefacts. He has a clutch of memories and shows me a story he'd written for *Time Out* magazine based on a conversation with Charlie Nicholas not long after he'd scored arguably the best goal of his Celtic career against Ajax in 1982. Broughan also ran a minibus to Old Trafford shortly before Christmas in 1984 for the ill-fated quarter-final of the European Cup-Winners' Cup, as well as witnessing Brian Clough's Nottingham Forest take on Celtic in the UEFA Cup the previous year.

Broughan's career has allowed him a surreal number of experiences that include breaking away from filming a Hollywood blockbuster starring Liam Neeson and Jessica Lange to lead the singing at Ibrox against a dominant Rangers team in the mid-1990s. Perhaps the most bizarre was taking Lisbon Story director and German film luminary Wim Wenders to Celtic Park in 1977 for a match against Motherwell. 'It was during the Edinburgh film festival at the end of August, there was a major retrospective of his work on and he was here for that and the premiere of his film *The American Friend*. Wenders was my hero at the time, I was working for the Scottish Film Council and asked them if there was anything I could do to help. I knew he was a bit of a football fan so I suggested taking him to Celtic Park which people thought was a great idea. I called the club and they were very helpful with tickets and we bought Celtic scarves on the way to the ground. As well as Wenders we were accompanied by his then wife Lisa Kreuser who was also in the movie alongside Dennis Hopper. We were greeted by the commissioner at Celtic Park who handed us tickets for the directors' box and then we were introduced to Kevin Kelly who was one of the main men at that point. The ladies were taken into a different room, which is how it was back then. Wim was big and tall and very director-like, he turned to me at one point and said: "Bobby Lennox is ze last of ze Lisbon Lions, no?" It was a strange moment and I thought: "Wim, you really know your football!" '

Like the echoes on the old stair landing from childhood, Celtic Park is full of memories of our own unique past, both on and off the pitch. As well as the patter and the glory, it is filled with the voices of family and friends passing over generations. Says Broughan: 'There are times in my life when I have just gone to Celtic Park when I haven't known what else to do. My sister was a principal teacher of English; she was my only sister and was taken into hospital in a critical condition. She had to get quite a complicated operation that didn't work out and she passed away. After leaving the hospital I dropped my father off and then his sister. I popped into Cullens bar to see a friend but he wasn't there and I didn't have a penny in my pocket. I just ended up driving to Celtic Park on that occasion, I persuaded one of the guys to let me in, they were working on the new stadium at the time, it was a very bright, clear sort of day and I just sat there and stared at the park. I've followed Celtic for good or for ill all my life, I'm still a season ticket holder and I never miss a home game. I've certainly seen a lot of good following this club.'

On the northern shores of the Firth of Forth, film director Richard Jobson was born in Dunfermline in October 1960. From Irish and German ancestry Jobson was raised with a strong socialist and political ethos informed by his Catholic upbringing. His life in the east of Scotland seemed less affected by the sectarian tensions associated with life in the west. As with Peter Broughan, the Celtic bus became a passport to another world from an early age: 'My identity in football came from my father who was a Hibs supporter and that's where he took me first as a very young kid so I have a soft spot for them, but it was with Celtic that you got a sense of community, home and identity. I would go straight from Saturday morning Mass to the Lochgelly Celtic supporters' bus which was run by an amazing guy called Arthur McKenna, this was the period just after Lisbon when the team were beginning to have a ragged edge but were still exceptional. You were watching players like Jimmy Johnstone, Bobby Lennox and Billy McNeill but it was also a time of emerging talent like Kenny Dalglish and Danny McGrain. For me McGrain became emblematic of a kind of Celtic humility, a much-loved player.

'The guys on the bus stuck together, which was always in the lower part of the Jungle. Home or away on a Saturday morning that experience exposed you to a camaraderie that I wasn't really party to in my own world, you were mixing with an array of different ages and generations. Essentially most of the people were from an Irish Catholic heritage and had mostly come from mining communities. They all had lives that were somewhat troubled but at the same time you got this incredible sense of warmth and a self-deprecating kind of humour. You were among people with very different views of the world, it wasn't just going to a football match; part of it was listening to an older generation talking in an informed way about current affairs. I think the politics was always on the left and it introduced me to this Celtic tradition of always siding with the oppressed. I'd never heard of the Palestinians' plight but I became aware of it because of that bus. At the time I thought: "What's that got to do with us in this cold, damp, dark, bleak, eastern part of the world?" The supporters on the Celtic bus were talking about political and human issues like what was going on in Gaza and on the West Bank, which has stayed with me to this day and I still take an interest in it. On the Monday after the game I'd ask the teacher about issues the Celtic fans were talking about; I began to understand that there was a collective sense of hurt on these issues. Primarily I look over my shoulder at the communities around me but certainly my sympathies are with the way those human beings are treated. For me the fans waving the Palestinian flags, that's exactly what Celtic is all about because its people who understand politics on the bigger stage and at the same time have a fantastic sense of humour about it all. I have friends in Beirut; they absolutely loved this idea of football fans in Glasgow waving the flag. I think that's the kind of stuff that attracts a lot of people to Celtic.'

Prior to this book I'd interviewed Jobson over the years for a number of publications such as the *Celtic View*, the *Irish Post* and *Scotland on Sunday* and he rarely failed to articulate the profound in a very uncomplicated manner. Never fitting into a neat slot, he's straddled the boundaries of punk rock, television, poetry and fashion before settling down in life as a film-maker. His first band, Skids, found a new generation of fans when U2 and Green Day covered their 1978 single 'The Saints are Coming' for the Hurricane Katrina appeal in 2006. Since then Jobson has sporadically resurrected their high-energy punk rock anthems for some memorable gigs including T in the Park, Homecoming Live and a few notable one-off shows in Glasgow and his hometown of Fife. Despite lucrative offers to go on tour Jobson has been reluctant to reform the act long-term due to his film career.

The youngest of five brothers, Jobson's father was a coalminer and his mother a dock-worker. His brother Michael was named after Mick McGahey, the Scottish trade union leader. Undoubtedly the psyche of Jobson and his family was shaped by some influential Catholic socialists and political firebrands of the era: 'During my formative years socialism was really at the heart of the Catholicism I grew up with and it was there with the mining community that no longer exists. I was an altar boy and we had a priest, Father Wilson, who was sort of like a union man. He never had an authoritarian presence; he was very much a community figure. The other important thing was although I'm from a Catholic back-ground, all my friends were Protestant. My best friend was a guy called Budgie, he had Rangers tattoos on his arm but we never had the problems that are so endemic in the west of Scotland, even around the big Old Firm games there was never anything extreme. I remember Budgie's brother Jim missed the Rangers bus, they'd get picked up a hundred yards from us, we knew them all so we gave them a lift. Some of the guys at the back of the bus that were known for singing the more Republican or Nationalist songs weren't too happy about this guy down the front with King William of Orange tattooed on his arm but our sense of a divide was not as ruthless and vicious as it was and still is in the west. I've never had that sense of I'm a Catholic and you're a Protestant.'

While many of his friends were joining the armed forces, Jobson channelled the culture around him when joining Skids at the age of sixteen. His lyrics quickly showed a grasp of the complex issues around the Troubles and his Catholic faith, issues he continues to grapple with today: 'I think if you listen to the Skids songs they have an anthemic quality and choruses that could have been born on a football terrace. There's the triumphalism of the football chant and the moroseness of the hymns. Evidently a sense of that collective sound comes from my Catholic upbringing and from the terrace at Parkhead. I was an altar boy here in Fife right up until I was about thirteen, the hymns and the chants on the terraces certainly informed the music a lot, and that world certainly cut a big swathe into what I was doing.

'On the song "Fields" there is a mournful and rather melancholy feel, a lot of it references a form of Christianity, although in my current state I'm probably closer to atheist than Christian. I'm the only one in my family that doesn't go to Mass, my brothers do, and I'm married to an Italian Catholic. I don't fight it but I don't shout from the pulpit, it gave me a sense of community and identity and Celtic fall into that grouping, no doubt about it. I wrote 'Into the Valley' about young guys in this part of the world who couldn't get jobs in 1977, they joined the army to become car mechanics or engineers but in a short space of time they ended up stationed on the Falls Road or Andersonstown and it changed them. They were not the same people.

'With my family and my background that was simply not an option. It's interesting for me as a Celtic fan, that culture is anti-army because of the Troubles in Northern Ireland and in some cases quite rightly. Derry comes to mind that fateful day those people went to exercise their right by saying we will not be treated like this and what do they do? They shoot them; that's what happened. There is a film I was involved in that has been shown at various football grounds in Scotland showing some of the fallen soldiers from Iraq along with an acoustic version of 'Into the Valley'. Quite a few clubs put the film on at their grounds but Celtic said it wouldn't go down well at Parkhead. I think they need to move on from that point of view because if you look at the statistics of who's joining the army it's not one community or another, it's everyone. The Troubles are not finished but we have to move on and I know it's still raw for people who have had terrible things happen to their family and friends, but we need to collectively move on together.'

The Troubles in Northern Ireland and the reverberations in his own community is something that deeply affected

Jobson and those around him: 'What it really was about was an association. People talked a lot about the Troubles in Northern Ireland but not in a negative way, this was the early 1970s, each week you were hearing about something awful that was happening either to innocent people or to the armed forces. Certainly I rejected some aspects of that identity; I didn't participate in any sectarian element but I knew all the songs. I just didn't want to sing them. Growing up my sympathy lay with the Nationalist community; I knew what they had gone through and how they had been treated. In terms of the hatred, I didn't understand any of that, it's just not the way I think. When you become aware that you have an enemy it just gives you an excuse to hate. I don't subscribe to any of that. My mother and various people in the community sang all the old Irish songs and some of them were beautiful. I preferred the ones about community, not the ones about going out and killing people, that's not in my soul. The idea of using an ideology to kill innocent people is not something I could support but I could support and subscribe to the community. For me it's a way of joining the dots of diaspora along with an egalitarian way of looking at the world.'

Jobson's work as a songwriter and film-maker has displayed strong and defining references to his own coming of age Catholic life. Those distinctions are perhaps most obvious in his debut feature *16 Years of Alcohol*, which delivered an exhilarating and poetic study of Scottish identity and masculinity with a particular East Coast and Edinburgh nuance. 'I use a lot of working-class Irish Catholic songs like 'One Day at a Time', 'You'll Never Walk Alone' and 'The Fields of Athenry' which sounds like an ancient song but it was actually written in the late 1970s. They are all fairly iconic songs that put the message across clearly. The colours I used were Celtic and Hibs; it put those characters in context and gives an idea what their story might be.'

Significantly Jobson splices the violence he experienced and participated in as a teenager with Catholic theology and a more profound search for meaning and understanding: 'In *16 Years of Alcohol* the speech in the church is taken from St Paul's letter to the Corinthians, I know this stuff off by heart, it's theologically imprinted on me and the good bits have stuck. Christ's teachings were amazing, the ideas around a common decency I still subscribe to for sure. The spiritual zone is very much alive for me, science provides some answers but religion provides solace.'

The values Jobson grew up with have positively bled into his film work as well as a consciousness of the wider world. *New Town Killers*, made in 2008, visualised some of the grotesque greed associated with the banking crisis that was anathema to his background and the beliefs that went with it. Although the film was inspired by Jobson's charity work with teenagers in the Oxgangs area of Edinburgh, many of whom were from extremely troubled backgrounds, he steered clear of the hopeless social realism that is often associated with film-making in this part of the world. This visceral punk thriller depicts a decadent private banker who by night becomes a sociopathic murderer, hunting down the poorest and most invisible members of society for kicks.

Essentially it explores the same themes that Jobson

WELCOME TO THE JUNGLE

wrestled with in his teens albeit in a more grown up fashion: 'I think that film captured a dark nihilistic world that is very popular today; it reflects that culture. These bankers presented people who have nothing and always will have nothing as having something. They abused their positions so brutally that now the people in the margins can't afford to live; that's not an invented story, it's there for all to see. I wanted to show that world and all its vileness and that is absolutely influenced by my background. The film brings two polar opposites together, in many ways they are both invisible members of society, and ordinarily their paths would never cross. It's a kind of apotheosis because everything is going against this young character being hunted down so brutally, but he sticks to the plan and the plan is to be as good as he can despite being thrown into a living hell with all kinds of shit being thrown at him. That was exactly the same kind of world my brothers and I were born into; we came from humble Irish Catholic origins but we've kept up a sense of moral decency. It's essentially a David and Goliath type of story.

'*16 Years of Alcohol* is a much more religious film. I created a character that crucifies himself. He creates his own self-destruction in order to re-invent himself. The character moves from one world to another through a kind of redemption, which is a very Catholic idea. It was an ambitious movie influenced by the kind of teachings I had when I was a kid, which is love and what you can do with it. That is a very single-minded Christian idea. At the end of the film he finds a perfect place, which is love.'

I leave Jobson to sort out the guest list for what might well be one of his last performances as front man of the Skids. He suggests that Paul McStay might be in attendance at the Glasgow show. The Celtic players he identified with throughout his teens and twenties remain as important as ever: 'Paul McStay is still a great hero of mine; it's so rare that a player with his talent would spend his career at one club. He is one of the most elegant players I have ever seen on any pitch; he could have played for Real Madrid, he had that indescribable thing. You look at the great midfielders of the current era such as Michael Carrick, Fabregas, Arteta and Menez; these players seem to have more time with the ball, time seems to slow down around them, they play at their own pace. Paul McStay was like that at Celtic and he could have fitted into any team in the world but he chose to stay. I think that says a lot about the man.'

Working as a television presenter for Sky Jobson befriended another of his Celtic heroes: 'Charlie Nicholas never had much pace but the things he managed to do with the ball were unbelievable, when he managed to pull it off it was just amazing. I followed Arsenal because of him.'

The politics of modern football have showed a widening gap between clubs and the more traditional aspects of a home-grown support. Historically British football managers such as Bill Shankly, Jock Stein, Matt Busby, Alex Ferguson and Brian Clough all would have described themselves as socialists and modelled their teams on the ethics and philosophies of that culture. The crippling effect from the recession of the late 2000s appears to have highlighted a player culture around Celtic that many supporters have struggled with. The feeling between the average Celtic fan and a new breed of aloof, inaccessible multi-million pound players seems to have grown wider in a new era of Tory cuts on public spending and education.

Here, at the start of a new decade, we are at a fascinating point in the club's history. For previous generations the idea of booing the team, as Peter Broughan suggested, would be considered beyond the pale. With the advent of digital technology it is no longer possible for the club to suppress the wider opinions of its support who write blogs or upload footage onto websites such as YouTube, which currently holds a clip of supporters booing the team after the Scottish Cup semi-final exit against Ross County in April 2010. In the footage Walfrid's statue appears to watch events unfold, begging the question, what would he make of the club today? Also posted on the site was a clip of fans interviewed for STV cameras. Many shared the view that this team was 'the worst in Celtic's history.' The opinions all centred on 'not playing for the badge,' suggesting a further meaning behind the day's result, namely professionals making millions from the club with no deeper interest other than money. It's hard to imagine a day when supporting Celtic doesn't mean anything beyond the confines of the game. After all the cultural differences around the club are what make Celtic attractive on a global level.

Gordon Strachan has called for a rejection of what he calls the 'Keyboard Cowboys'. Undoubtedly there are forums and blogs full of hate-filled bile worthy of zero attention rightly attracting the attention of the relevant authorities and politicians keen to issue jail sentences to the perpetrators but it would be churlish to ignore a measured, educated and articulate group of Celtic supporters who are voicing valid opinions and arguments through a variety of new media. Says Jobson: 'When Rangers went through that tough period in the 1970s when they couldn't touch Celtic, their crowd was dwindling to nothing. That would never happen with Celtic. There's been a feeling around the fans in recent years that the club are not delivering what Celtic fans expect but it's not changing what you do on a Saturday because you've got nowhere else to go. Rangers fans can go and see some other Scottish team if they don't like what is going on at the club. I remember Celtic beating Hibs 5–3 in the Drybrough Cup, no matter how many the opposition scored Celtic would come back more with more. That would never happen now.'

Jobson talks with a warmth and affection about the people he grew up with. His connection and sense of carrying the torch is not necessarily related to the institutions of Celtic Football Club or the Catholic Church and not necessarily fans of the club today but the people he grew up with. The elements that Jobson harnessed from the culture were as important as the ones he discarded. This is something he continues to do. 'My son has begun to get into Celtic, I took him to Man United v Celtic at Old Trafford. I'm still a Celtic supporter but I'm not connected with it in the same way that I was. I was in the stand at the old Celtic end at Parkhead and there were some guys from Somalia there, they all had Celtic scarves on. I was upset to see some nutters behind were shouting racist stuff at them. Growing up I didn't hear one racist thing at Celtic. You might have heard ten priests all swearing at John Grieg but nothing racist, that makes me angry and it really disgusts me. In saying that I know a lot of Celtic fans that still hold true to what it's really all about. I went on the pitch at Dunfermline v Celtic a few weeks ago and the fans that were there were very generous towards me. They gave me a tremendous reception. To get that from fellow supporters was a very special moment. I'm still attracted to the mystery of Celtic. It's tied up with my youth and who I am; I don't think that will ever change.'

CHAPTER EIGHT WHEN YOU WALK THROUGH A STORM

He's got useful players and he trains them the right way and he gets them all to do what they can do well, the little things they can do, and he merges them all together, it's a form of socialism you know, without the politics of course and they are all helping each other.

BILL SHANKLY ON JOCK STEIN

OWNERSHIP OF THE ANTHEMS shared by Celtic and Liverpool football clubs have been hotly contested between supporters over the years. 'You'll Never Walk Alone' started life in 1945 as a Broadway show tune by Rogers and Hammerstein, written for *Carousel.* Named by *Time* magazine as the best musical of the twentieth century, the story has continued to capture the zeitgeist due to the constant themes of class politics, tragedy and redemption; themes that would undoubtedly appear in the history of Liverpool Football Club. Some Celtic supporters claim that they heard the song sung in the Jungle as early as the 1950s and there is anecdotal evidence that it showed up at various other grounds too. Liverpool's claim became more 'official' when Gerry and the Pacemakers popularised the song in 1963. This was made flesh the following year when the city of Liverpool became the centre of a cultural shift.

The sound of Merseybeat was dominating the hit parade just as Bill Shankly was building a football empire at Anfield. The BBC's *Panorama* programme makers travelled north to Anfield for Liverpool v Arsenal and recorded a league clinching 5–0 annihilation of the north London team. Generations of Koppites were filmed singing a string of Merseybeat anthems: The Beatles' 'She Loves You', Cilla Black's 'Anyone Who Had a Heart' and, of course, the song that would become something of a hymn for both Liverpool and Celtic 'You'll Never Walk Alone'. The grainy black and white footage shows a city dominating the football field and the pop charts; Liverpool was repositioning itself as the cultural centre of the universe.

The sharing of songs is undoubtedly part of the friendship between these two clubs. 'The Fields of Athenry' first sung by Celtic fans in the early 1990s had been a familiar staple in Catholic homes for over a decade before its appearance at Parkhead. Liverpool's take on the ballad soon followed with 'The Fields of Anfield Road' reflecting their history and further expressing the Irish cultural link between these two sets of supporters. While Liverpool actually stems from the Methodist origins of neighbours Everton, the club retains an overwhelmingly Catholic identity in its support.

Beyond these two anthems the history and friendship between Celtic and Liverpool runs deeper than the shared ethos between most other 'associated' clubs. Paul Holleran is the organiser for the NUJ in Scotland and has lived in Glasgow since 1976. From the centre of the Kop, and subsequently the Jungle, he's followed both clubs fervently throughout his life. Born in Walton, an area set between the grounds of Anfield and Goodison, on 31 March 1956, the future trade union organiser and journalist would listen to the echoes of football supporters chanting their way to the grounds and watch bustling spectators on their way to Aintree for a day at the races. 'I came from a typical Liverpool background, my mother said I was born at five to midnight, my dad said five past, which would have made me an April Fool. My dad's father was Irish, he claimed that our jet black hair came from survivors of Spanish Armada ships that were wrecked on the west coast of Ireland, which is where he came from. The name Holleran means foreigner in Gaelic. On my mother's side my grandfather was a Swedish seafarer and he married my granny who came from Scottish ancestry. My sympathies are quite wide ranging. Both grandfathers worked on the docks, the Mersey Tunnel and at the Tate and Lyle sugar refinery.

'My earliest recollection was looking out the back window of our house. Outside was a playing field, the Catholic Church and next to that was The Crown pub, which was renowned for being a bit of a rough boozer. On a Saturday night you'd hear the singing from the pub and then the church bells on Sunday morning. Whole families and communities would get together for weddings, christenings and funerals and then gather round the cubby hole in the pub for a sing-song, you'd have big nights with the dancing at Christmas and New Year, it was typical of the time.'

Although his first football trip took him to Goodison, Holleran soon found his real allegiances in the Kop and a visiting team from Glasgow playing Liverpool during a match in the 1966 European Cup-Winners' Cup: 'My dad took me to Everton first, I think he thought there was less swearing. Coming from a staunch Catholic family, even though he was a Liverpool supporter himself, I suppose he didn't want to force it on me. I grew up through the Merseybeat explosion when the Kop would be singing Beatles', Gerry and the Pacemakers' or Searchers' songs, whichever Liverpool band had a hit at the time. You had to catch the movement of the sway, it was wild. So many people would go that they often shut the gates at half past twelve for a three o'clock kick-off; you'd be there for the next two and a half hours having to catch the movement of the sway. The dockers would share out the whiskey, the old timers would veer off to the side and there would be an almighty sing-song.

'I became a Celtic supporter the night of the European Cup-Winners' Cup semi-final and I think that's where the connection with Celtic for a lot of Liverpool fans started, especially after seeing that team which went on to win the European Cup the following season. What I clearly remember about that night was seeing Bobby Lennox scoring a perfectly good goal that was disallowed. It stands out to me to this day. That was my first experience of bad refereeing against Celtic, something I've become more aware of over the many years following them in Glasgow. After the incident it was a wild night, there were bottles getting thrown onto the pitch but there was no animosity between the fans, the foundations of the relationship were already in place because of Stein and Shankly.

'Shankly laid the brass tacks at Liverpool in exactly the same way Stein did at Celtic. He went to Liverpool and fell in love with the place and his priority was turning the club into something the fans could be proud of; he believed in the importance of municipal pride and focusing positively on where you come from and where you live. If you are perceived as coming from a culture that is all about rogues and scallies, that people only take the piss out of, then someone comes along and makes you the best football team in the world, wants to create a new training ground for the players, a new roof for the fans and bring in the best players, it completely changes the psyche of the whole community. He brought in a confident working-class ethos. Jock Stein and Matt Busby came from the same mining culture in Scotland and they built football dynasties with that philosophy. Busby and Shankly felt at home in the culture of the North West; their ideas of how the game should be played were easily able to cross over. It was that distinctly Scottish working-class essence where many Celtic and Liverpool supporters found common ground.

'Shankly immediately created a team of Scots and Scousers. The Scots put a spine into the team: Tommy Lawrence in goal, Ron Yeats centre half and Ian St John in attack. The best Liverpool teams have always had Scots: the list is endless, from a post-war player like Billy Liddell, who spent his career at the club, to Dalglish, Hansen and Souness who all played a major role in Liverpool's most successful period. "Team of all the Macs" was Liverpool's original nickname after Irish founder John McKenna used his business connections to sign thirteen Scottish players from across the border in 1892, the year of Liverpool's formation after breaking away from Everton. The Shankly Gate, erected in 1982, displays a saltire and thistle flanked between the Liver Bird and the iconic "You'll Never Walk Alone" calligraphy.'

Like the bronze statue of Walfrid outside Parkhead's gates, the similarly placed Shankly statue with fists in the air decked in a supporters scarf gives prominence to a philosophy, values, character and an attitude towards the game where there was no separation between club and supporter: 'I think what was also important was Shankly going into the dressing room after the match in Lisbon and saying to Stein: "John, you're immortal now", that's a historical moment which has retained a significance for anyone who has come to appreciate what happened that night in 1967. I think in some ways that must have been a hard thing for Shankly because he had been thwarted from getting his hands on European silverware in 1965 because of some dodgy decision in a match against Inter Milan. He was able to put that aside because of the solidarity with Stein that transcended football. People say you shouldn't bring politics into football but I think that's rubbish, their whole approach was based on a socialist philosophy. Next to the statue of Shankly it simply says: "He made people happy." Shankly built on that tradition of having Scottish players and local lads. He brought in the "boot room" where the coaching staff would sit with a whiskey and figure out a winning strategy, the red strips and the "This Is Anfield" sign that hangs above the entrance to the pitch, that was all from his attitudes and ideas which was more about a way of life than an actual technical system.

'Shankly talked about the importance of honesty but he also believed in entertainment, and he wanted success with that. Celtic and Liverpool came from a philanthropist ideology, the clubs were set up for those in need and for communities to have a place to go and be part of something. The clubs have that ingrained in them; they were formed by members of the clergy to improve lives. Liverpool and Everton both have Methodist origins, the denomination is not what's important; it's that the clubs were given a Christian ideology.'

Testimonial matches can often lack competitive edge, leaving supporters in a state of mind-numbing languor. On the other hand they can also give a sense of occasion, one that surpasses the conventional routine. The six matches honouring Ron Yeats, Ian Rush and Ronnie Moran at Liverpool and Billy McNeill, Jock Stein and Tommy Burns at Celtic have further bolstered the relationships between fans of both clubs. These games have often been infused by events that surrounded them and have been preserved in the consciousness of supporters ever since. Bill Shankly's last game in charge at Liverpool was McNeill's testimonial in 1974; during Stein's testimonial four years later Kenny Dalglish was booed for ninety minutes as it came soon after his move to Anfield in 1977. Boot-room graduate Ronnie Moran led out Liverpool against a Celtic team that was managed by Dalglish after the disastrous appointment of John Barnes. Reinforcement work began on the Anfield Road stand after eyewitnesses reported it moving under the weight of the Celtic support.

For Paul Holleran the first of those testimonials, for Ron Yeats in 1974, provided a memorable encounter with the Celtic support: 'Bobby Charlton played for Celtic that night and the team paraded the Scottish Cup in Liverpool shirts. Of course both sets of fans sang "You'll Never Walk Alone". I know that Celtic claim to have sung it first; if they did it was the *Carousel* version, which is one of my favourite songs. Liverpool got beat 4–1. After the game I was walking down the road and this rickety old coach pulled up, the bus doors flapped open and a Celtic supporter shouted over "Where's the best pub round here mate?" I ended up taking them to The Crown, which was my local about two or three miles down the road, it was on the way home for them on the East Lancashire motorway. On the way I began to wonder if it was a good idea, a couple of my mates were like, "What are you doing bringing them in here?" The atmosphere can get a bit territorial between supporters, but it turned out a great night, scarves and numbers were swapped after a few beers.

'I remember having a lengthy discussion about the pub name, in Liverpool a lot of the bars have royal names like The Crown or King George, with Scousers there's not the same awareness of imperialism and the forces of the crown, pub names wouldn't really be associated with a religious affinity. Perhaps because there is such a high percentage of Catholics in Liverpool, you grow up not knowing any different, everybody was Catholic so we didn't experience the same problems. When they left the bus wouldn't start so we all had to go out, get the sleeves rolled up and give them a push to get them on the road again. The next week those Celtic supporters sent a plaque to the pub in commemoration of a great night. The lads left saying any time you are in Glasgow, just let us know you're from The Crown in Liverpool and, of course, we all went back up for Billy McNeill's testimonial in the August later that same year.

'I was eighteen at the time, it was a Monday night and dark by the time we got there, which seemed to take forever. I was quite shocked at first, there were a lot of rundown tenements. Liverpool was more like Dublin with a lot of brick houses; tenements were more in the South Side. You could still see the old tramlines in the East End, everything was black, dark and thick with soot. What I remember most clearly was the intense thumping of the Parkhead Forge, all you could hear was the 'boom chissshhh, boom chissshhh' of the big steam hammer as you made your way towards the ground which added to the intensity and the anticipation of seeing the ground for the first time. It was like Fritz Lang's *Metropolis*; I had this vision in my head of a massive dark satanic mill and all the workers in this underground drudgery. The other things that stood out were the big green pylons; I remember thinking if that was Liverpool all the scallies would be up them. Those two games and the fans I got to know etched onto me the Glasgow psyche which I felt an immediate affinity with.'

Two years later Holleran moved to Glasgow permanently after serving his apprenticeship as a printer in Liverpool. The first part of this interview took place shortly after hearing about the sad death of NUJ leader and journalist, Harry Conroy. From my own experiences dealing with Harry as editor of the *Scottish Catholic Observer* he was a class apart from the vast majority of other editors. As a Christian socialist he was quick to assist others in an environment perpetually frothing with ego and self-interest. Said Holleran: 'Harry always tried to build bridges, always tried to get on with people, even when he disagreed with them. He would always talk to people, negotiate. When I first moved to Glasgow, Harry was something of a leading light and a mentor for me.

'In many ways my life in Glasgow felt like a progression from my life in Liverpool where Catholic life was everything. There was one local priest, Tom Bradley, who had trained as a boxer and played football for Tranmere. He would arrange trips to Lourdes, the camaraderie and the teaching built you up, gave you the tools you needed for life. The only difference with Glasgow was the sectarian tensions, I was friends with both Celtic and Rangers supporters but I kept it out of the workplace. On a Monday morning someone would come in and say: "What about the Tims or the Huns?" I just kept out of it, outside my allegiances lay with Celtic but you couldn't bring that into work.

'One of the first games that I saw was Celtic v Hearts and I was gobsmacked by the biased decision making, the fans were almost philosophical about it; their response was "The ref is a Mason; what do you expect?" The support at Anfield wouldn't have put up with that. The other thing I learned very quickly was not to clap the opposition no matter how good they were. Being a football supporter if I saw something spectacular I would applaud, even it was Manchester United and George Best scored or Everton I would applaud. Watching Celtic I learned very quickly to put my hands in my pockets. I picked that up after I was about to clap a Davie Cooper goal, he scored with a volley; of course the blue end erupted. All that felt like a real culture shock to me. In Liverpool you had many cultures, because it was one of the biggest ports in the world with miles of dockyard and from that you ended up with a massive Chinese community, a huge Nigerian population, there were also Orange areas and streets. Although there was a history of violence I didn't experience the sectarian problems that you would find in Glasgow, perhaps because there was a Catholic dominance.

'Harry Conroy was a Catholic and a Celtic fan but he didn't view people from those narrow confines, he saw the person not the affiliation to a political party, class, football team or a religion. I found myself in the company of guys like Jimmy Reed and Mick McGahey, these were men that somehow transcended their backgrounds and the divide to get better housing, better working conditions and better lives for people working in industry, in the mines and in the shipyards. Just listening to these men was a pleasure. Their aim was to preserve a working-class dignity and that is something that I strongly identified with. Where Glasgow and Liverpool are very similar is in the political and trade union cultures. There's something about these two cities that produces leaders, people that are prepared to stick their heads above the parapet and argue for the rights of workers, even today you look at all the big trade unions, they continue to be dominated by Glaswegians and Scousers.'

The 1976–77 season saw Celtic secure a Scottish league and cup double as well as making it to the final of the League Cup against Aberdeen, but it was something of a bittersweet time for Celtic supporters. At the end of the season they lost their leading marksman, their captain and all-round star player Kenny Dalglish. 'King Kenny' had achieved the status of hero among the Celtic support for his unique blend of imagination, charisma, dignity and goal scoring ability. For two seasons he wanted to achieve a lifelong ambition by signing for Liverpool. On returning to the helm after a serious accident, Jock Stein eventually granted Dalglish's wish and in August 1977 the Celtic manager handed the player over to his friend Bob Paisley with a final bear hug and offer of 'good luck you wee bastard'. Kenny had left Paradise as a Celtic player for the last time.

Paul Holleran had just turned twenty when he returned to the city with a romantic inclination: 'I had been working as a DJ in Italy where I met this bunch of mad Glaswegians. In those days you seemed to be forever getting invited to a twenty-first or an engagement party. One of the girls that I met in Italy invited me up to a party in Glasgow, it was like one of those stories that you hear of Scousers going for a loaf and not coming back. This girl ended up becoming my wife and I got a job in Glasgow. Watching Kenny Dalglish that year I was mesmerised, he was joint top scorer that season with Ronnie Glavin. I was well aware what he could do and told my mates in Liverpool to expect something exceptional when he arrived on Merseyside, although they were big Kevin Keegan fans and very sceptical at the time. In the end, of course, Kenny became as big a folk hero, if not bigger, in Liverpool. Obviously I was still travelling back and forward to see the family and going to the Kop so I was able to keep up with Dalglish in his zenith under Bob Paisley.

WHEN YOU WALK THROUGH A STORM

'When he left Celtic it was a shock to the system for the fans, people were genuinely gutted; it was the end of that optimistic "Quality Street" era, any Celtic fan at the time would have had posters of this new generation of Celtic players on their wall, including me. Dalglish was the real star of the show, in those days people were not used to seeing their star player leave his club. It was the same with Keegan and Souness at Liverpool, they were the first guys that we called mercenaries; it was the start of that whole shift in the culture where multi-million pound clubs would buy your best players and the players would put their own interest before the club's.'

A further marked shift in the culture can be traced back to Liverpool's European Cup adventures in Europe. After jaunts to the likes of St Etienne, Paris, Rome and Madrid the appearance on British streets of the three parallel Adidas bars on colourful canvas and leather trainers was the beginning of the 'casual' subculture. European fashions that were all about the cut, collar, cloth and colours were often shoplifted, looted or filched on European trips by a new style-conscious, counter-culture generation of football supporters. An association with thugs, thieves and wide-boys initially marred the casual movement; the aesthetics, however, have prevailed to dominate male working-class fashion and tastes ever since, bleeding into the iconic and confident look of the Manchester bands of the late 1980s and the associated Britpop movement of the mid-1990s. The post-punk explosion of Liverpool bands in the late 1970s, along with further visibility on television drama such as the mainstream soap *Brookside* in

1982 and the award-winning drama *Boys from the Blackstuff* by Alan Bleasdale (first transmitted as *The Black Stuff* in 1980), showed the city in a full-blown cultural and sporting renaissance despite economic turmoil, crippling cuts and privatisation. As Liverpool squared up to mass unemployment, urban riots and grinding poverty, the city bucked with the strength of its community identity, rooted firmly in the local. Outsider pride increased and notions of English national identity in sport and politics represented an alien way of life. These responses formed by the city's history as Europe's most significant port looking across the North Atlantic to the New World perhaps finds more common ground with New York than London.

For Holleran this was something innate in the culture and its people: 'There had always been what you could call resourcefulness in the Liverpool support that predated 1977. In the days of Shankly I hitchhiked all over Britain. My parents would find my football kit behind the door and by that time I would be on my way down the East Lancashire motorway to Leeds, Huddersfield or across the Pennines. During the power cuts of 1973 I met two lads with ladders and shammies who were making their way to a League Cup game down south to "clean the windows". There was always that scally element where you'd meet lads you knew on the way home who had went on the rob for bars of chocolate wherever they were and were handing it out on the journey home; that was just carried on into the big European trips.'

With the club's supporters lampooned by Harry Enfield's moustached and permed 'Scousers' and the city written off by the wider media as a drugs and latterly gun hinterland, Liverpool fans continued to express their separation from the rest of England. The 'We're Not English; We Are Scouse' banner comes from the idea that Scousers believe that they are different from anywhere else in England in a similar way to Celtic, coming from an Irish tradition and having a separate identity from the rest of Scotland. There is also a tradition among Rangers fans of supporting England. These traits are not always appreciated by the rest of the country, or the media. When Celtic won the European Cup they achieved the most phenomenal feat that everyone else could only aspire to and they did it with local lads, a tremendous self worth comes from that.

Says Holleran: 'The humour of Glasgow and Liverpool is very similar; I don't think it translates outside of those cities. That comes from history, both being port cities with high immigration looking to Ireland and often America rather than London. We watched the UEFA Cup final in 2003 at a place called Olivers in Drumchapel. A couple of mates who are Rangers fans came in with policemen's helmets on in reference to the "We'll be Over in Seville; You'll be Watching *The Bill*" chant. Outside of Glasgow or Liverpool, you just wouldn't get that.' Liverpool was the stop-off point from Ireland, Scotland and Wales, so people would sail from Liverpool to where they were going but quite often they would stay. Growing up you would hear about uncles that went off to sea and came back with all kinds of books and records that fed into the culture.

'When something kicks against your identity, that identity

gets stronger. Players like Steven Gerrard and Jamie Carragher could have went anywhere in the world; it's a throwback to another time, that kind of loyalty to a club. If you watched them in Istanbul, those players are literally dying of cramp and putting their bodies on the line. That's how much it means to them; you don't get that same commitment from players that come and go in a season or two. When trainer Rudolfo Borrell arrived to develop youth at Liverpool he was asked about bringing in Spanish players, what he talked about was the importance of local talent, players that understood the club and its fans. He understood that local pride and understanding of the fans brings a more determined spirit. In Liverpool our focus was always the club and the city; we didn't want our best players coming back injured from playing for England, part of that attitude came from a London centric media.

'It was also partly due to a political backlash that fed the creativity of the city. There was an explosion of bands from Echo and the Bunnymen to The La's. I've two younger sisters and they ended up making the costumes for the film *Letter to Brezhnev*. You had writers like Jimmy McGovern breaking through on *Brookside* along with Alan Bleasdale and Willy Russell, who were all profoundly inspired by what was going on politically. Liverpool was targeted in the 1980s by the Thatcher government and the city defended itself in a number of ways. The council fought a campaign to stop Tory cuts and joint ecumenical services between Derek Worlock, the Catholic archbishop, and the Church of England bishop David Sheppard set themselves up in opposition to the Thatcher government, and in particular that individualist ethos which disregarded the most vulnerable, the poorest and the weakest in society.'

I arranged a second meeting with Paul Holleran just prior to a Hearts v Celtic midweek league fixture in November. We arrive outside the *Scotsman* in Edinburgh in the aftermath of the 'No Bloodstained Poppy on our Hoops' banner being unfurled at Parkhead the week prior to Remembrance Sunday. Entering Tynecastle one home supporter unravelled a Red Hand of Ulster alongside a self-made banner that read: 'Celtic Fans Ashamed of Nothing; Offended By Everything.' As I stood next to a former member of the services now in his seventies, the anti-poppy chanting started from a group of mostly young fans, aged eighteen to twenty-four. There were varying degrees of trouble outside the ground of a tribal nature, altercations with the police at half-time and a physical barrier was raised after the game. It's not the first time we've witnessed hostile anti-Celtic fractions outside of Tynecastle. The media were finally forced to acknowledge the aggression at the ground after Neil Lennon was physically attacked in the dugout by a Hearts supporter in 2011. Talking in the aftermath to Celtic supporters from various backgrounds and ages who were at the games, it's obvious that a widening schism has emerged.

Due to extensive media coverage the most widely referenced episode of football violence involving Celtic is the 1980 Old Firm Scottish Cup final. A post-match riot ensued leading to a ban on alcohol in grounds that still stands to this day. Holleran believes the wider media have a responsibility to explore the issues around a new wave of emerging trouble: 'In Scotland the tribal has come back in and there will always be people that want it to be there and keep the bitterness going ... but what about the rest of us? Working in the media it's obvious that they are part of the problem because there is such a lack of coverage and a failure to explore what these issues are about. People are not being educated on these subjects in Scotland and so the perpetrators are going underground. We need people in the media who are not dogmatic, someone in the mould of Jimmy Reed or Tony Benn; we need people with a broad philosophical approach. In the late 1950s and early 1960s you had a television series called Face to Face with John Freeman. On these programmes you would get one-to-one interviews in a darkened room with left-wing radicals, comedians, top actors. It was top-notch journalism with people who really knew their stuff. It was also an opportunity for them to talk about issues they felt strongly about. I think that's what's lacking now, that's why figures like James MacMillan are so important because he speaks out on issues that no one else will address in an intelligent and informed way.

'History changes and people need to move on. If you look at the history of political organisations such as ETA and the IRA they were formed as defence organisations; they wanted their country back against an oppressor. In Spain's case General Franco wanted to wipe out the Basque culture. You could look at the plantations in Ireland and the forces of the Crown in that context but what is equally important is to understand that the majority of people want to get on with their lives without living in fear of violence or oppression. When one side refuses to compromise or move on it becomes tribal and conflict remains. If there are still areas of conflict then maybe more reconciliation work is needed. If you look at the Truth and Reconciliation commission of South Africa, it's widely regarded as a successful development in the culture. It's the same in Belfast, which is unrecognisable from the city and situation it was in forty years ago, and you have to take the last forty years into context.

'It's not part of Celtic's history to keep conflict on the boil. If Walfrid thought that's what was being carried on in his name he would be affronted. A lot of credit is given to Tony Blair but to be fair John Major deserves credit for paving the way for the Good Friday Agreement. It all boils down to the question, who fights your wars? There's that whole question of why people joined the army, in some cases it's a profession, people were in the worst conditions and used as cannon fodder. Today you find an anti-war sentiment which throws up another question: what's a good war and what's a bad one, what about the people that died to stop Nazism? People are made up of many different influences in their lives, if you look at someone like James Connolly he is most widely associated with the Irish Republican movement, yet he represents many things. He was born in Scotland and was an essential part of the trade union movement here and in America. He was a Hibs Supporter, a writer, a husband and a father. He flitted between many different things in his life, he was an atheist then questioned faith at the end of his life. He asked on his deathbed if he would be remembered as an Irishman . . . but at the end of the day, what does it matter? I was born in Liverpool but I feel Scottish now, my five kids were born here, my wife and my ex wife come from Glasgow. It's naive to suggest that every Celtic fan has a blanket ideology but it is worth considering what ideas have a place at the club.

'Of course, there are positive traditions associated with Celtic but there will always be individuals who don't represent those ideas. I know that because I was there in 1980 when Celtic played Real Madrid in the European Cup. A fantastic night for the club was marred by a couple of lads shouting racist abuse at Laurie Cunningham. In 1973 I saw the same thing at Anfield when Liverpool were playing Ipswich who had a number of black players in the team, some idiots started shouting "kill a nigger". These guys get shouted down, but it still happens. More recently there have been stories in Liverpool of fans stealing tickets out of the hands of fellow supporters; you can't get much lower than that but, equally, if someone feels society has let them down, people become feral, it becomes about survival.'

While working as an investigative journalist in the early 1990s Holleran uncovered more than sixty chromium waste sites throughout Scotland, one of which was viewed as a possible location for a new Celtic Park. His discovery forced the government to act. Today Paul represents over 4,000 journalists in Scotland. He has written about and lectured on events such as the Heysel and Hillsborough stadium disasters in relation to the media's responsibility in reporting the facts. The City of Liverpool and supporters of Liverpool FC continue to boycott the *Sun* newspaper due to the unfounded stories it published in the aftermath of the Hillsborough disaster in 1989. The police's attitude was arguably shaped by the spirit of the times, riots and casual violence led to a pessimistic and disapproving view of football supporters. Poor policing, stewarding, organisation at the grounds as well as a hooligan element had all played a part in destroying the game's reputation. That aside, questions continue to be asked about the treatment of the ninety-six Liverpool supporters who lost their lives in the crush at Hillsborough and pressure from the 'Justice for the 96' association of football supporters and families of the bereaved continue the campaign for a full enquiry.

The Hillsborough tragedy continues to be a live topic for supporters of Liverpool and Celtic who have kept up a sustained and visible focus on the issue. In October 2006 Celtic fans produced a twenty-six-foot banner with both clubs crests intertwined with the words: 'Justice for the 96' and 'You'll Never Walk Alone' emblazoned across it. Celtic supporters were later invited to Anfield to present the banner to Liverpool at half-time during a Champions League match against PSV. The response from Liverpool was a streamer that read: 'Thank You Celtic Fans; We've Never Walked Alone.'

After the tragedy in 1989 attitudes towards football supporters drastically changed, all-seater stadiums were introduced as a safety mechanism and slowly the violence associated with the casual movement began to fade. In the decade that followed football entered a new era of commercialism, star players and media dominance. Clubs began aggressive marketing campaigns that treated supporters as customers. For Holleran the Hillsborough disaster remains a personal memory and the tragic outcome of neglect for decades: 'There was always a danger attached to going to football in those days. If you look at the Bolton (1946) and Ibrox (1971) disasters then the Bradford fire in 1985, the signs were there. It wasn't unusual to see someone get a few broken ribs with all the swaying in the Kop. Before Heysel there had been an attitude to certain football supporters. I was aware Liverpool complained and put a dossier together condemning the ground at Heysel in 1985 before the European Cup final with Juventus. The security and the arrangements for that game were unsuitable. There is also evidence to suggest the Liverpool support was infiltrated that night, casual arrangements with right-wing groups had been planned months in advance. I understand health and safety, it's part of my job, and it was a disgraceful decision to go ahead with that game in Brussels. Had it been Manchester United I doubt whether it would have. I'm not suggesting anything overtly sinister but I'm talking about the way fans of some clubs are treated. There is a history of bad blood between Celtic and the SFA. Why were Celtic fans in the uncovered part of Hampden for years?

'When Hillsborough happened I had two girls from Liverpool staying at my house, they were friends of my sister and had been accepted for university in Glasgow. We tuned into the wireless to hear the game, which was an FA Cup semi-final against Nottingham Forest. I remember hearing events unfold. One of the girls had a brother at the game so you can imagine the tension before we knew he was all right.

'It was an extraordinarily emotional time for me. My mother had died in March, I had friends die at Hillsborough in the April and then my father died the following month. Over those three months the level of emotion was phenomenal because I was travelling back and forward to Liverpool from Glasgow for the funerals.

'The English authorities put intense pressure on Liverpool to start playing football again after the tragedy and they forced us to play four games in eight days at the end of the season. The players and fans response was, "We'll start when we're ready." We attempted to win the double for the fans that had died and their families, but the emotional drain of the funerals was too much. I think Kenny Dalglish eventually packed it in as manager because of the stress associated with what happened that day.

'The memorial match against Celtic (30 April 1989) was so important because it allowed us to finish the season but, more important than that, it kick-started people's lives again. It could only have been Celtic that Liverpool chose for that; you knew you could trust the support. The day remains clear in my mind. It was a Sunday afternoon; I knew whole families that came up from Liverpool to stay in Glasgow. On the day I dug out my old scarf from the Ron Yeats' testimonial all those years before from when I was just a teenage lad in Liverpool. There was no separation, you couldn't tell who was Liverpool and who was Celtic. People walked in arm in arm hugging each other. It was much bigger than football; it was like nothing I've ever seen. During "You'll Never Walk

Alone" you could literally see people's spirits lift. It was then I remember thinking the Shankly quote has been so misunderstood about football being "bigger than life and death". I think what Shankly was talking about was what we saw that day. These clubs have a meaning that is passed on from generation to generation, there's a continuation that feeds into a community of supporters, you saw that feeling of family and community extended to another club that day. It's something we'll never forget.'

CHAPTER NINE TRANS-EUROPE EXPRESS

ARRIVING IN NUREMBERG I am greeted by German Celtic fan Matthias Kist for the first in a series of discussions about his relationship with the club. We drive by the Palace of Justice where the Nuremberg Trials were held after the Second World War. Night is falling as we pass the Zeppelin Field and the accompanying gigantic stone mast where Hitler would address Nazi party rallies. I notice the eerie sight emerge as Matthias makes a right-hand turn, revealing the Star of David tattooed on his arm. Although not Jewish, the tattoo is about an association and an identity. An avid football fan, Kist has travelled the world collecting memorabilia and photographing stadiums while encountering supporters at both ends of the political spectrum. Today his replica football top sports green and white Hoops with a shamrock on the badge but it's not Celtic. While his local team Greuther Fürth have an identical kit, Kist's allegiance to the Glasgow club is a lot more sophisticated than an indulgent association with his local team.

Matthias is one of the most travelled football supporters I've encountered on my own Celtic journey. Although from a background he describes as Catholic and Christian with political leanings on the left, his support of Celtic doesn't necessarily have anything do with either. You get the feeling Matthias is keen to avoid any kind of clichéd religious or political sloganeering in his support of the club. 'I am a Catholic but it has nothing to do with why I am a Celtic supporter. In Scotland the Catholic and Protestant culture is very different from Germany; we don't have that feeling of segregation and separation. In Glasgow if you are a Catholic it usually means you have an Irish background. The association and history is very different here; it has more to do with Martin Luther and the particular history of the area or the town you are from.'

In a new century and decade Kist is revitalising proof of what it means to be a football supporter in modern times. For the German football fan songs of hatred and discrimination are out of synchronisation from the time in which they were written and are something he would rather keep at a distance. 'I'm not a patriotic, at least not in football. I only support Germany when they play England and then I'm one hundred per cent German. When it comes to the big tournaments it's everybody supporting Germany, not the real football fans that are standing on the terraces every week. It has begun to change in recent years but because of Germany's history, getting behind a national flag in a large group and seeing the flag plastered up on buildings is not something I could relate to growing up. It's a bizarre feeling and situation to be in and, of course, not everyone getting behind Germany is a Nazi but a lot of people here, me included are still getting used to that feeling today.

'My local team in Germany is Greuther Fürth and I am equally a Celtic supporter. I've followed Celtic around Europe since the mid-1990s. I've been to Scotland but in Europe it's different. I've travelled to football grounds all over the world and encountered a lot of supporters, their politics, their passion and their behaviour. Where Celtic is different for me is the fans, yes they have an association with St Pauli, I suppose for the left-wing political identity, but it's not like Celtic have this heavy political burden dragging them down, there is ultimately something more joyous and celebratory about Celtic supporters. The fans know how to have a party, they don't take themselves too seriously, they have a sense of humour.'

Kist's first Celtic match was against Hamburg SV in 1996. The experience found him following the club as fledgling independent nations were forming in Europe in the aftermath of perestroika, glasnost and the Cold War. A new generation of Celtic supporters established themselves, visiting European locations in the aftermath of wars and Soviet oppression. 'When I first saw Celtic it was simply magic, totally outstanding. I'm talking about the fans. In Europe you see thousands in the green and white singing together and enjoying the moment, the supporters bring the party to places where life is tough. What first stood out to me was the sense of caring about your fellow fans. That was a strong feeling among the supporters; everybody is together. No matter where they go, no matter if they get beat, Celtic supporters want to make friends with the opposition. If someone is causing a problem or getting out of line, everyone goes out their way to stop it from escalating and reason with the person involved. This is unusual for football supporters; Celtic are not typical. I know about the history, it's important but wasn't all that important to me, it was the experiences I had among the travelling support.

'I was aware of Celtic from an early age and I heard about the support being one of the most likeable and friendly in Europe. I couldn't have started to support Celtic if I'd had a really bad experience. If the fans had been a bunch of idiots smashing the place up after getting beat, that would have been it. The fans I travel with support a variety of German teams. Of course, St Pauli but there's also Dortmund and Bayern Munich fans. If you are travelling from Scotland, it's a long way but because of where we are situated, it's more of a road trip following Celtic in the big European competitions. I'd never been to Russia or the Soviet Union so a few us decided to travel over for the FK Suduva game in Lithuania. It was the first round of the UEFA Cup competition where we, of course, reached the final in 2003. Lithuania had only been independent about ten years so there was still a big hangover from Soviet control. It was different from anything I'd known in the West, there were a lot of kids begging in the street, they were desperate for any kind of souvenir from us, it was like we had come from another world.

'About two seasons after the Hamburg game we travelled to Croatia for the Zagreb match, it was not long after the war and all the political unrest. They were also leaving a time of communism. There were only about 700 Celtic fans but typically they descended on the market square for a party.

You could see the Zagreb fans standing on the outside just studying and carefully observing us, slowly they started to trickle in, by the end of the day it was a sea of green, white and blue celebrating together.'

After the drive through Nuremberg we arrive in Kist's home of city of Erlangen. Negotiating an endless row of bicycles we finally arrive at the apartment he shares with his partner Carmen and son Raul. Thumbing through his vinyl collection, Matthias opts for Fischer-Z and *Red Skies Over Paradise*; the needle hits the groove over a crackly 'Luton to Lisbon' which gently floats from the turntable. The walls feature immaculately framed mementos of his years following Celtic. Ticket stubs, photographs and signed souvenirs make up an impressive and preserved reminder of some memorable treks. Centre stage is a photograph showing a dreadlocked Henrik Larsson with his arm around Kist. For a generation that grew up in the shadow of the Lisbon story, Larsson gifted Celtic supporters the experience of watching a modern football genius at work and was arguably the most complete player ever to wear a Celtic jersey.

The picture in front of me reveals Larsson at a time of deep uncertainty, after a troublesome time at Feyenoord the Swede accidentally set up a goal for opposition player Chic Charnley in his debut against Hibs at Easter Road. Dating back to 11 August 1997, the shot shows Larsson in the ground of Austrian club Tirol Innsbruck, the evening before an encounter with Celtic. Celtic would lose the game 2–1 and Larsson would score an own goal in the second leg at Parkhead. Despite a shaky start, the meeting proved to be an insightful experience for Kist: 'it was a great moment and time in my life captured in the photo. We arrived in Innsbruck and noticed the stadium's floodlights were on, I thought it would be worth taking a chance to see if Celtic were training. It was easy to get through the gates and in front of me the team was there on the park. We decided to go over and say hello to Andy Thom, having the German connection got us talking. Tommy Boyd was fantastic, along with Larsson he is probably my favourite Celtic player. Tommy showed us what the fans mean to Celtic players, as soon as he saw us he came straight over and welcomed us, he made you feel that it was important to be a Celtic supporter. For me Tommy was a strong captain and defender for Celtic at an important time for the club, he was a reliable player for Martin O'Neill when he first arrived as manager and part of the change that O'Neill created. He left a lasting impression. Boyd gave us time and had a laugh with us; it's a great thing for the fans to feel valued, he was very genuine. No one could have known what kind of player Henrik Larsson was going to be; he was standing there very quiet but always smiling and very cool with the Rasta hair. Larsson was very charismatic even then; he shook my hand and posed for the picture. I remember that Celtic won the return leg in Glasgow, Innsbruck were a really crap team and went out of business a few years later.'

If Celtic ever officially decides to initiate 'the top ten Celtic villains' a good chunk of the slots would understandably be filled by referees. For many Celtic supporters the man that could justifiably top that list is German whistler Helmut Heinz Krugg. His shocking performance in the Juventus v

Celtic European Cup match in September 2001 led to an emotional Martin O'Neill, on camera, voicing exactly how every aggrieved Celtic supporter was feeling at the award of a ridiculous penalty to the Italians three minutes from full time. 'No Celtic fan could ever forget this German referee; the chant was, "Are you Dallas in disguise?"' Remembers Kist: 'Celtic completely went on the attack that night; Sutton and Larsson were magnificent. Edgar Davids was just back from failing a drugs test, and committed foul after foul, which Krugg refused to acknowledge until he was eventually sent off but it was too late. That Celtic team were simply magnificent; we've not seen anything like it since Martin O'Neill left. They wanted to win every game and they had the skill and determination to give it a try. When you watched Celtic under Gordon Strachan it was very different. In Germany we call it "one way football", it's like the game was down to chance; they might win 5–0 but they also might get beat 2–1. Where is the conviction to win the game? Where is the structure?

'In 2001 Juventus thought we were a formality and that is the biggest mistake you could make against that team. We came back from 2–0 down, two great goals from Petrov and Larsson made it 2–2 and after that Celtic just kept coming at them. It was very unfortunate because Sutton nearly scored on the final whistle. It took a shameful performance from the referee, a dodgy penalty and a lot of cheating to defeat Celtic that night. Martin O'Neill's Celtic team didn't know when they were beaten and when they did lose, they were as devastated as us.

'What I remember about that game is the Italian people because some countries don't really understand Celtic, they don't see any difference between Celtic fans and other British teams like Chelsea or Manchester United. In Italy people know about Celtic because of the history in the European Cup. As usual we made our way to the town centre but the police in Italy are a different story, they descended on us like we were wild pigs and rammed us on about twelve buses, which meant a lot of friends were separated. No one informed Celtic that this would be happening but as soon as we got on the bus, the singing, dancing and clapping started again with 'Hail Hail the Celts are here'. As the twelve buses made their way some Italian people started to line the streets of Turin and applaud us, the feeling was extraordinary. To be part of this support and part of that experience; it turned out to be the best bus journey of my life.'

Perhaps the most evident German association with Celtic is with St Pauli. Fans of the Hamburg club are famous for their leftist anti-Nazi stance, particularly in the 1980s when neo-Nazi groups and far-right extremists seemed to gain a foothold on the terraces of Europe. Much is made of St Pauli and Celtic's leftist connections, in truth while there's a crossover of values, the emphasis is really on far more pressing issues such as, 'where's the party'. Over the years St Pauli have retained a strong punk rock and metal ethos. As well as being left wing there's a strong sway towards anarchy and hedonism. The team even run out to AC/DC's 'Hells Bells' with fans ranging from New Jersey's Gaslight Anthem to Norway's Turbonegro. Unsurprisingly it's not something that sits well with the more traditional cornerstones of the Celtic support and those who pledge their support to Celtic alone.

For the main part our away travellers are a non-judgemental bunch, intent on having a good time which is what seems to have united both sets of supporters on Celtic's German tour back in 1995. Fifteen years later and a St Pauli hoody can now be found among the racks of the Celtic Superstore. For Matthias the connection has lost a bit of clout over the last few years: 'I think St Pauli has become a bit of a trend thing, you know what I mean; it's cool to like St Pauli. It's become famous for being leftist and cool to like but what does that mean apart from being fashionable? Don't get me wrong I think the political history of anti-fascism is very important and there is that connection with Celtic, but people have got into St Pauli because it's a fashion statement. The people that go to the games go once or twice a season, they live in different parts of Germany. It's the same with Celtic. I follow them less in the pub now because it used to be a special event with everyone gathering together in one place. Now you can drift into any Irish bar and find the Celtic game, it's nothing special. You could compare it to twenty years ago when people collected vinyl records and they would find something rare in some second-hand record shop. Now you can find anything you want on the internet but it's not the same feeling or emotion. When Celtic stopped Rangers from winning ten-in-a-row I was going frantic in Mexico. The internet didn't have the same reach at that time and I was using this crappy phone-card trying to call a friend in Germany to find out the score. I couldn't sleep that night with anticipation, wondering what happened. I raced out of bed in the morning hunting down internet cafes, but everywhere was closed. I felt like I was in the middle of the desert; the anticipation nearly killed me it was so intense. Now you get the score sent by text: bang.'

While the digital age has bolstered various expatriate communities, the convenience of satellite broadcasting and internet coverage has given many supporters the option of staying in to watch the game. For Matthias Celtic has lost its cult appeal, a bit like your favourite band selling out and wearing that passé St Pauli hoody. In contrast to the majority of New York Celtic supporters who drink in The Parlour, the relationship lacks an ethnic bond with Scotland or Ireland. Says Kist: 'The feeling of going to watch Celtic in Scotland and in Europe are very different things. The first time I saw Celtic in Glasgow was February 1998 towards the end of Larsson's first season. We thrashed Kilmarnock 4–0; it was amazing, the songs in the stadium, the atmosphere, brilliant. I went with my friend Brian who lives in Airdrie. But what I find strange is the rivalry with Rangers. For instance, when we arrived in the area I had to hide the Celtic scarf in my pocket. I find that whole experience very difficult. My friend would say, "Get that out the road." It's hard to explain why the experience is so different but I think this is part of it. I work in a hotel, when guests arrive from Glasgow I ask them: "Are you supporting Celtic or Rangers?" I play the stupid German. If they say Rangers I tell them to have a nice stay and if they say Celtic the party begins!

'I understand rival supporters but having to hide what team you support is not something I like. In Glasgow I was told not to start talking about Celtic in the pub as it's seen as common sense not to ask someone what team they support. That was all very different to the feeling in Europe, where you wouldn't think twice about these things. My home team, Fürth, actually played a friendly against Rangers a few years ago. They had to do a double take when they arrived to see the green and white Hoops, shamrocks and Ireland flags. I don't think their fans had any idea about our colours. There was one guy going mad at us jumping up and down, when he realised we were German he started laughing. Another guy was the double of Martin O'Neill so we gave him a few bars of the 'Martin O'Neill' chant. A few of my friends went for a beer with them; it wasn't really a problem, it was mostly just a bit of fun.'

With the recent reversal of Celtic's fortunes abroad Matthias' rambling days around Europe are temporarily on hold. His focus remains with Greuther Fürth and while they have retained something of a reputation for being a people's club, Kist admits the corridor between corporate enterprise and retaining an individual ethos is a tight passage especially when clubs are desperate for revenue just to survive. 'With Fürth it's more familiar, it's more social; every supporter is important. You can get a word with the manager if you want to say something. It's got the feeling of a big family, people are reachable, the fans get a fair hearing. At the same time you have to be realistic; football in general is becoming more commercial and distant from the fans, the focus is on money. We are trying to find the middle of these two extremes. I feel a sense of frustration that Celtic did not build on the UEFA Cup final place. A great many of us who followed Celtic in the 1990s and the O'Neill years have family now; it's harder to get to games but the main reason we're not going is that Celtic aren't in Europe.

'The other thing is that there is nobody special for me in the current team. Where is the Tom Boyd type of player, the guys that love Celtic and love the fans? There is no one with the fight or spirit of Johnny Hartson, there is no talisman like Larsson. You can tell when a player is only at Celtic for the cheque. The feeling changed after Martin O'Neill. The players and the manager had a strong awareness of the fans and the past but they put their own stamp on the history. Is anyone doing that now? The memories of Turin are fresh in my mind. I also have to say, who out there could do a better job than Neil Lennon? He is doing the best he can with what he has and I support him as a manager, he was a great servant as a player.'

I call Matthias again as my deadline approaches. What stands out in my memory is his vast collection of memorabilia from the mid-1990s through to the O'Neill years. I wonder what his most prized possession is. Perhaps his ticket from Turin, maybe it's a programme from when we travelled to Seville or Milan together, what now seems like a lifetime ago? Naw, it surely must be that early picture with Matthias alongside an uber cool dreadlocked Henrik Larsson in Austria. Matthias laughs down the phone: 'It's none of those but I'm looking at it right now. You remember the story I told you about playing the stupid German? I had a call one day from a lady in Airdrie called Cecile. She was preparing for a trip with her swimming club who were visiting the Christmas market in Nuremberg. So I asked her the question, "Are you supporting Celtic or Rangers?" Cecile was a massive Celtic fan and during the lead-up to her visit we ended up talking most days. It turned out she had a rare illness and was assigned a special doctor in Glasgow who also worked with the Celtic team. On the night she arrived there was a long delay with their flight but I wanted to stay so I could welcome her to Germany. We exchanged presents and of course, she had brought me shortbread from Scotland. Once we got everyone settled down it was really late so I said my goodbyes to Cecile. There was a moment's silence and then she said, "Wait a minute; I have one more present for you." I unwrapped this massive frame and inside was a Celtic shirt; it was signed to Matthias Kist from Henrik Larsson. I was fighting back tears and smiling at the same time, I just couldn't believe it. I called Cecile about a month or two later to see how she was doing but she had passed away from the illness. She gave me this special gift and a memory I'll never forget as long as I live.'

On 28 December 1983 Mario Gil Soriano was born in Zaragoza, one of seventeen devolved autonomous communities in the Spanish constitution created in 1978. Since the mid-1990s Soriano has been on a journey, discovering his links to the Aragon community located in north-eastern Spain. Soriano and a number of like-minded friends went on a collective journey of self-discovery keen to learn more of the

Aragonese language and history. Significantly, it was the green and white Hoops of Celtic that united a bunch of teenagers, eager to be educated on their own local culture, heritage and history.

Today, taking a break from his work as a microbiologist Mario explains the deep connection he formed with Celtic as a teenager: 'I discovered Celtic when I was about fifteen. I was in a tavern and there was a fan with a Celtic top on and a few others with scarves. I started to ask him about Celtic and what the club meant in relation to Scotland and I was hooked. Celtic has become important for minority communities here in Spain because we share the same human values and ideas of freedom. It relates to a representation of a people without a fixed state and we share a lot of the same beliefs. We identify with Celtic because it is about not being repressed and expressing your politics, your culture and your point of view through football, language and music. For me it is more about politics and culture than religion. In Scotland I know this is different but I am not Catholic; I don't mind that but for me it is important that Celtic represent Scottish and Irish culture, they express difference in the UK the way we do in Spain.

'When I watch Celtic it is a very strange feeling for me, Glasgow is not my city and Scotland or Ireland is not my home, but the Celtic supporters are my people, we are the same. When I first watched the Celtic supporters it was like they represented me. I pay more attention sometimes to the fans in the stadium than to the field because I like the passion of the songs and the spirit of the supporters.'

It's a surreal notion to imagine a collection of rival fans coming together in a Zaragoza pub to watch Celtic. In contrast to Matthias in Germany who suggests the media retain an open hostility towards Celtic, their Spanish counterparts are widely aware of the club's hospitable reputation in Europe. 'When I watched the final in Seville I was going absolutely crazy; I was devastated we did not win the match against Porto. Many Spanish people support Celtic because they are the only British team we feel something for. In Spain people who know about football know that Celtic is famous for being the first non-Latin club to win the European Cup. Seville was a big event in Europe because of how we feel about this club. I've since watched Celtic play Barcelona and Villarreal in Europe; these nights have been very special. It's painful not to see Celtic go as far since Seville and fall away in European competition.

'Those games with Villarreal and Barcelona have made our connections stronger with supporters here in Spain. The Celtic Submari is a Villarreal Celtic supporters' club called after their own 'Yellow Submarine' nickname and they have arranged some charity events with Celtic. In the pub you will find Athletic Bilbao supporters from the Basque country; their roots come from British working-class miners and steel workers that came to Spain in the late nineteenth century. There's also a Celta Vigo fan from the time they played in 2002. Many people around the country identify with Celtic because when they play Spanish clubs the fans make friends. I myself have a good friend, Ronnie, from East Kilbride.

'The other thing Celtic has in common with these clubs is

the left-wing politics. In Spain there are ultra groups, which often have a right-wing identity. Even if there's a small group in a club like Real Madrid it gives the entire club a bad reputation but not every Real Madrid supporter is a right-wing fascist. The culture around Celtic is the most important thing to me, the fans are always having fun, they have a lot more in common with the Mediterranean character than English clubs. For me those clubs bring a very different feeling when they come here. I think people have a separate opinion on Chelsea and even Manchester United. The ethos with Barcelona is more than a club; the same is true of Celtic. The media here understand Celtic. In the press they talk about the openness of the supporters, they are well known for being a friendly and welcoming people. When other clubs come over it can get ugly and there is a lot of street fighting but when the Hoops come to the cities here and people from Spain go to Parkhead this never happens. The Celtic thing brings like-minded people together; it's joyful celebration. I was wearing my Celtic top and scarf today when I saw a guy at the university where I work wearing the Hoops and we struck up a conversation. It's not unusual to see that here. Celtic is not a team like Manchester United, you know popular for winning trophies. The kind of people who wear a Celtic top don't wear it because of trophies; it's more about the ethos; it's a very different thing. On St Patrick's Day people here would wear the Hoops and they would relate it to having affection for Ireland, there is a feeling for Ireland in Spain because we share a similar history and way of life.'

After years of watching Celtic from afar in Zaragoza,

Mario decided to make a trip to Glasgow, intent on sampling the ground and local culture for himself. 'Last year I travelled to Scotland at Easter time. I spent about a week there and the first place I went to was Celtic Park for a tour. I felt a bit wary and didn't really want to talk about my support of Celtic to strangers, I know this is something you have to be careful about. I felt strange walking along past the cemetery and then finally I reached the ground. It was an amazing feeling to be at the place where all this history has taken place. When I arrived at the stadium it was like being a small boy because I've spent so many years supporting this club from very far away. I got to meet Nakamura and had my picture taken with the European Cup.'

Aside from his visit to Parkhead, Mario struggled to find obvious examples of the Celts. Keen to hear traditional songs and poetry in Scotland's native tongue he decided to travel further north: 'I wanted to find out more about Scottish culture when I visited and it was very difficult. It wasn't until I reached Skye that I heard people singing traditional songs. I wanted to hear them sing in their own language, this kind of connection made me feel close to Celtic. Psychologically it's good to know your roots, your language and where you come from; both British and Spanish oppressors have tried to eradicate the culture of the Celtic races. Supporting Celtic keeps our way of life and our culture alive.'

Like many Celtic supporters Mario feels a sense of displacement in his home country: 'I don't feel Spanish, I am part of the Aragon community in the way that some Scottish people don't feel British or want be part of the UK. In Spain you have the Catalonian and Basque communities. They were all here long before the kingdom of Spain came into existence, our history goes back thousands of years. I don't support the Spanish national team, I don't care what they do but I prefer it if they lose because I don't want to listen to the media and people around me boast about them. My national football team is Aragon. The Aragon culture is not something I was taught in school but something I had to discover for myself. I got talking to some friends and it was obvious we had a strong feeling for the language. I suppose it would be like learning to speak Gaelic in Scotland. By learning the language you learn about yourself, it's like a light being switched on. For many years the Aragonese language was dying and nobody was doing anything about it. I think it's getting stronger again. Many people in my generation believe we need to learn our own tongue because it brings us closer to who we really are. When my ancestors spoke Aragonese they were hit with a stick by the teacher for not speaking correctly, this generated a feeling of hatred towards what they called Spanish culture. We are starting to recover our own culture and traditions now.

'To me it is stupid to say there is only one culture, one tradition and one language. If you take something like Halloween, it's a Celtic tradition. People seem to think it's American but it comes from us, the same with Christmas. In the last fifteen years the awareness of the language, cuisine and culture is growing. I feel positive about the future, people are studying and getting educated, I grew up not knowing anything about my culture, I thought I was the same as someone from Madrid but we are very different as are other parts of the Spanish estate. We are not better than others but what I'm talking about is celebrating the difference and viewing yourself alongside other cultures not against them.'

CHAPTER TEN A WALK ACROSS THE ROOFTOPS

THERE'S SOMETHING FUNDAMENTALLY Celtic in the anecdote where Jim Kerr reveals his burning unease at the late Jimmy Johnstone's ambition to record a version of Bon Jovi's 'Bed of Roses' with Simple Minds, the request reaching the band's front man led his heart to sink like quicksand. On the one hand here's the chance to combine Kerr's twin passions of football and rock 'n' roll with arguably the greatest Celtic player that's ever graced the green and white, not only that, he's famed as a bit of a chanter. On the other there's the impending dread of being associated with an overworked American power ballad for the rest of his life. Ultimately, what can Jim do? The track's purpose was to raise awareness and funds for motor neurone disease, the illness that would ultimately claim Jimmy's life. However, the song that was finally cut: 'Dirty Old Town' written by Ewan MacColl and made famous by The Pogues couldn't have been a more fitting tribute and has now firmly established itself as a welcome blast on the Tannoy at Celtic Park. A sprinkling of magic dust falls over Paradise particularly where Kerr pays tribute to Jinky with the amended line: 'Saw Jimmy Johnstone set the night on fire!' In reference to the player's single-handed demolition of Red Star Belgrade.

Penned by a second-generation, self-educated, communist Scot, the song stands firm as a hymn to industrial Britain and mainlines straight to the core of the culture and wealth of ideas that have traditionally surrounded the Celtic support. Written in 1949 and widely associated with the folk revival of the 1950s 'Dirty Old Town' evokes a distinctive and dangerous working-class romance and masculinity from a bygone era. While the characteristics of an Irish immigrant support have always been palpable, the media often overlooks interpretations of Celtic's wider Scottish identity. The Scottish journalist and broadcaster Gerry McNee once suggested Celtic fans sing 'The Fields of Athenry' 'for all the wrong reasons'. The theme of an Irish struggle and famine are apparent but they are only there to set the scene of a typical Irish ballad. To suggest that its purpose is to 'wind up the opposition' shows a refusal to try and get to grips or understand the ethnicity of the club's support. The areas of discussion around the Celtic support have traditionally carried the voice of opposition and an alternative choice in Scotland. Much of the culture around Celtic has been as much about preserving the merits of an urban working-class Scotland as well as maintaining a relation to Ireland. Since the mid-eighteenth century Scottish working-class masculinity was shaped by the politics and ideas of an industrial workforce supported by the trade union movement; undoubtedly the same culture that shaped Celtic's support from the club's formation in the late Victorian era until the death knells of industrial decline in the late 1970s.

Since then, in the face of market forces, the dominance of the service industry, high unemployment and a drift towards gang culture, Scottish males have struggled to hang their identity on a definitive pillar causing something of a personality crisis. For many, Celtic has proved to be a healthy psychological gateway to the past and to the previous generations that put their stamp on Scotland's industrial cities where their toil, effort and contribution instilled a pride and enduring association in the land where they lived and worked. In many ways Celtic has functioned as a baton for ideas, stories, passions, folk songs and feelings to be passed on as mainstream working-class culture has shifted beyond all recognition.

The arrival of all-seater stadiums and the commercial impetus of modern football have paved the way for a family and female friendly environment in what was previously the domain of working men. When discussing Celtic with a number of well-known Scottish women in the area of entertainment, politics and public life, born somewhere between the late 1950s and early 1960s, what is obvious is the club's permanence in their life despite at times feeling separation or alienation in a previously male arena. Their relationship with Celtic reflects changes in the expectations, traditional responsibilities and perceptions of women in Scottish society. Since the mid-1990s women have asserted a mainstream ownership of Celtic and wrestled it away from a traditional working-class male preserve. Today's stories, traditions, politics and the now familial nature of the club belong in their narratives as much as their fathers, brothers, uncles, husbands and boyfriends in the generation before, when Glasgow was the workshop of the world.

Born in Glasgow and the eldest of seven children, Eddi Reader initially cut her teeth as a pop singer fronting Fairground Attraction. The band are largely remembered for their UK chart topper 'Perfect', which was significantly adopted by Celtic supporters in the club's centenary year. Today Reader is better known for earthy folk songs and interpretations from the works of Robert Burns. Her earliest memories are of the songs and parties associated with tenement life in the early 1960s. Her father, a welder and fervent Celtic supporter, would bring home an array of characters for a Glasgow sing-song after last orders as a buffer for hitting the pub on wages night. Says Reader: 'At that time we lived at 7 Anthony Street in Anderston. My da had this Phillips reel-to-reel tape recorder on which he recorded a lot of our house parties from 1960 to 1965, when the tenements came down. It's helped me remember a lot of stuff. You'd have this wait for the green light to come on and away somebody went with a song like "The Glasgow Barrowlands". One of the first things I heard was my uncle teaching a few of my siblings "The Celtic Song".

'It was different in those days because I was in the women's club; male and female were segregated. The mothers, grannies and aunties would be moaning and getting on with things while the men watched Celtic on the television or listened on the wireless. What I understood early on was that this thing, the game and this team in the green and white stripes, or grey and white on our black and white portable television, were of massive importance. When Celtic scored you were hit with this impact of emotion. Something amazing happened, you felt that thunder in your living room, everybody was on their feet, roaring with their fists in the air.

'I have two clear memories involving Celtic from when I was really young. The first is of Jimmy Johnstone, watching the power and skill of this wee fella taking on all comers while running the length of the park, no one could get the ball. I'd sit fascinated and infected by my da's enthusiasm. The other is the Atletico Madrid game where players were literally getting battered stupid on the park. I was a bit older by this stage, I was in my teens and this was the early 1970s. What still stands out is seeing how appalled people were over that game; my da was disgusted. The sentiment of the day was how could anyone call themselves sportsmen behaving like that; no one could believe that kind of violence on a football pitch. It really went against what the game was about and pretty shocking at the time.'

In the 1960s Celtic songs were sung alongside political anthems of the day. Undoubtedly the late Matt McGinn was something of a local hero capturing the spirit and humour of the times through his work anthems and protest songs, often lampooning the religious divide. Today McGinn remains the only Scot in the Smithsonian Institute's top 100 folk songs, alongside the likes of Bob Dylan and Pete Seeger. In 1961 McGinn found himself in the company of both men when he appeared at Carnegie Hall in New York after an invitation from Seeger. Although he's received a variety of plaudits, McGinn remains something of a cult figure and his songs about the shipyards, sectarianism and Glasgow life are arguably kept alive in Celtic pubs, particularly 'The Two Heided Man' on Hope Street, which stands as something of a modern tribute. In the same way that Ewan MacColl summons Salford and all that goes with it in his music, McGinn, more than any other songwriter, soundtracks Glasgow. Both writers in their songs captured a native way of life particular to their area, suggesting differences from the British conservative model and from a mainstream saturated by transient American consumerism and pop culture.

Raised on the music of McGinn, Reader believes Celtic is not only tied to the culture of Glasgow, rather than to a perceived Irishness, but also to typical Scottish folk traditions: 'I see Celtic as a Glasgow team not an Irish team. Again it's connected to the songs; it's folk music. A folk tune that belongs to you should come from your town, your street even if you can get away with it. Celtic was a working-man's team; it belonged to Glasgow shipyard workers, corporation bus drivers, miners and iron turners. The club created a sense of belonging for working people and I think that's what the founder, Walfrid, was trying to do. In one sense I grew up with Celtic songs and Irish rebel songs, there was none of the lunacy that you sometimes get with that culture in terms of the rebel stuff, if there was they would have been kicked out my mother's house.

'The men in my family that support Celtic probably have more ancestral links to Fife and Germany than they do Ireland. Had I not had that deep connection to my Irish granny from Tralee I don't know what my link to Ireland would have been. When I think of what the Irish side means to me, certainly the matriarchal side, I think of her lilting Irish tongue, creamy teas, she seemed to smell nicer, those heartbreaking hymns about Jesus; it's a quiet and peaceful kind of feeling. Irish Catholic culture in Glasgow wasn't like that; for the young guys that supported Celtic it was about pop culture. Around 1968 it would be your cousin's boyfriend coming round to a tenement party with a carry out and a guitar to play Beatles' songs, before that it was just singing. It was more about getting off with lassies, it was louder, it was violent and whiskey drenched; it was Glasgow.

'When I got a bit older I realised that I had no idea what a Scot was, but there was something very Scottish about Celtic and part of that was the songs. I was at Celtic Connections with a friend recently; he's an intelligent, educated guy from a Presbyterian background but he started referring to some old traditional Scottish tunes as "aw this Irish stuff". I thought how weird that you don't feel ownership of your own culture. I discovered the same thing in England one night when I played an old folk heartbreaker called 'The Blacksmith'. There was a girl after the gig came over and asked me where it came from. I was like: "It's yours, it's an old English folk song." I talk to friends in London and they get very embarrassed by morris dancing. My attitude is why? Because these are the things that pin us to this planet, it's like Irish dancing or Scottish country dancing here. What supporting Celtic gave to people was an ownership of the songs that go with it. Those rousing anthems I heard in the living room when I was growing up stir something very deep inside and that's different from other teams, largely because folk culture was being swept away by the end of the industrial revolution all over Britain. Celtic didn't just provide you with a love of the team, supporting Celtic is connected to an overblown love of the culture, the expression and feeling when you were singing those songs wasn't just about the team. It was an expression of who you were! The other thing is the way Celtic fans take ownership of songs. When they began to sing 'Perfect' and changed it to "It's got to be Celtic", it made the connection even stronger for me and it made my da immensely proud.

'For a long time the association was different, it was part of a very male world. Glasgow in 1978 was a very different place. There were no toilets in the pubs or grounds for women. It was a violent city and women were viewed and treated differently. Now Celtic is back in my life, my partner John will come from the pub with a story about wee Shaun Maloney. As much as I own Celtic, Celtic owns me, whether it's going back to my family in the living room, or the fans singing 'Perfect'. I'm always going to be involved with it. I'm connected to this thing that's bigger than me and it's bigger than the football club.'

As much as Reader's generation of women have had to reclaim Celtic, they have equally had to reclaim and discover their Scottishness. For previous generations the ethnicity of Celtic supporters seemed to sit in a cultural no-man's-land. Fear of an association with the Irish Troubles led many to keep any expression of Irish identification hidden. Many felt alienated from the predominant culture of Scotland and the significance of the General Assembly of the Church of Scotland. (Pre-parliament the Church gave Scotland a strong sense of independent identity and authority.) Those feelings undoubtedly conferred greater prominence to Celtic for those in Scotland's Irish Catholic community, and supporting Celtic undoubtedly became the arena of another Scottish expression. (The experiences of that culture are wonderfully articulated by author Andrew O'Hagan in his book *The Missing* – see chapter 11.)

For Reader, as much as it was a celebration, there was always a strong awareness of the disappeared: 'If you are talking about the history of Celtic and Glasgow you can't not talk about the sectarian problems because it's part of the experience. I come from a very mixed background on both sides, a mix that was both devout Irish Catholic and staunch Orange Protestant. At family gatherings you were always aware that people were missing and there were things that didn't get talked about. Around 1915 some relatives of mine, two brothers, had joined the struggle in Ireland. These guys were regarded as outlaws and wanted by the authorities. I can't relate to the celebration of murder and hatred that you have in violent Republican culture now, but when I think of my relatives that went to fight in that struggle nearly a hundred years ago, there are some similarities with the struggle we have for independence in Scotland today. The difference is that over there it got violent. While I think we have to celebrate both cultures, I would struggle in a Scotland that celebrated King William of Orange for the simple reason that he wanted to sterilise Scottish women.

There were some family members with strong Orange allegiances that completely removed themselves because they didn't agree with mixed marriages. Also, there were stories of half-siblings in my family that didn't talk to each other because of those cultural allegiances.'

Arguably sectarian rivalry with Rangers supporters today rests on a tribal perspective rather than a strong religious faith. The Scottish government pointed to some degree of success in tackling the problem, going on record with their attempt to work with related offenders in prisons, experimenting with public banning orders and supporting anti-sectarian organisations such as Nil By Mouth. But others have suggested that SNP ministers simply didn't do enough. Violent attacks relating to sectarianism in the 2010–11 season and related tensions between the teams, management and fans in a Scottish Cup game at Parkhead led to a government summit in March 2011. Two months later Professor Tom Devine suggested that SNP 'took their foot off the pedal' on sectarianism which had reached its most 'explicit' and 'extreme' peak in recent times following letter bombs being sent to Neil Lennon and others. More positively Reader believes the problem is changing: 'It will probably take about another generation, I think this generation that are coming through now really have the chance to change it. I come from a culture that says, "but for the grace of God go I"; we needed help and somebody helped us. Glasgow people are kind hearted; the people that adopt it become kind hearted. The Asian community have integrated and love it as much as I love it and it belongs to them as much as it belongs to me.

My kids told me a story about these Buckfast guys who were being racist to a young Asian boy in a skate park; they were suddenly surrounded. To me that is Glasgow; that is the culture. I lived through changes in this city, the violence in the 1970s, I saw the fighting, the wife beating but I also saw the tremendous generosity of the city.

'It's interesting the innocent way in which you view it all when you're young. My Irish Catholic granny's birthday was 12 July, and I always thought that the Orange Walk was part of her birthday celebrations. To me it's all linked in some way and I've written about this most of my life on songs like 'Glasgow Star' where I'm sitting on a Glasgow bus and there's a guy singing a Rangers song. My response is "Shut yer bloody mouth and kiss us." For all the sectarian problems there is also a connectedness, which is a Glasgow thing. For years my da talked about his best pal who owned a pub up in Skye. After he died I went through that thing where I was missing my da and wanted to follow his trail a bit. I was playing some gigs further north and decided that I wanted to try and find this pub. I eventually found the bar. It was near a harbour, obviously a fisherman's pub. When I walked in I felt a bit self-conscious, the place was covered in red, white and blue with FTP on the wall. It was obviously a Rangers pub and I could see the punters were thinking, "It's that bird, the singer" sort of thing. I walked up to the bar and there was this guy with a silver duck's arse haircut behind the pumps, just like ma da. So I went forward kind of self-consciously: "I'm looking for Harry Dick; I'm Danny Reader's daughter." To which he shouted: "Elvis's kid". Harry and my da were big rock 'n' roll fans and that's how they originally became pals growing up in Glasgow. Seeing the funny side I was like: "You know my da was a big Celtic man Harry?" He then pointed to an old picture and there was Harry in green and white Hoops and my dad smiling at me as if from the other side in a Rangers top. It's moments like that which makes a life without Celtic or Rangers unimaginable to me.'

Before its implosion the Scottish Socialist Party brought a much-needed shot in the arm to left-wing and working-class thinking in the late 1990s. Into the new century the party's presence in the Scottish parliament tapped into Scotland's rich, socialist heritage. Rosie Kane, in particular, marked her territory in an overwhelmingly middle-class male environment, shaking up the Edinburgh bourgeoisie with her wide girl swagger and sassy charisma. Her strong Glaswegian brogue was a reminder of Scotland's working-class achievers from the past, particularly those that talked with confidence and intelligence in their native tongue, with one obvious difference. While politicians are often reluctant to reveal their football devotion, Rosie eventually regained her allegiance to Celtic after an initial hesitation while in the public eye: 'For me it was a bit about reclaiming my past because football has always been a big part of my life, growing up I was a bit of a tomboy having a kick about with my four brothers. I once worked as a football coach alongside former Scotland manager Andy Roxburgh and as a sports organiser in the community.'

My first interview with Rosie was arranged while she was

still an MSP collecting money outside Hampden at the Celtic end exchanging banter with the green and white horde. Significantly Rosie started going to games long before it became fashionable for women: 'I've seen a lot of emotional days at Parkhead; I was at the Jungle's Last Stand and the game against Liverpool after Hillsborough. There were times when it wasn't really a place for a woman to be so I was away from it for a while. I'm not ashamed of the association with Celtic. It's no secret that it's instilled a confidence in me. Getting into politics you hear things like "You'll alienate half the city" but my feeling is you can still support your team, of course you can. I've had to think about it more deeply at times, my first game back after a bit of time away was Celtic v Aberdeen at Parkhead and it was just a magic day, it brought back a lot of feelings from my childhood, it was a very freeing experience.'

Undoubtedly the folklore around Celtic players and the imaginative and literary components of Irish culture softened the harder and craggier edges of Scottish football. Jimmy McGrory, the son of Irish parents, was famously known as the Mermaid by fans due to his unique heading ability, despite his height. It's not outlandish to suggest a player being called the Mermaid at Kilmarnock or Rangers just wouldn't have the same ring or meaning. It's unquestionably Celtic because there's a cheek and a mischief attached that's not particularly present elsewhere. Similarly the Irish-born Celtic player Charlie Tully remains a cult figure as much for his persona as for his skills. While mothers and children didn't have a strong presence at the games in the days of the Jungle, they undoubtedly felt a connection and support of Celtic because of the club's personality. Says Kane: 'Celtic was my mother's greatest love; if Celtic was on the wireless you didn't dare walk in the way of it. Every week she would go to Parkhead and collect the tickets for the Celtic Pools. We lived in Pollock and it felt like a day out on the bus going to the East End and collecting the book from Sean Fallon. We would wait for players to arrive and collect autographs, when the Lisbon Lions came out everyone would be pushing for Jimmy Johnstone and Billy McNeill. It went right through to the next generations of young players like Kenny Dalglish and Danny McGrain then Paul McStay and Roy Aitken. When I think back it makes me laugh. I remember waving to Bobby Lennox at Barrhead Road, he was driving in from Ayr. My mother would take us down to cheer him on as he drove to training. She was on first name terms with all the players and would write letters congratulating or commiserating with them. She had contacts that nobody else had. I remember she got Bobby Murdoch to go to the school for a prize-giving.

'The other thing I would say is there is something attractive about the colour green, and you can understand why it's used in a lot of advertising. In our house the door was painted green, the frame painted white, the furniture and carpets green, the colour of everything had to be considered. We were quite countrified although we lived in the city. My mother came from a wee mining village. I remember the differences in Pollock and all the women that lived there and came to the house seemed to be fashion queens with bee-hive hairdos, jewellery, ears pierced, short skirts and black tights.

My dad was Irish and looked like a very typical Celt. We were treated to many a ballad and hymn from his repertoire, he would often start with "Forty Shades of Green" and he'd sing these old heartbroken country songs usually about the wife dying and the weans being left with the dad. I know these songs meant a great deal to him, the rebel songs would start up but my mother would hush him up because of the neighbours, once you got into the 1970s you could have got done under anti-terror laws.'

Since her emergence in Scottish politics Kane's private life has been well documented by the media: surviving a breakdown, time in prison for her political beliefs, the sudden death of her parents and the demise of her party amid much controversy. From the ashes Kane has emerged as something of a trooper. The times I've bumped into her at McChuills on the High Street or collecting outside the grounds, Rosie always emerges with a smile and a story. Her connection with Celtic doesn't strike me as overtly political, there's something more primal and innate that connects her to the club. The songs and attitude has become an essential part of her survival: 'Part of the attraction is that rallying cry that goes on even after some of the worst defeats. There's a buoyancy where people pull together. I often watch games in McChuills and there is an almost unspoken communication between people that says, "Get your head right up" and that's contagious. There's feeling you get when you hear the fans sing: "It's enough to make your heart go woooooaahhhhh." I've seen it many times and it comes from that feeling of picking yourself up out of whatever situation you're in. It's about transferring those feelings of rejection, especially when you look at the background of poverty in the creation of Celtic and its support. You have to keep yourself buoyant because it's about digging yourself out of a hole and finding a courage and an inner strength.'

Throughout the twentieth century Celtic provided some kind of cultural stability in what were particularly nomadic times for Irish families crossing the Atlantic or even just moving around Scotland. For actress and Deacon Blue singer Lorraine McIntosh Celtic offered her maternal Irish family a sense of connectedness and cohesion. Now married to the band's front man Ricky Ross and with children of her own, the vocalist stresses the importance of passing on that bond to the next generation. 'It was very important. My mum was one of ten children; most of them were Celtic fans and most of them ended up in Glasgow at some point in their lives before going to various places. I had one aunt who ended up in New York and she was a huge Celtic fan. For me growing up it was part of the cultural landscape; it's a connection to the past, to your roots. We moved from Glasgow to Ayrshire and there weren't many Celtic fans there. My brothers used to get the bus every Saturday and that was the highlight of their week. I would never be included in that trip because it was a very male thing but you wanted Celtic to win because it would be a happy house that night. Today the world has changed and my daughter's generation go to games and think nothing of that but back then it was a different thing.

'Now I'm married to a Dundee United supporter and we've

got a wee boy. He decided he was going to support Dundee United but I told him, "You need a Celtic strip; you need to be aware of your heritage." Ricky's response was: "C'mon; it's football." He's ended up with three teams: Celtic, Man U and Dundee United. When you have a parent that comes from a different country, that country becomes idealised and longed for, it's the place you go on your holidays. I think so much of it is tied up in who you are, from the way you talk to the songs that you sing and the places you want to go. Celtic was one way of expressing the culture and there weren't many other outlets to do that, Celtic became about much more than football. My mum died when I was eleven. Very quickly I realised that her influence in the house was gone but I was always in touch with her family who looked after me. I still go back to my mum's house in Ireland. I don't know if my kids will feel the same but Ireland was always very important to me. I'm equally proud of my Scottish heritage but growing up that didn't seem important because you were living it.'

Star of stage and screen, Celtic season ticket holder and patron of the club's women's academy, Elaine C. Smith spins the typical Irish story of scarcity and hardship on its head. Although born in Glasgow her identity was strongly informed by her Irish family in Midlothian: 'My link with Celtic came from my grandfather, there's a big Irish connection through a relative called John McGarry who was from the north of Ireland. His great uncle was John McCormack, the Papal Count. My Irish papa came over to Scotland and met a girl from Dalkeith. The Irish side of the family was quite middle class, but I think he had a personal struggle because he couldn't get a promotion above a works manager and in those days it really did come down to religion. The Catholic side of the family were all university educated, professional and middle class. Although he was a Protestant, my dad's story read more like a traditional Catholic upbringing. He was a miner and came from a family of ten but he had no interest in football whatsoever.'

Although following local side Motherwell for a time, the family links with Celtic proved to be a stronger attraction for the budding entertainer in her teens. 'I suppose you could say that the Catholic mafia in my family turned me onto it. I had an uncle, Nicky Avaloni, who used to drive a lorry for Tunnocks. He got me tickets for a game and that was it. We also had a connection with Billy McNeill who knew my mother. Whenever I saw Billy he would always ask for the family. I remember him telling a story about being pushed on by the rest of the team to knock on Jock Stein's door and ask for a pay rise. Eventually Billy worked himself up into asking Stein for a £2 pay rise for the players. Without lifting his head, Stein replied: "Fuck off." Billy turned around with a: "Thanks Boss" and then had to go back to the dressing room and tell the boys how hard he fought but that it wasn't happening.

'The link came through my Irish family even though I've always felt intrinsically Scottish. My husband is a Celtic supporter from the East End of Glasgow. His heroes were always Irish, he's always felt split about the Scottish thing and he knew more about James Connolly and Ireland than he did about typical Scottish heroes like William Wallace or Robert the Bruce. I went to a non-denominational school, which really means I went to a Protestant school, but everyone supported Rangers and the Rangers bus left from the end of our street in Muirhill. When I heard anything anti-Catholic, I used to think, "Do they mean my papa or my granny or my uncle" so that's why I started to support Celtic. I think it's different now. I don't think Rangers is seen as this Protestant bastion anymore and I don't see Celtic as the underdogs, I think we can look at things a bit through rose-tinted glasses. For the majority of people the culture has moved on from what it was in the 1970s.

'Today my daughter goes to the game and can read it as well as my husband but thirty or forty years ago women that went to the football were not regarded as the most attractive or intelligent; they were seen as weird. As a woman the nostalgia around going to the games doesn't work for me because I didn't want to be in the middle of the Jungle peeing into a cup. Today Celtic Park can be one of the greatest amphitheatres in the world and that works a lot better for me than a cold wet Wednesday watching Cowdenbeath with forty-two other punters.'

CHAPTER ELEVEN
THOUSANDS ARE SAILING

BEFORE THE GAME THERE'S a collective power and an explosion of human electricity that generates and crackles along the spirited streets of Glasgow as splashes of green and white dot the city. It spills out of hectic pubs, underground trains, docked ferries, cheap flights, minibuses and even chapels before it reaches Paradise. The pilgrims have travelled the length and breadth of the country and beyond to feel something communal, a joint strength that's no longer tied to the workplace, the union or necessarily the Catholic Church but to Celtic Park, where a victory is celebrated long before the ball spins from the halfway line. For generations a sense of self and self worth for Irish derived Catholics was garnered from supporting the club and equally to those that stood beside them on the terraces and walked home blethering, chanting and singing through sodium-lit housing schemes. Essentially what they had in common was their connection to something that granted collective value and helped make sense of the world beyond themselves.

The Celtic supporters that once lived in single ends and worked in the city's shipyards would no doubt feel a strong sense of alienation in the full-blown age of player power and the twenty-first-century corporate entrepreneur. Change and progression, however, have always been the nature of Celtic and the club has undoubtedly embraced modernity whole-heartedly in order to survive, but at what cost to the club's traditions? In the mid-1990s new lights set flame to an old Scotland where Catholics felt invisible, the expressions of a new intelligentsia in the arts and in public life challenged and addressed the old prejudices that needed lancing from Scottish life. Voices called for a new beginning, one that bolstered the confidence of the diaspora.

One of those voices, writer Andrew O'Hagan, here discusses a fresh set of challenges for the Celtic support, challenges that no longer come from a perceived outside but from within. He considers the sense of social urgency rooted deep in Celtic's origins and the genesis that created its existence. Unlike most football clubs, the core identity and evolution of Celtic has always been in synch with the social progression of its supporters. O'Hagan realistically considers the club's future without that link to the people that follow it, or at least without a relationship to the community it was founded to serve. Celtic also remains inextricably tied to notions of politics and religion but for many those beliefs have become dead symbols of a bygone age, old causes and beliefs that fail to engage with modernity or further progression. Have some of us perhaps become victims, victims of religious and political nostalgia, self-interest with no concern for our fellow supporter and tribal purveyors of past wrongs? For many the answer is a resounding no. Victim is not even in our vocabulary, while there have been injustices, prejudices and misconceptions, to remain broken and beaten down permanently would suggest victimhood. It's not a word that could ever be used to describe the nature of the Celtic support. Perhaps it's got something to do with Walfridism, Catholicism and those Sermon on the Mount religious education teachers that created a support that for many suggests not victimhood but survival and triumph. Here Andrew O' Hagan discusses the spiritual nature of the club, the ideas that have defined us and the responsibilities that lie ahead if we are concerned about sustaining our identity, our core beliefs and our politics in relation to Celtic Football Club.

O'Hagan is a regular turn at the Edinburgh International Book Festival, and it's here in the Georgian splendour of Edinburgh's Old Town that we meet. Although it's only a train ride away, we are a million miles from the evocations summoned from O'Hagan's Glasgow and Ayrshire childhood in *The Missing* and *Our Fathers*. His current book *The Life and Opinions of Maf the Dog and of his friend Marilyn Monroe* is currently the subject of a major Hollywood picture while *The Missing* has been adapted as a play by the National Theatre of Scotland. It's a volume I've noticed on the bookshelves of countless Celtic supporters, spanning class and generations. When I interviewed Peter Mullan in 2002 he cited it as a major influence on his debut feature film *Orphans*, released in 1998. *The Missing* revealed something about where we came from long before the internet reached critical mass and researching your family history became a leisure pursuit. People simply didn't know, have the time or were afraid to discover what they'd find. *The Missing* should be compulsory reading for anyone interested in the world that created Celtic.

O'Hagan's research for the book revealed an Irish population that were determined to survive what life had thrown at them. It's a story that pre-dates the club, of a people that raised a communal hand to the elements and succeeded. Undoubtedly an essential ingredient in their endurance was Celtic's success. Says O'Hagan: '1888 was a good year because within a time period of about forty years since coming to Scotland in some of the worst conditions imaginable on ships such as the SS *Londonderry*, the Irish had laid the foundations of a world-class football club. They arrived, faces purple with breathlessness and hunger, and in 1847 something like 35,000 Irish people appeared at the Broomielaw. These people, skeletal and desperate, had escaped famine to create Celtic as part of a new way of life. The infrastructure, team, support, streets and communities all happened in a very short period of time. Celtic came not just to represent a Saturday leisure pursuit but existence itself was embodied in that team and it still is in the minds of people who respect its traditions. It would probably mean nothing to those who are caught up in the digital premier league television sports world where "history doesn't matter; it's all about money".

'Walfrid remains a fascinating and enduring figure for me because I think that finding a very novel and original way to access people's enthusiasm is sometimes brilliant and sometimes sinister. In Walfrid's case it was a very clever move, not just on a spiritual level but in an everyday sense he gave people a cause and a focus for their feelings, he gave them a sense of each other in a much wider community.'

In the course of writing this book and travelling around the globe to speak to Celtic supporters, it's apparent how much the club represents something beyond the exterior shallow rooted values of the day. That doesn't mean to say the club can't exist in the modern game, every Celtic supporter I've met wants to see the club compete at the highest level possible but it shouldn't be done with the exclusion of those who can least afford it. The main reason for the club's formation was to attend to the needs of the poorest in society. Says O'Hagan: 'Of course there is joy, good humour and a real blessing in just the sport, people don't have to be soaked in Walfridism every Saturday in order to enjoy themselves but if you are interested in human affairs and interested in people in this part of the world you'd want Celtic to remain in tune with certain ideals and I would say a socialist expression of people's needs. There are still a lot of poor people in this country; there are still a lot of prejudices against Irish derived Catholics. The football club at its best would never be pushy or ideological or boring about these things but it should always be aware that part of its duty and obligation to my mind is not just to make a winning team and a very lucrative international business, which of course are great interests of theirs, but over and above all those money-making concerns they should be educating constantly, this captive audience. There's a generation of kids in this country whose only sense of history is what they will glean from this football club.'

John Reid has arguably been the most visible chairman in the club's history. Along with Gordon Brown, a former

Cabinet colleague in the Blair government, both men were shaped by their lives and experiences at a major point in Scotland's recent history. Brown accompanied his father, a Church of Scotland minister, on visits to the homes of unemployed miners. Reid in particular, while working in the East End of Glasgow as an insurance man, was inspired to move into politics after being shocked by the extremity of poverty he witnessed first-hand. The former Secretary of State for Scotland and subsequently Northern Ireland became a divisive figure for Celtic supporters, largely because he is viewed as having strayed far from the ideals that informed his early life. It's particularly his association with the Iraq War that led many supporters to question his appointment between 2007 and 2011. For others he represented someone from a Celtic background who used his political fire and skill to meet the needs of the club in a period of severe economic decline.

Said O'Hagan: 'Those men travelled a long way in their own conscience, sometimes pressed by economic and political responsibilities and realities. They are politicians after all, it's a bit hopeful to expect them to represent the best in human idealism and beliefs. They are animals of a particular sort, they respond to voting patterns and economic pressure as we've seen. Having said that we like leaders who not only respect but also embolden tradition. We've always liked politicians who stayed true to their original principles. In response to the politicians we are talking about, that's a problem because they didn't stay true, they attached themselves to policies and ideas that actually undermined the community they used to serve. I don't like condemnatory language; I'm always ready for redemption. I'm a good Catholic like that, if only in that respect. In the spirit of redemption I still believe that these men have a lot of good in them, if they can afford that community some of their experience and time then good. These men are organisationally brilliant and they have a lot to offer, it would need to be borne in mind that today with a team like Celtic there's a pressure to remember why they exist, we are at the 50–50 stage and it's slipping to towards 40–60 against the people who care for, remember and indeed know the reason for that club's existence.'

In his research for *The Missing* Andrew O'Hagan discovered his family had significant links to the IRA and Sinn Fein. It's one of the many complexities that face Celtic supporters when examining their past and putting the present into context. Significantly, Scottish national identity, like Ireland's, has been characterised in victories against the English in folk songs such as 'Scots Wha Hae' and 'Flower of Scotland', both of which celebrate the Battle of Bannockburn. For O'Hagan the distinction is time, as these songs are not being sung in the aftermath of a war or in the days of newly found peace and reconciliation. Perhaps the time has come to reshape and remodel certain expressions of Irish identity: 'I think you display that sense of your own history by overcoming it, you wouldn't want to frame your life today according to dead heroes. That is a mistake in any context. I come from a direct ancestry with people who were in Sinn Fein and fought, they were involved in the slashing of the van incident in Glasgow. They were gun-wielding individuals in terms of Irish

Republicanism and it was on Scottish soil. As much as I respect the legacy, I think that struggle is over. I think there are new and deep struggles still going on both in Ireland and Scotland about identity and about rights. We must attend to them now and we make heroes of ourselves in the attempt to address them. There is no guide to life in the sweat and blood of the dead. James Joyce suggested the past hinders the present and I think literature has a role to play in reviving the past in order not to repeat its mistakes.

'We have new Irish heroes, if we are into hero worship – Seamus Heaney and John Hume in particular. Heaney is an example of grace and tolerance under fire, there is a man who had a strong humanitarian feeling for his community throughout the Troubles yet remained a contributor to common tolerant values. The title of his current book is *Human Chain*, and that is what he was always about. Even those of us who have been subject to sectarian delight over the years have to remember that you're human before you're Catholic; you're a citizen of the world before you are a citizen of Scotland. There are six billion people in the world and five million in Scotland, around 800,000 of which are Catholics; you've got to keep breaking it down.'

Some writers have criticised Celtic's support for the oppressed, suggesting it's tokenistic and self-serving. That's one way to sear their conscience in a time when major television networks such as the BBC fail to accurately report the suffering in Gaza. When Celtic fans raise a Palestinian flag and world-class writers and artists discuss the associated problems then the issues blaze into a wider public consciousness: 'I don't think that we should be cut adrift from the isolation and oppression endured in Gaza. These are very human values about basic issues such as identity, rights, freedom and housing. If we have any true understanding of what these issues meant in the lives of our parents and grandparents and what part it played in the formation of our moral character then that would cause us automatically to feel for those people. It's as simple as that. The subjection of those people under a colonial power pressing on into their land and houses and denying them basic rights is a reminder of what we went through and survived. In certain parts of Britain people are still struggling to survive. Any kind of violent extremism is out of bounds except where people are involved for a struggle for their very survival against an oppressive power.

'A figure like Walfrid would have opposed, I'm sure, dictatorship and people hating wherever it existed in the world. Unfortunately religious figures have a luxury that the rest of us in the laity don't have, which is that they can forge an alliance with peace in their own mind that can be satisfying to them. But not everyone is gifted in that way. The rest of us have to struggle for the patch of land and the rights for change. There are people all over the world struggling in the same way the people coming from Ireland to Scotland struggled. I would be on their side if I could be, although I wouldn't want armed terrorists blowing themselves up in busy markets full of innocent people. We always have to be specific when talking about these issues. You can protect people's rights and the decency of a community without wanting to send kids strapped with bombs. That was always an issue in Ireland when people wanted rights for Catholics in the community to be respected and upheld. We felt that very strongly but we also felt very strongly, some of us, that walking into chip shops with bombs and what happened in Enniskillen was a disaster for the cause as much as the individuals that the cause was supposed to represent.

'I come from a family where at least two of my three brothers are Celtic season ticket holders. They believe very deeply in the traditions of Celtic Football Club politically and emotionally. The goals of the founding fathers remain very important to them. They, like many of the club's supporters, have travelled some distance over this argument. They've travelled with history and are probably much less hardcore than they were in the 1970s and 1980s. They have grown to accept the political reality that violence is out of the question in Northern Ireland and it was certainly always out of the question here. The idea of sectarian abuses would be anathema now. I certainly believe the idea of a struggle has come to an end. That battle has been won with certain accommodations made and with certain rights being agreed and shared. I would be shocked if I stood in a Glasgow pub now and heard violent struggle speak or bomb speak in relation to Protestants. I would find that absolutely horrendous, the idea that there could still be people that want to bomb others into shaping their frame of mind. That would be to deny history because they effectively won that struggle and it would be a denial of those who gave their lives to get to where we are today.'

Today the club is represented by a support that transcends

the old working-class barriers. Among the faithful that sit inside Celtic Park are supporters who have successfully entered the top positions in the land, from business and academia to politics and law. Perhaps most visibly, two of the world's most popular and wealthiest entertainers from humble beginnings, Rod Stewart and Billy Connolly, sat side by side on the 25th anniversary of Jock Stein's death during a game against Hearts in September 2010. The club's majority shareholder Dermot Desmond is estimated to be one of the wealthiest men on the planet with an approximate fortune of over 145 billion euro. In a new century and decade Andrew O'Hagan argues we need to turn our attention away from being an 'injured party', suggesting our history doesn't grant us special status but instead gives us a fresh set of responsibilities. 'It's always a mistake when anyone becomes addicted to its injured state or takes a certain pride in its downtrodden history. There lies folly. Adopting a kind of minority resentment and then taking pride in it, that's reactionary thinking and you want to get rid of it. I absolutely want to see that community go from strength to strength. I want to see it run the country in top political positions addressing the economic well-being of the nation and trans-forming the country. I want to see it bring grace and imaginative life to the arts, sporting excellence and innovation. I want to see brilliant things in that community; I'm not interested in their downtrodden state in the slightest. I'm fucking sick of it. It's a step back to wallow in the squalid conditions of our ancestors at the point of arrival; the terrible iniquities of that experience are not something to be pleased about. These people suffered. They had to overcome bad luck and the bad decision making of governments that cared too little for human life. Their survival and their triumph is our reason for being and we are evidence of their triumph because they got on with it. They had families; they had futures. The idea that we would take pride in their pain is disgusting, they were brought here on coffin ships because they had nowhere else to go and treated like shite. They invented the ground on which they stand to create a platform for self-respect and Celtic was an essential part of that. Thirty or forty years after arriving they had the beginnings of a respectable society. For groups of us to wipe that away and say, "Wha's like us when we're downtrodden; we were great then" is a massive mistake. Our greatness is a potential and those people would be ashamed if they thought some were holding up their pain as a badge of honour for themselves. It's immodest and if people want to honour that community they should realise their prosperity and increase it for others.'

Among the Celtic support today is a generation that established itself in a period of industrial decline. While many have transcended their background, Celtic maintains a relationship to their class and spiritual home, the experience keeps them tuned to an atmosphere in which they've grown and developed. It could be argued that Dermot Desmond's financial stake in Celtic isn't just business, he's suggested a feeling and connection to the club that transcends his normal interest. Similarly Rod Stewart doesn't charter a flight from the other side of the globe just for the football alone. What they both want is to remain a part of something communal, and like everyone else in the ground they form part of that pre-match electricity that, unlike some of its English equivalents, continues to span class boundaries; but for how long will this community exist?

Says O'Hagan: 'I think traditionally with Celtic the sense of personal well-being was about the community doing well. It has always had its entrepreneurial heroes that made a mint, their pockets jingling with change. They'd come back and build a library or a hospital like the missionaries that would come back and serve their local community. There was a sense of the people and not just a person. I think that is the great distinction in that community and that always fascinated me as a writer. E.M. Forster said that great writing should be about creating bridges between periods, time, class and individuals. I think that's something Celtic supporters have to bear in mind because there are so many challenges still. It's so baffling that people are sentimental and reactionary in wanting to solve the past's problems or prolong the agonies of yesterday because the present difficulties are so fascinating and gigantic in the community today. There are still far too many living in poverty in this country, too many working-class Catholic individuals are suffering a bad education and too many of those kids are going into life ill equipped and unable to fulfil themselves or play a part in their society. That's happening now in Glasgow and throughout the country, there's so much to be done to improve the fortunes in that society and also there are spiritual challenges. The Catholic Church's role in our lives is changing as we speak, in my view the Church itself and the Papacy particularly is refusing to engage with the changes of modernity and the spiritual life of the faithful in this country is suffering as a result. That will be a real challenge for people to overcome, there's a generation whose sense of spirituality has been rocked by the behaviour of the clergy and this draconian, dysfunctional institution. People are going to have to work hard to hang onto their faith and to transform their church to make it fully modern and fully functioning, if they are interested in preserving those values and some of that sense of ancientness.

'As John McGahern once said, the great thing about the Church, even if you don't believe, is that it points to a sense of your existence. It derives from something beyond sense in that it takes us out of pure reason and makes us look at something magical and wondrous at the foundation of our lives. If that alone can be a definition of what Catholicism is, then it's an ancient invitation to a mystical party. Without it there is no mystery in our lives, there is only pure rational science and that's simply not enough for many people. If people want to preserve it and continue to question it then they need to engage with it now and continue with the argument of ages while they are here on earth. A concern for me is children's education. I worry that there is a whole generation of Catholics here and more coming that have no idea of the questions that might matter in their lives. There's a commercial ethos that has been absorbed thoughtlessly by that generation. I look at the old school I went to, which has been pulled down and another built in its place, in Ardrossan. I look at the kids in a school like that now and I think they are utterly commercially minded with no sense of trade unions or faith-based communities or a common economic struggle. They have an idea of their own personal economic struggle doused in a sense of what they want from life, but none of their wants, wishes and desires are tied to the wishes of others and that's a real problem. The challenge is how to inculcate a tolerance in kids towards a genuine accept-ance of others and otherness rather than a continuous celebration of selfhood. You hear a lot of rights speak today but no responsibility; they must go together, everyone is aware of their rights in this society but who is aware of their responsibilities?'

The social world around Celtic supporters in the 1970s was one that is arguably unrecognisable from today. O'Hagan explains it was a world of 'no writers and very few books'. The blend of Irish and Scottish was present in William McIlvanney's 1975 novel *Docherty* but Irish life in Scotland was largely invisible outside of your own world. It was an unrecorded and unseen existence, outside of those living it. While that community delivered footballers, singers such as Frankie Miller, and world-class comedians like Billy Connolly who 'busked the patter of the shipyards on a world stage', the inner experiences of those hidden lives floated by unseen. Following *The Missing*, O'Hagan's Booker-nominated *Our Fathers* successfully managed to further resonate a partic-ularly male Irish Catholic experience and its relationship to Celtic, left-wing politics, domestic life and social mobility for a particular generation. Significantly 'the green and white bars of a Celtic strip' are the only constant in a dramatically changing world. Remembers O'Hagan: 'If you look at pictures of the terraces from that period it was a very male culture. They were used to having a bevvy, someone would have a slash at the back of your legs. I went to enough games to know what it was like and it smelt of piss. I found everything interesting, examining the conversation, the dress, language, the behaviour, even at that age. It could appear overwhelming, threatening or a bit imposing but I was able to overcome it. When I was taken to watch Celtic I was thrilled to have the opportunity to see something new. I'd buy these big fat notebooks from Woolworths for eighty pence and fill them up with descriptions of Celtic Park or my gran's block of flats. It was a start because you never found descriptions in your local library. Now you can walk into a library and pick up books by writers like me or Des Dillon talking about Catholic life on a working-class housing estate in the early 1970s. You can hear the voices that their families spoke in and discover a whole community of Irish derived Catholics struggling with socialism, municipal housing and the future. *The Missing*, whatever its faults, filled a gap in the market.

'I was always amazed when I was taken into Glasgow; all the Irish derived families, the O'Hagans and the Dochertys, they would all be there in some pub or club. On my mother's side the songs they sang weren't Irish; they were always American. Their sense of freedom was about being glamorous and prosperous in an American sense: it was Frank Sinatra, Doris Day and the songs of Sarah Vaughan. In the East End Catholic socialist clubs someone would break out into 'Boolavouge' or some great rebel song but part of the business of being Irish was to get to another place and that always interested me. Part of the liturgy in the Catholic upbringing presents you with a lot of challenges, nowadays especially, but one of the things is a sense of transposing yourself from one place to another, there in the Mass is transubstantiation. I think that exists for people on an everyday level in their own lives. They want to go from one place to the next, in a sense raising themselves up. That was so natural and evident in the Glasgow that I grew up in; it seemed natural to think America was a suburb of Glasgow.'

O'Hagan's work brings insight into the complex nature of the community in a transitional period. The world that he inherited from his parents, grandparents and great grand-parents no longer exists. He brings to life a working-class Scotland on the ropes where the Labour movement that informed the politics of previous generations is fatally tied to industrial decline. A new right-wing mainstream ideology is emerging that undermines an Irish community which fought in two world wars and invested their lives in an empire of coal, ships and steel, effectively keeping the country punching above its weight. Throughout the 20th century, alongside these strivings, Irish Nationalism undoubtedly led to a schizophrenic relationship with Britain and the contradictions have been strongly played out in Scottish life and culture. The imagination that O'Hagan describes, which celebrated the glamour of American culture, was an important escape from the everyday Irish and Scottish inner conflict, contradictions and struggles that often led to violent and chaotic behaviour: 'It's complicated and that's what I like about Celtic, it becomes fascinating when they get more integrated into the complexities of Scotland, this is a country that is not one thing. It's a divisive country: Highlander or Lowlander, Mainlander or Islander, Catholic or Protestant, Glasgow or Edinburgh, Scottish or British. It goes on and on. Celtic has absorbed a lot of that complexity and chaotic mix; the club has always been open to the winds of fortune in one way or another.

'On both sides of my family they brought a lot of the old Irish clichés into Scotland: alcoholism, mental disturbance, suicide and profound poverty. My mother's grandmother and aunts were hawkers at Paddy's market. That was my mother's granny, whatever was found was opened onto the pavement to sell and that's only two generations ago. That's a first generation Irish girl in Glasgow all almost within living memory. Celtic was incredibly important to these women; it was so much more than the sport. In my childhood and before, the people who exuded the Celtic ethos the most were women, but they didn't go to the game and didn't play football either. My paternal grandmother, Granny O'Hagan, and her daughter were the most Celtic promoting people you could've met. All that mattered was where the ball went, how it got there was of no interest as long as it went in the back of the net. They weren't mindful of athleticism or technique, their interest overrode the game itself. It was symbolic of a larger struggle which was about their very existence, visibility and self-respect. The very idea of an Irish club in Scotland presents a contradiction before you go any further. This is a Protestant country where a team of Irish navvies kicking a ball about a park eventually got truly respectable, not just in sporting terms but in political terms they achieved a focus for their excellence.'

There's a certain British superiority that has failed to understand the significance of Celtic in Scotland, viewing the club with the confidence of ignorance. In 2010 newly released government papers revealed that during the Troubles the Tory government considered the removal of the tricolour from Celtic Park after a public request. In times of dramatic unemployment, poverty and a growing drug subculture, Celtic Football Club gained further significance as a new wave of unrest and anxiety swept across society. Support of the club was one way of passing an ethos and traditions to a new generation of supporters in a time of social turmoil and civil conflict. O'Hagan was sanguine when he heard the news: 'Thatcher never understood: not only that "no such thing as society" are some of the most chilling words spoken by any British politician of the twentieth century. She valued nothing beyond individualism and the individual greed that rules in the market place. Everything else is sentimental; that was her view. The tricolour at Celtic Park represents an entire community, their beliefs and their values but that idea was nonsense to her and that is why she came a cropper. Those ideas are not nonsense and they will never be nonsense to the people in that community. I've always thought if there was a revolution in Scotland it would be caused by something very small and by an outside power. Had the tricolour been taken down from Celtic Park that could have been a very real trigger. It would have caused the kind uprising in Glasgow that wouldn't have been seen since the Calton Weavers. If we had a referendum tomorrow I don't think even thirty per cent of the nation would be for independence but if Scotland won the World Cup independent fervour would sweep over the land. It's that kind of country, it can become quite savage over events that are quite small or insignificant in themselves but it's the symbolic power of those things that get people's dander up and those of us who care about Celtic understand that because the club means more than the country.'

It's now over a decade since Andrew O'Hagan defended James MacMillan at the end of the 1990s after his Scotland's Shame speech at the Edinburgh Festival. The address made way for government changes, prison initiatives and media attitudes when understanding of the community was at best vague and at worst, hostile. While the merits of the lecture have been examined elsewhere, MacMillan's position and clout allowed a clean sweep for the community, a chance to rediscover its own sense of Scotland. The Scotland's Shame speech gave the country a psychological reboot, challenging outdated mindsets while giving those of Irish stock, Celtic supporters and Catholics an establishment figure who was ready to fight their corner, intellectually at least. Significantly O'Hagan swaggered into the debate to defend his friend and strengthen the argument further: 'There was a certain savagery with which he and I were dragged onto the front page of the *Scotsman*. I was hauled on for defending him and I was absolutely right. I didn't even make the speech but I said he was right. At that time the Booker was in the news and *Our Fathers* was in the air. I supported Jimmy whole-heartedly because I had grown up with that same experience. I was told that I was a really good writer but that I would never get a job at a Scottish paper with a name like O'Hagan. I had just won a Scottish writing prize, beating candidates from all over the country. I was just setting out but the paper of record in the city where I was born, grew up and fundamentally came from dismissed me to London. That's a fact, a newspaper which was supposedly a bastion of the liberal arts.

'Jimmy spoke up for his people, in a nation he loves and cares about, he wanted to address its problems. It's the responsibility of the artist and he was treated like a wee diddy who opened his mouth and upset the people in power. The *Scotsman* cover had us as public enemy number one and two; we were the Bonnie and Clyde of truth telling. I was delighted because I'm a complete bring it on merchant, I was like, "Come ahead every one of you." My attitude towards Jimmy was, "C'mon, hauners." I was ready to wipe the deck with every one of them because I'd had enough of it. I was living in London by then, not feeling either exiled or compromised having left Scotland. I'm a Scottish person and proud but I've made the journey Scottish people have made through history to find a peace and distance and a landing spot for themselves. That didn't mean Scotland was behind me, it was at my desk and in my mind every day. It was on my tongue and in my DNA. I'd had enough of victim talk and victimisation and the notion that you could have an equitable legal system, education system, parliamentary system and journalistic system that was based on the idea that somehow Catholics were inferior. It had become time to say come ahead because

I'm smarter than you and I'll wipe the fucking deck with every single one of you. And I said it to them because these papers are racist, misogynist and stupid, you abuse the common language and you abuse spiritual well-being in this country every day so my response was "Come ahead" and, of course they all ran away. But Jimmy was the biggest come-ahead merchant because he lives in this country and he's a very sensitive artist. It's very hard as an artist trying to live in a state of peace and contemplation especially as a musician, to step out of that, to dive into the melee at the centre of the storm.'

Perhaps most positively the speech allowed Celtic fans to reclaim Scotland. Hostile attitudes towards Catholics and Celtic supporters had soured relations with the land of their birth. While transcendence and a connectedness with Europe, the Americas and naturally Ireland remain significant, the speech allowed a healthy reconciliation: 'Denying Scotland is one of those negative fantasies that creates a form of self-denial and repression. It poisons the soul because it denies the sweat and toil we've put into this country over generations. We made this; we built it up. These men weren't just earning their pay; they were creating a world for us to inherit. To deny that for an Ireland that isn't even a real Ireland, is reactionary thinking. Ireland becomes this absurd misty Germanic emerald place in the mind, like something out of a weird fairy story. I was born here, paid taxes and worked with my mind and my hands and lived among my people. To deny that makes no sense. You hear people ask, "Why did it take so long for us to emerge," but it takes about the time that it takes. The great Polish Scottish novel: it could take a hundred years and because those hundred years are spent in economic difficulty, they are spent pulling themselves up through life. They didn't just arrive and become writers, journalists, lawyers and artists, that's the way it works.'

Our time is drawing to a close. O'Hagan has a meeting with the National Theatre of Scotland and an event to host at the book festival. When discussing Celtic, it's obviously a return home to a place in his mind and spirit which continues to inspire and enthuse. O'Hagan's reflections of the culture are not sorrowful or sentimental but a celebration of the rougher edges missing from today's luxurious and Americanised experience: 'There's something smooth, slick and international about the game today, it's so mediated. That's different from watching a bunch of wee bauchles: stocky, over-fagged, hung-over, charging toward the goal with a certain genetic disposition. You looked into the eyes of those players and they looked like your pal, your brother, the boys you went to school with. At a certain point in the club's history every player on the team was born within thirty miles of the ground. That's a different world now: we have super-models, these slick hairless guys covered in gel full of self-belief. It's like comparing a gang of scabby alley cats to a group of panthers. They could be playing for anybody, they have a different bearing on their feet and in their face. You couldn't imagine Bobby Lennox in Milan or Argentina, he had that completely home-grown appeal and that's what people miss. I don't want to be one of the nostalgists but there's something to be said for a shite ground, really horrible Bovril and the smell of piss on the terrace. That was a particular Celtic experience which has gone. When you look at Leeds United in the early 1970s you can see the steam of a lager hangover, but it didn't make them less exciting players.

'The threat to the game in the face of all this corporatisation and a po-faced media is that it will lose its charm and saltiness. The corporate life of the club has squeezed some of the humanity and small time humour out of the game and I'm sure that is as true of Tottenham as it is of Celtic. Pat Nevin is right, you would need to go in search of a smaller stall in order not to feel the pinch but it's worth sticking with the club and laughing it off, you can still have a very naked relationship with the field of play and say "Fuck it" to the corporate noise of which there is too much. I've always felt both part of it and away from it, I wasn't a natural footballer and not a football fan in the way that my brothers were but I was at the dead centre of that culture, it affected me in every way, it was everywhere in the house and in the school I went to. I remember my uncle calling me "a fucking Jonah" after a Celtic-Rangers game where we got beat because I had blue trousers on. Even now, colours matter. I find myself in a strange position sometimes, I wouldn't think twice about pulling on a wee blue Ben Sherman in London but I'd think twice in Glasgow. I'm a forty-two-year-old man but I'd still think again before walking through the centre of Glasgow wearing a particular shade of blue. That stuff is bred in the bone. My girlfriend and the mother of my daughter thought that was evidence of insanity, the fact that you'd be so repelled by the idea that people would be thinking you were wearing a Rangers top. That kind of thing is in your DNA and I suppose I'm victim of that separatist thinking.

'For me Celtic remains the only interesting team in the world; I don't have time for anything else. I don't have three lives so how can I have three teams – one life, one team. If you are truly interested in a team, the fans, the traditions, and the trials and tribulations in the present day then that is a life in itself. The culture of Celtic represents the universe and no other football team is interesting to me in that way because I don't have the connection with it. I can admire other teams and these panthers running up the park in this or that team or ground but they don't carry my DNA up the park, I know there are a lot of foreign players now but the bones of this club represents something that really captivates me and it's in a city that really interests me. It's the only team that will ever have my full and undivided attention.'

Des Dillon throws a few shadow punches before he walks on stage, retaining the same build from his days of fighting and working construction. He's a long way from his time in the ring but there's still something of the boxer wrapped in Dillon's persona as he plays to the crowd: bounding up and down the stage, arms exploding into windmills and adrenalin coursing through his veins as he gleefully delivers a vivid collection of stories. The tales feature a cast of old school hard men, neds, schemers and hustlers all based on his early life in Coatbridge. It's often an absurd, violent and surreal place but not without hope and redemption – the essential components of any good fight story.

Dillon's work on the Irish diaspora in Scotland has gained the writer international recognition with a clutch of literary awards and translations into numerous languages including Catalonian, Russian, Spanish, French and Swedish. His play *Singin' I'm No a Billy, He's a Tim* is currently the most performed and bestselling play of the last five years in Scotland, successfully pulling in a mainstream working-class audience, over seventy per cent of which hadn't been to a theatre in their lives. A critical and commercial success story, the work was discovered by actor Scott Kyle in his local library, where the authenticity of a Celtic and Rangers fan locked up in a prison cell shortly before their teams kick off motivated Kyle, a Rangers fan with a Celtic supporting brother, to set up his own production company. In 2010 the play completed a sell-out run at the Edinburgh Fringe with Kyle scooping *The Stage* best actor award for his role of Billy.

In writing the play Dillon was inspired by the rival supporters he once knew and worked alongside in the 1970s, often using humour to curb a descent into violence. 'In those days you always pushed humour. Sometimes it worked and sometimes it failed miserably. Going back to about 1979 I worked with this guy Alan from Ruchazie. He was as staunch Orange as you could get, he knew I was an uber Fenian but we got on great. Anyway on the night of the 4–2 game when Celtic won the league against Rangers he asked me to go for a pint. I wasn't going to the game because I was more interested in women and drink at this point so I decided to go with him. He took me to the Louden Tavern. I had no idea it was a Rangers pub until I saw the red, white and blue decor outside. As soon as we reached the bar one of his mate's came over: "Where you from? Coatbridge? Are you a Mick?" I downed the pint and left. When *Billy and Tim* was on at the SECC one of the best moments for me was when I heard this voice behind me shout: "Alright Des; how's it going?" It was Alan. I hadn't seen him in over twenty years, he just hugged me and said: "Des you brought us all the gither in there the night."

'When you knock all the evil out the bottom of it I thought, "We're nothing without each other." It's like that scene in *Billy and Tim* when the character refuses to continue the argument: when he doesn't play, there's fuck all else for him to do. If someone wants to run a Fenian flute band or an Orange parade you can't stop them. It's been going on for thousands of years and if you do stop them, you'll never stop the bigotry because they'll just move on to something else, it's part of the human condition. That's why I wouldn't boo during a minute's silence, even if I disagreed with a war or whatever it might be. I might not agree with someone's traditions and arguments but if they've went to their death believing in an idea then I'm going to respect that even I don't agree with it. It's two traditions and two ways of life.'

As we journey back to his childhood home in Coatbridge, Dillon talks frankly about the Irish community and the town's influence on his work. The language he grew up with: Scots voices with an Irish vernacular along with Catholics and Celtic supporters, are running constants in his novels, plays, comedy routines and work for television. Coatbridge and Celtic are to Dillon what Hibs and Leith are to Irvine Welsh or Little Italy and small-town gangsters to Martin Scorsese. 'Celtic was as much a part of life as the stove in the scullery. When you're a boy the big city, Glasgow is this distant far off place, so getting the bus from Coatbridge to Celtic Park is a big deal. Hundreds of us, brothers, cousins and pals left on buses, it was like a flotilla of cars and buses carrying you off down the motorway. It didn't cost you anything because you were lifted over the turnstile. Glasgow in the 1960s looked like Dresden after the bomb had dropped. To me it was this wild place: I think of big dookits, demonic railways and the smell of piss on the bus. In terms of poverty this place took the biscuit. In Coatbridge we were cut off from the rest of Scotland; the Irish immigrant culture was so concentrated. When we went to Parkhead you felt part of something bigger, you were connected to all these other satellite Irish communities coming together. When you got home the person who was the most encouraging is always your granny saying, "Did you enjoy it son?" that was because the grannies knew that Celtic was the hook for the culture, it was a like a loch running into a sea with a thousand years of history and tradition.'

After a time of hard living it was literature that reconnected Dillon with the culture, his roots, childhood and his future. While studying English at Strathclyde a lecturer handed the budding writer a copy of Sean O'Casey's *Juno and the Paycock*. It opened up a new but strangely familiar world to Dillon, one in which the phrasing, body language, linguistics and pulse of the storytelling were identical to his life growing up in Coatbridge. 'When I first read that book it sent a shiver down my spine, it was set in Dublin but that could've been my house. It tuned me back into the culture, because you weren't used to seeing that in Scotland. I also love William McIlvaney's writing. *Docherty* told you about that Scottish Irish experience in relation to industrial life, but those days were over and it had been twenty years since anyone had written about that way of life. Literature helped me rediscover my Irish roots and my relationship to Celtic. I never went through the Republican phase, which a lot of people did, although my brother tells me when I was drunk I would sing the songs. You'd hear them on the buses and at games but when I got a bit older I stopped going. I can understand how rebel songs became part of the community spirit. If you take somewhere like Little Italy in New York, the culture didn't have a Bloody Sunday to impact the society in the way such events affected Irish communities in Scotland. If Italy had been taken over by another country then maybe they would have had an immigrant culture that would look very different.

'Irish culture in particular is very musical so the songs become a springboard for the political ideas that are flying about but I think people need to look beyond that too. Ireland gave us a lot more that bled into life here. In Irish literature and songs there is a strong emphasis on transforming your culture and your reality, it's very theatrical, very dramatic; it flexes your imagination. It gives people a sense of something grand in everyday life. If you take Simple Minds as an example, they came right out of that Glasgow Irish working-class Catholic world. On 'Belfast Child' they captured an everyday experience in Belfast but they turned it into something epic, which resonated on an international level. A writer like Bruce Springsteen also has a very working-class Catholic approach, he takes a very obvious subject like a guy getting his girlfriend pregnant and then wandering down to the river. For a few moments he takes you to this magical place; he transforms your reality.'

For his stand-up routine tonight Dillon will pay a mental visit around the doors of his youth where tales from his living room will take on the significance of a Greek tragedy. The narratives around Celtic, the support and the rival relationship with Rangers have brought a particular dramatic tension, social currency and sense of place to Dillon's work. In his plays, poems and novels the writer delves into the afterlife of the 'Iron Burgh' where stories and humour are as essential as food and oxygen. 'Celtic became so important for Catholics in Scotland because of the underdog thing in the community, which the team exemplified in Europe. It's almost like a folktale. What happened in Lisbon will always be an inspiration to people. The victory brought a confidence, this was very important in a working-class culture. I was born at the bottom of an ocean of Irish low self-esteem. When I got to the surface I thought, this must be Scotland then, we felt as if we had the double dunt. Looking back I can see how winning the European Cup was the start of you being able to openly say you were Irish and hold your head up but within three years of winning it the Troubles in Northern Ireland had flared up. We used to have this code where you would touch your nose if a Protestant was in the house, not because we were bigoted, it was out of politeness. We didn't want to talk about Celtic, chapel or anything Irish during that time. The Troubles were at their peak when Celtic was running riot in Europe. It took your focus away from what was going on in Ireland, Celtic was a movement in itself. After Sunday Bloody Sunday Coatbridge was silent, but after the funerals people got drunk and violent, the place was wrecked, that's how the emotions came out.'

Published in the same year as Andrew O'Hagan's *The Missing*, Dillon's *Me and Ma Gal* set the Scottish literary establishment aflame. The late Edwin Morgan said the work 'reminded me of Twain and Kerouac . . . a story told with wonderful verve immediacy and warmth.' Critics went on to herald the work as a classic. What remained a point of frustration for Dillon was reviewers' failure to engage with the book's Catholicism, sending his future writing in a more determined direction. 'There is a lot of Catholic symbolism in that book, I think it was the first Scottish novel to print the Hail Mary in its entirety,' he explains. 'It's about a young boy's way of looking at the world which was essentially Catholic and religious. He runs to the water looking for fishers to help him, a shaft of light hits the loch in a certain way and he says a Hail Mary. Nobody picked up on it, nobody mentioned the Catholicism and it's an overtly Catholic book. The other thing in Irish culture, it's the women who run the society, I think that's why Mary is such a central figure. We needed that focus.'

Walking around Coatbridge, Scotland's former industrial heartland, we meet Dillon's dad and later his sister who leads us to the now common sight of flowers and football tops paying homage to yet another victim of street violence. The murders are often random, sometimes sectarian but always undoubtedly relate to a strange feral void. The row of Celtic tops, the dotted Rangers tops, various banners and a few flickering candles pay tribute to a life that walked around these same streets 24 hours before.

For Dillon this is not the hometown he writes about in his work; his Coatbridge flexes more of a sub-cultural muscle in his imagination and remains locked into another time. Today the sense of Irishness is more obvious, the Catholicism less fervent and the violence less tolerable. 'I think in Coatbridge now it's changed. It's too aware of its Irishness; it's like an Irish theme park. We didn't have the kind of celebrations of Irishness that you have now. It's like the Boston Irish or something and that's not something I can relate to. The numbers in the chapels are diminishing, it's only a matter of time before that fades completely. I went to Ireland thinking I would get the whimsical thing but it was freezing and raining, I could have been in Mull of Kintyre. What I realised is that Coatbridge is my Ireland. I'm an emigrant from that now because I live in Galloway. I've got the love/hate relationship with Coatbridge that some guys get with Dublin. A lot of people are like, "I can't wait to get out of this place" and that can happen for a variety of reasons but generally it's only when I'm not there that I write about it in this whimsical way. A lot of the writing is about a certain type of communication that I remember from my youth. When I wrote *Six Black Candles* I wanted to capture how my sisters talked, I

253

wanted the chaos and energy of six women and six conversations, I wanted that energy of the old house.'

Dillon has written for his audience, sometimes narrowing it down to writing for his own family and community. In doing so he's translated feelings and beliefs often overlooked by the mainstream. He's led us to laugh at the more extreme and bitter elements within ourselves and in wider society. The Catholic life he portrays, which is often described as insular, has successfully translated on an international stage. Significantly for the Lanarkshire writer it's the peculiarities and the differences in the culture that have been the essential element in the translation of his work for other territories: 'there's a lot that is particular to Scotland. In *Billy and Tim* I was trying to show both the similarities and how the rest of society view Celtic and Rangers fans. At the same time I wanted to look at the more universal themes in Irish life. The Irish are known for digging roads here and there is a strong physical element to the culture. I know if I don't do something physical I feel crap. There seem to be things built into our DNA and when you unlock them, there's an explosion. I think it's the same with storytelling and flexing those creative muscles; that is a big part of who we are, without it we become depressed.

'The other thing is the spirituality; one of the ideas is sticking by a kind of morality against all odds. There is a pride in the culture but it has to be clean, otherwise it's arrogance. The Billy character asks Tim, "What have you, the Irish, ever brought to this country?" He rhymes off all the clichés about junkies and alcoholics. When Tim responds about the infrastructure he finishes by saying: "Celtic, for fuck sake". Celtic wouldn't be here if it weren't for that influx of Irish and not only that, Rangers wouldn't be the team that it became with the traditions that it has. The creation of Celtic was about service to others when you take it down to its basic roots. When I've acted for others it's the most blissful feeling and yet I don't do it often enough. When you lose your own ego you feel more positive about the world. Those ideas completely impacted my writing; there's a scene in *The Blue Hen* where the characters are frying eggs on shovels in the sun. It's a kind of communion, a last supper if you like because one of those friends goes on to be a right evil bastard. When that character is reminded of the past, they talk about the eggs frying in the sun, the sense of togetherness, the eating together; it's all packed into that scene. His mates don't condemn this guy, even though he's a really vile bastard, they try to empathise with him by telling him, "There's an evil in us all", in the hope that it will pull him out the darkness. That idea is very Catholic.

'After *Me and Ma Gal* I got fed up of people not seeing what I was about. With *Six Black Candles* I thought they [the critics] can't fail to see the Irishness, that we are from Donegal, we wear Celtic tops, we have priests round the house, that we do Irish things and sing Irish songs. We speak with Irish language in a Scottish accent. There is a great love in Irish communities for the sound of language, and growing up that was my apprenticeship. You could walk into a room and there would be ten of the best storytellers in Coatbridge. I laid it on so thick that maybe it wouldn't work in Ireland.

It's really a play about emigrants for emigrants. Some critics said there wasn't a lot of substance but any Catholics I spoke to were stunned by how much it moved them, if you were not from that background then it wouldn't get you. That play was a way of transmitting the culture right from the moment the play began with the old hymn 'Bind Us Together'. Putting a character in a Celtic top was a deliberate move because in that you are declaring a lot of things: a Catholic morality, whether you've got it or not because that's the root, you're declaring tribalism, anti-racism and you are declaring that you are not completely locked into this country, your own town and your local team.'

CHAPTER TWELVE HAIL! HAIL! ROCK 'N' ROLL

Football was the only thing and suddenly there was this cross fertilisation with pop culture. I guess it was the glamour of both, when you saw that first Ajax team they were hippies; football players that looked like proper rock stars. I suppose it started with the jack the lad players like Best; he was the first soccer pop star and after him the cultures seemed to complement each other. **JIM KERR**

IN MY MIND CELTIC IS inexplicably coupled with rock 'n' roll, particularly David Bowie's *Aladdin Sane* and Iggy and the Stooges' *Raw Power*. My uncle Terry's curtains were always drawn, even on fresh spring days at the end of winter. The yellow lamp would glow over pictures of Ziggy Stardust and Kenny Dalglish in all their 1973 pomp. A few spaces were reserved for the essential side-men Danny McGrain and Mick Ronson but nothing that pre-dated 1970. These were my uncle's heroes, they were claimed and they represented him, not his big brothers or the big boys at school, they were his clean start. In the years that followed Terry's walls would fill with other heroes, but none would ever burn as brightly as Ziggy and Kenny in 1973. His relationship with Celtic would have intermittent breaks in the years that followed: jobs, women, musical ambitions and a move to London sometimes got in between him and Celtic, but when one of the above imploded he would always return to that original comforter, identifier and friend.

At nine years of age Terry got his first Celtic top, it was a few days before the European Cup final against Feyenoord.

For Terry the green and white Hoops was a 'proper' football top because it was immediately recognisable and definitive. He had been disappointed with the gift of a Real Madrid kit from my uncle Brian on his return from Spain, complaining it was just a plain white T-shirt and gym shorts. The Hoops were bold, magnetic and wearing them was a statement of intent. Brian knew what he had to do. When Terry did finally pull the green and white over his head for the first time there was a sense of the passing the baton on to the next generation. My grandad passed away the following year and Terry's big brothers stopped going to games. For Brian and Angus in particular their experiences of watching Celtic, living through the triumphs and telling stories about what happened on Saturday were fundamentally tied up with 'father'. My gran moved to Edinburgh and worked as a nurse at the Western General, Terry was living something of a nomadic life spending summers and weekends with the families of his big brothers and sisters in Glasgow, Lanarkshire and West Lothian. On 24 October 1970, he made his first Celtic game, a League Cup final against Rangers. Arriving at the national stadium he entered a Hampden filled with thousands of men roaring and shouting abuse, some ten foot high on shoulders, others cheering wildly when a young Derek Johnstone scored the game's only goal for Rangers.

Football had always been important among the men in my family. My uncle Brian had played for a string of junior clubs but there was always a certain twinkle in his eye and an air of satisfaction when he regaled us with stories of his time in the green and white Hoops at Blantyre Celtic. My uncle Sonny had also been a keen footballer at junior level and in the army. His tactical awareness and knowledge also led to a spell in amateur management. On Sonny's mantelpiece was a picture of my grandad from his days in the Royal Scots Fusiliers playing football for a British Army select in the Himalayas. In his youth Andrew Purden had also played for Caledonian FC. His brother Peter played for Galston. An opportunity called him to America and in Pennsylvania he joined Bethlehem Steel. The steel corporation from which the club was formed was the second largest steel producer in the United States and one of the largest shipbuilding companies in the world. The area's subsequent struggles were later the subject of Billy Joel's 1982 single "Allentown" and the track brought to light memories of my great uncle. Long before industrial decline, a piece of family folklore told of Peter scoring from a penalty in the 1925 National Challenge Cup final for the Shawsheen Indians after a move to Massachusetts.

The identities around manual labour and the armed services that informed my grandad and uncles didn't inform my uncle Terry or his generation. An explosion of political unrest in the north of Ireland would dissuade many young Catholics from considering a life in the services. Under my grandad's supervision Terry had shown keen academic leanings. After moving to Edinburgh, his social world split in two between Oxgangs in the south west of Edinburgh and Shotts in North Lanarkshire. Throughout the decade Celtic became a constant in his life: home, away, weeknights and European fixtures he would travel with the St Patrick's Shotts Celtic supporters' bus and members of the 'Young

Mental Bar Ox'. They'd meet up at their head office, The Good Companions bar, or after jumping on an Edinburgh supporters' bus at Ryries pub in Haymarket.

On reflection today, Terry explains the cultural gap that was already widening between himself and the previous generation: 'In the early 1970s my big brother or sister would get the older boys to look after me on the bus going to and from the game. At the front of the bus there were older, austere gentlemen in suits who would have worked in the town's mining and ironworks industries. Often they had been in the armed services; it was only 25 years since the end of the war. As always the head cases were up the back. That was the young team; everyone wanted to be a hard man. The talk was always about their social lives and usually girls. The big difference was we would be decked out in scarves around the wrists and waist; it was like an explosion in a supporters shop. Helmets became a big thing in the 1970s, probably because of the flying missiles. I found an old German helmet from the war in an antique shop, painted it white and covered it in Kenny Dalglish stickers. I had a Bowie haircut, Celtic top, Oxford bags and fourteen-hole Doc Marten boots. The Oxford bags were ideal for hiding cans of beer. I remember someone on the bus wearing their mammy's tights just so they could get extra cans into the ground. The guy was slagged to death but everyone wanted a can off him once they got in the ground.

'On the way back everyone would be talking about the game. That's what connected us. For the young guys Kenny Dalglish was a hero; even girls liked Kenny. One of my favourite pictures of the time is a shot of him at Celtic, there's a girl who somehow managed to get on the pitch and is behind him in tears like she's at a Bowie or Marc Bolan gig, he had that kind of effect. There hadn't been a player like him before, he was a total star and he changed a lot of things. We loved him because he was cool but I think the older guys liked him because he was a family man, he didn't have much time for the media; he wasn't a playboy like George Best or Peter Marinello. He was very serious until he scored and then he'd give the double fisted salute. He bridged that gap and it's what he's always done, he's doing the exact same thing now with his return as manager of Liverpool. He's the guy that grandads will talk to their sons and grandsons about. The game has changed beyond recognition but Kenny is still fundamentally the same and he's loved and respected for it. Strangely enough my favourite Kenny moment in the Hoops was a game we lost 3–2 to Rangers. It was the 1973 Scottish Cup final; there were over 122,000 fans in the ground. I was in a fantastic position for his goal, which he volleyed into the top right-hand corner of the net. It was one of life's perfect moments. I can close my eyes and I'm back in the crowd with the boys watching that goal hit the net right in front of me.'

For a generation of rock 'n' rollers that grew up in the 1970s and 1980s Celtic became an essential way of expressing youthful ideals while retaining a healthy and captivating link to the past. Primal Scream front man Bobby Gillespie has often put his views and opinions in context by discussing the violent city he grew up in during the 1970s where political thought, conversations and beliefs were rife. His interviews are often highly charged affairs: deadly serious and tongue-in-cheek in the same breath. Throughout his career Gillespie has been consistent in his support of human rights for the Palestinian people. When asked by the NME in 2006 if he supported Hamas or Hezbollah, he replied, 'No, I support Celtic'. The answer might have seemed contrite to many but it shows just how entwined support for Celtic and this particular political cause are. Gillespie's political character was formed watching Celtic throughout the 1970s and early 1980s and his often uncompromising views have remained clearly visible throughout his rock 'n' roll adventures with Primal Scream. Using his affiliation with Celtic in many of his interviews with the English rock press was one way that Gillespie could get journalists to understand his political beliefs and his working-class background. A student of Johnny Rotten and Jock Stein, he typifies the punk generation where the environment around popular music and football kicked open the door to fresh possibilities and ideas. He said in 2006 that Jock Stein's vision of football 'inspires him to this day'.

Born in 1962, Gillespie grew up in Springburn before moving to Cathcart near Hampden Park. At the turn of the decade he became a fanatic, covering his walls, collecting metal badges, imitation silk scarves and filling scrapbooks of his heroes Kenny Dalglish and Johnny Doyle. 'My earliest memory was the 1970 Feyenoord game on television. I guess what got me into football was the Mexico World Cup the same year. We moved up near Mount Florida close to

Hampden Park in the 1970s. I got the chance to go on a Celtic supporters' bus. Boys got in for free and you'd get lifted over the turnstile; when I got a bit older I knew ways to get in for free. My dad wasn't into football; he was too busy because he was a trade unionist. I didn't go with guys from school because I went to a Protestant school and my classmates supported Rangers. My neighbour was a Celtic fan, a guy called Jimmy Cowen. Jimmy was a fireman; he was down the stair in the council block where we lived. He was a lifelong Celtic fan and so were his sons but they had left home so he'd give me a run to the game. I started off in the stand and then I'd go in the Jungle by myself, he'd also take me to the away games. As a teenager I got the bus from Derry Traynor's pub in the Gorbals. You'd wait outside the pub and give the guy money and we'd travel away to Perth, Aberdeen or Edinburgh. It was when a lot of the Gorbals was being knocked down; about the only thing left standing was this pub.

'I seen a lot of good games. I saw the end of the Lisbon Lions: Jimmy Johnstone, Bobby Lennox and Billy McNeill. I saw crowds of 130,000 against Rangers on a Wednesday at Hampden. There was a good long period of ten to twelve years where I was going all the time. I was a fanatic. Kenny Dalglish was my idol and I saw him in his ascendancy. You look at him now and still see a strong powerful guy. The Old Firm games were the best. I don't know what an Old Firm derby means now with all the foreign players but I remember what it meant when we went down to ten men against Rangers in 1979 and still beat them 4–2 to win the league. In those days you would see Johnny Doyle jumping over the advertising boards and crossing himself in the Rangers end. You'd be watching him thinking: "I'd love to dae that; I'd fucking dae that!" The whole Jungle would cheer for Doyle. He was like a guy that had ran straight off the terrace and onto the pitch. In those games I respected guys like Willie Johnston because he was playing for his people or John Grieg because they meant it. It wasn't about money for those guys. I support Celtic because it's an underdog thing. At that time it was a Protestant ruling class that ran everything. Celtic was about the Catholic population standing up for itself but doing it in a beautiful way. I always hated the sectarian stuff; you would see a guy with his son shouting about an Orange bastard or a Fenian bastard. I hated that because the young guy isn't learning anything. It's going to be the next generation of hate and someone ends up getting stabbed. I don't know if that has changed; probably not.'

During the 1970s and early 1980s Gillespie witnessed some of the most violent games in the club's recent history. Post-match he would watch running street battles descend into chaos outside Hampden. Unlike the casual movement that followed a few years later, that was largely associated with Aberdeen and Hibernian, the fighting was often territorial: 'There were a lot of old guys on the bus and there was me and a couple of pals, there weren't really any hooligans but I saw a lot of madness and violence at the games. I was there at the pitch invasion during the 1980 Scottish Cup final. The Celtic end was pretty mad that day, a lot of guys I knew were involved. There were a lot of inter-gang rivalries so you had Celtic fans fighting with their fellow supporters, which I thought was fucking odd. A lot of people went onto the pitch to escape trouble. I remember this kid turning round with his da and he got hit full on in the face with a bottle of wine and crumbled. There were always drunken psychopaths at the games. I'd sit on the hill and watch the fans come down from the Rangers end and then the Celtic end would come out and they would meet in the middle, bottles and fists would start flying. You seen it all but it didn't faze me. It'd faze me now but then I'd watch it to the finish and walk home, hiding my scarf so I wouldn't get stabbed. I kept going into the 1980s but it got less and tapered off about 1985. I remember thinking at one point "This isn't how a Celtic team should be playing", after Jock Stein left. I loved his whole attitude to the game; he knew how a team should play. After Stein it all fell apart slowly and I don't think they ever replaced him. His values came through in the team's attitude, the players loved him.'

Historically Manchester United and Celtic have shared the common bond of Catholicism. United's affairs were run for many years by influential Catholics Louis Rocca and Matt Busby. When interviewing a number of well-known rock 'n' rollers from the city for a variety of football club publications and monthlies almost a decade ago, a case was made for Manchester City joining this select band. Although cut adrift from football in the current climate Johnny Marr was an Irish descendant City and Celtic fan in the 1970s before he went on to establish himself in The Smiths.

The beginning of the 1960s saw a final mass exodus of Irish migrants arrive in Britain and many provided essential labour for the construction industry. As Britain went into a further post-industrial decline the children of those immigrants formed new sub-cultural identities relating to life on the football terraces and popular music. As Johnny Marr explained to me: 'In the 1972–73 season there was a movement where City fans wore Celtic scarves and the United support were in Rangers ones. It was a spin-off from going to away grounds and claiming scarves. I heard stories about violence and was more aware of it coming from a Catholic background. There was a bit of woefully misinformed religious stuff going on but we took it as more of a fashion thing. It was confined especially to the derbies and for many it was about whether you were a Catholic or a Protestant.

'The City fans had a bit of a Bay City Rollers vibe, tying their scarves round their wrists and through their belts. I had a big thick woolly Celtic one that was too thick to get round my wrists. The United fans were a bit more androgynous; they had a David Bowie thing going on with the shaved eyebrows and Ziggy Stardust haircuts. I used to argue with a mate who was a United fan. He said they (Celtic) looked like a rugby team but I thought they appeared almost continental. I remember watching the highlights of Celtic games. I thought, "Is this the same sport I was watching earlier on?" It was so fast it almost became a different game. In the 1980s I liked Charlie Nicholas, what was there not to like? Charlie was someone you wanted to hang out with and he delivered as well, that was the great thing about him. He had a good haircut, which is always important, and the right attitude. There was the crowd-pleasing thing a lot of flash players have but he was consistent and tough with it. In England there wasn't the same fervour, passion or insanity except for City and United derbies maybe.'

Born in 1967 just days after Celtic lifted the European Cup, fellow City and Celtic supporter Noel Gallagher was in agreement with Marr when he added: 'The United v City derby is a great thing to go to but it's nothing compared to a Celtic–Rangers game. I've been to a few Manchester derbies and I'd put it second to Celtic and Rangers. There are a few Irish descendant City fans, like me, Johnny Marr and Billy Duffy in The Cult. I had a few mates who didn't have an Irish background and they all supported Celtic. I could never work that out.' Like Marr, Gallagher's parents were both Irish. For the offspring of that final influx that arrived from across the water, Celtic became an integral identifier, particularly in Britain's inner cities. Gallagher's older brother Paul ran a bus from Manchester to Celtic Park. Famously the former Oasis chief songwriter and guitarist attended the 6–2 victory over Rangers in August 2000. 'The greatest thing I've ever seen in my life was before the match. I was having a drink and this guy came up and said, "You better go and sit in your seat son, something special is about to happen.' As I walked into the stadium 'Roll With It' came out of the PA. They stopped it halfway and the fans stood up and began to sing it.

'I'm glad I got the chance to see Henrik Larsson score against Rangers when he looked especially cool with the dreadlocks. He scored with a magnificent chip over the keeper's head. Everyone thought the ball was over, even the ball boys, but he was already celebrating. My other favourite Celtic player was Kenny Dalglish. He was just a phenomenal footballer, he had the haircut, the big sideboards, the big collared shirts and the number on the shorts. I also liked Charlie Nicholas; anyone that comes with the prefix Champagne is all right by me.'

Both Manchester City fans have a particular reverence for Martin O'Neill, with Gallagher crediting the much celebrated manager with Celtic's revival on his arrival at the club in 2000. 'Celtic for a long time had some nondescript managers like John Barnes. When Martin O'Neill went to Celtic, I was pleased because I knew he was a proper Celt. I always liked him because he played at Manchester City for a while. I watch most games on Sky, the number of times I would sit in my bedroom or would sit in the house and watch Celtic fucking outplay Rangers for an hour and then bang, Ally McCoist. Every week it was like, "You bastard". He wasn't even on the pitch this geezer then he'd come on and pop up from the far post. Then all of a sudden it was scorelines like 6–2, 3–3 and 5–1.'

Throughout his career Noel Gallagher has made his allegiances to the Republic of Ireland national team and Celtic clear. His declarations helped obliterate the old clichés of not revealing your colours and splitting the Glasgow audience in half. Gallagher once told me that after Manchester, Oasis sold more records in Glasgow than anywhere else, pouring further cold water on the idea that identifying with Celtic loses you fans in Scotland. Said Gallagher: 'It's funny how a lot of it all stretches across to New York. We'd be playing there and it would be like Glasgow, a lot of straight up

American people can't believe it but the place would be all Irish and Scottish people. Scotland is a strange and beautiful place; one of the reasons is because of the drinking laws.

'Aside from the gigging I've went there on holiday and it's where my girlfriend [now wife] is from. I think the Scottish and Irish outlook is identical when comes to politics and family aspects; I really can't separate the two. When you're Irish Catholic you have to work for a living and you're usually working for someone else and it's usually on a building site. Irish Catholic people don't work in offices; they don't own their own businesses. They put gas mains in the fucking streets and they put roofs on houses. I worked for John Kennedy, an Irish subcontractor for the gas board, I'd be knee deep in shit five days a week but I wouldn't change that for the world because of the people that I met. When Liam and me became famous a lot of people were like, "Look at them two arrogant bastards" but we'd just signed off the dole and someone gave us half a million fucking quid. We could have been back on the dole in six months so we thought right we're going to enjoy this. When you come from that background, you're born with nothing, especially Irish working-class people. You don't make plans for the future because what are you fucking planning for? You've got more kids than everyone else and more cousins than you need so you just live for the moment.

'Manchester was a great place to be. Everybody I knew was second generation Irish; I didn't know anyone that wasn't. There has to be something in it, there's just a passion and sadness with Irish people, it's extremes all the time. They can make the saddest sentiment in the world sound like the most spiritually uplifting thing you've ever heard. I think that's why Oasis were so massive. *Definitely Maybe* will always be my favourite album because I was writing it in the centre of Manchester on the dole, I was writing about what it would be like to be a rock 'n' roll star escaping the city.

'We were all from working-class Irish backgrounds. We weren't the best looking band in the world, apart from Liam who's a good-looking lad, but the point is anyone could have been in the band. I remember Alan McGee said to me: "What are we going to do about Bonehead?" I said: "What about him?" He said: "Well, he's bald." I said: "Bonehead's Bonehead; he comes as he is." I've written some pretty good songs since but that album was from a different perspective. We had all lived through the shit of the 1980s, the Tories, football violence and all that but in the 1990s life got a bit better, the clothes were better, the music had got better. Life was quite cool for a few years, it was a good album because it hit the nail on the head, it just sums up the times. A lot of bands were singing about how miserable life was, we had fuck all but we could still go to the football and have a drink, we were just glad to be fucking alive.'

Bobby Gillespie's Mancunian band-mate Mani, also born in 1962, has retained an open Celtic affiliation alongside his support of Manchester United. For the Stone Roses bass player the two clubs share a unique bond stemming from what Mani describes as 'an inner city, anti-royal, anti-establishment, working-class sub-culture.' When Mani joined The Stone Roses, the clothes became looser, the bottom end funkier. His Northern Soul-influenced rhythms meshed with John Squire's guitar and Ian Brown's traditional folk harmonies and Aeolian melodies to create one of the most loved and celebrated debut albums of all time. The Stone Roses found an audience in Scotland long before they brought about a revival of guitar bands which followed in their wake after the second summer of love. After the band split in 1996 (reforming again in 2011) Mani joined Primal Scream while they were also on the ropes. Bobby Gillespie admitted that the former scooter boy's fervent enthusiasm, mental toughness and supreme talent lifted Primal Scream back into the premiership of rock 'n' roll while feeding them with his take on funk, dub, hip-hop and reggae. As contenders and comrades limped off to the sidelines and crashed behind the advert-ising boards, this musical Melchizedek has outlasted the competition since forming in 1982. Despite drugs casualties, stabbings and disillusionment with the industry, Primal Scream remain one of the last great rock 'n' roll bands of the last three decades.

Undoubtedly the support of both Celtic and Manchester United in the band has brought even greater concurrence within the ranks. Says Mani: 'For me Rod Stewart called it right. He didn't say "Celtic and Liverpool" or "United and Rangers"; he said "Celtic United". Bobby Charlton had his testimonial against Celtic in the early 1970s. I've been to Old Trafford for a few of the big games with Celtic. The game for Brian McClair was one of the best times I've ever had, for a testimonial there was well over 40,000 people there. Only

Celtic and United can bring those kinds of crowds for a friendly. Innes and Bob in the band are Celtic but they also have leanings towards United and had them long before I joined Primal Scream. It goes back to the impoverished Irish that formed both clubs. In Man United's case it was for the rail workers and a lot them would have been Irishmen that had to move to Manchester to get work and survive. Pat Crerand, who played for both clubs, has always had a big personality so there was a bit of cross fertilisation and that really strengthened the link for my generation. It was the same with Lou McCari, Choccy and Keano; they have all kept it going strong.

'I've nearly got in trouble a few times for my Celtic leanings. I've been handed Celtic/United scarves at gigs in Glasgow and things like that. I've got mates up in Glasgow and around the west that go back to the early days of the Roses, but it goes back a lot further than that. I was always conscious of Irish music because of my ma. There was no one musical in my family but you always knew the rebel songs and the songs of depravation from home, you were conscious of it. I come from an Irish family in north Manchester, I went to Catholic schools, most of my mates were Catholic and everyone supported Celtic and the Republic of Ireland. It was part of the Irish character. The "People's Republic of Mancunia" is how a lot of United fans feel about Manchester, the identity is with the city. There is apathy towards the English national side and the English press. It's exactly the same in Glasgow; people feel a loyalty to the city. There's always been an anti-royal thing, which is just a weird

Manchester trait. The royal family was very much something you associated with Cockneys and London. It meant nothing to us.

'Before Primal Scream plays in Glasgow I often go into Bairds Bar in the Gallowgate for a "wee nip". I had to re-record the bass for a BBC radio gig a few years ago because people kept buying me drinks: "Another wee nip Mani?" They weren't letting me out the door till I'd finished every one of them. I think the people in Glasgow and Manchester are exactly the same; both cities should be twinned. One of the best nights in Glasgow was when a pal managed to get me a ticket for the Boavista game at Parkhead. It was the UEFA Cup semi-final and a big deal at the time because Celtic hadn't got that far in Europe in over twenty years. Innes in the band made it over to the final in Seville and said it was bonkers; whole families were sleeping in doorways. I went to the European Cup final at the Nou Camp with United in 1999 and every pirate, vagabond and scally I'd ever known in my life made it there. Again I think that's something unique to Celtic and United; the fans intent is to support the team and have a good time doing it.'

Former front man with The Verve, Richard Ashcroft, reflects further on the historical friendship between the two clubs and how wider cultural shifts seems to have stemmed the flow of players pulling on colours for both teams: 'It used to be a lot more open in the early 1980s when I started to watch United. I used to have one of the Celtic/United splitter hats, which I swapped for an airgun. I remember meeting this lad on our bikes and changing over. There's always been massive links going back to players like Paddy Crerand; they're both glamour clubs, outsider clubs. Looking at it now the only Scottish international we have in the team is Darren Fletcher. If you compare that to years gone by it's unbelievable, the quality of the Scottish players not just at United but in English football was absolutely incredible, but it's been lost to Sega, PlayStation and the internet. Our greatest players were born out of a culture where there was nothing else going on, football was the universal game because of its simplicity, all you needed was a ball and a bit of space. Now dads are buying their kids plasma televisions. You need to go and make your own life. There's no Kenny Dalglish from this generation because kids are living vicariously through other things. You see it at gigs, they don't want to be there, they're filming it, watching it through a screen. It's become a removed thing and it's the same with football. Watching the World Cup you can see the hunger of African nations. We've become too sorted.'

The Celtic influence at Old Trafford was particularly present when Ashcroft began travelling to games from Wigan in 1981: 'It was much more tribal and hairy then and looking back quite scary in a way. The Celtic thing was more freely expressed then than it is now. You'd see the coaches line up and there was always a tremendous Irish contingent like at Liverpool; that influence was very strong. The other thing was the link with Ferguson and Stein. Fergie was on the bench the night he died during the Scotland–Wales World Cup qualifier. He's carried the same psychology as these great managers: Stein, Shankly, Busby. No one ever imagined there would be anyone after Matt Busby at Manchester United that could leave an impression like that. Statues have been built honouring these men. There's an immense power and history that goes back to those managers, a connection like that is so healthy because it takes the club in the right direction. It's not the sort of thing that after having a few bad seasons you just throw away. I think it's the same mindset that the greatest bands have come from. They have had a foot in that psychology and wanted to take you somewhere but even that seems to have changed. I look at groups now and they seem reluctant to have their foot in any camp.'

Shortly after this interview the singer will draw out a green and gold anti-Glazer scarf on stage in Manchester, throwing his weight behind the now famous fan-led protest against the American owners of Manchester United. The magnitude of the remonstration, with well known fans such as Mani and Ashcroft voicing their disapproval, has increased publicity around the cause which has strong echoes of the fan-led ousting of the Kelly and White dynasties organised by Celtic fans in the early 1990s paving the way for Fergus McCann's takeover of the club in 1994. Demonstrations, pickets and even the boycott of a home match against Kilmarnock brought the old guard crashing down as the threat of Celtic's existence hung over the heads of fans. The club was said to be minutes away from bankruptcy before McCann and his financial clout stepped in to save it. It's impossible to imagine what the outcome would have been without the Scottish-born Canadian businessman's intervention, but equally without the organisation of the Celtic support, the move might never have come to fruition.

For Ashcroft, fan-led movements have the power to change the outcome of Manchester United's future. The actions of the support have been projected into the public eye through merchandise, banners, phone-ins and media coverage which all now play a realistic role in determining the future of certain clubs. Undoubtedly Manchester United and Celtic in particular through their roots are resurrecting voices from the past in order to give weight to modern-day concerns. The original green and gold colours visible in the anti-Glazer protest is a firm nod to the many Irish workers that formed Newton Heath Lancashire & Yorkshire Railway Football Club in 1878. The club was renamed Manchester United in 1902 after the name Manchester Celtic was rejected for sounding too Scottish.

Today the community concerns of a Marist Brother and working-class railway football team at the end of the nineteenth century continue to drive the spirit and deter-mination of supporters in the modern game. Says Ashcroft: 'Celtic always seemed like that, a very fan-led club, you don't want to go in against the Celtic fans. You know what I'm saying because they still hold an influence in the decisions of the club. Other clubs are run in a completely different way. How many other supporters would even consider a protest about the situation in the West Bank. That is one example of football's power and having a collective ethos with a political standing. It blows my mind but in fan culture you have to be aware there is a fine line between tribalism and fascism or sectarianism ... and between nationalism and violence.

'There is a fine balance that goes on in Glasgow for me as a guy looking it from England. As a fan of these clubs your say, your shout and your voice is important. The protest we have at Man U right now is very powerful; it flows into the roots. I have no idea how a working-class man and his son can follow a club, buy a match programme, get something to eat and travel to the game. You add all that up in a man's wage once he's been taxed and it's an astonishing amount of money to put out. That's why everyone is looking at Barcelona and saying why can't my club be like that, why can't I have a stake in it and why can't the money I'm earning every week and putting into your club through season tickets and kits for my kids be part owned by me? Why can't I have a say in what's going on with my club? I think these ideas are very important.'

Returning to the west of Scotland, you couldn't really describe Mogwai as rock 'n' roll. In fact any attempt to describe Mogwai is a waste of time and often involves a lot of superlatives that are guaranteed to have the band howling with laughter. It's far better to just listen to the sonically brilliant and unpretentious Lanarkshire five-piece doing what they do best. In truth Mogwai are probably closer to the original counter-cultural guts and force of rock 'n' roll and punk rock than most and part of their outsider identity has been their unequivocal support of Celtic. The

Edinburgh Evening News once displayed a review headline that read: 'Mogwai play well despite Celtic loss', referring to the band's late arrival onstage after a 3–0 defeat to Manchester United in the Champions League.

Since forming in the mid-1990s various members of the band have captured the zeitgeist and humour for a post-industrial generation of Celtic supporters. Mogwai are the Celtic supporters' Celtic supporter, whether it be wearing the Hoops onstage and even on the cover of NME or referencing various narratives, issues and concerns among the support despite criticism from some. To their credit the band remain unapologetic towards those who fail to see the humour in the ludicrousness and absurd nature of Scottish football and its fan culture, which the band send up unrepentantly. Rather than making an overt political statement, titles and songs such as 'Scotland's Shame' and 'Hugh Dallas' are, by and large, referencing in-jokes between the members of the band and their wider community. 'Scotland's Shame' in particular from *The Hawk is Howling* album was widely read as a sober proclamation. In truth it was a reference to a Celtic banner that has become a part of recent folklore.

Stuart Braithwaite from the band explains: 'People have taken "Scotland's Shame" as a real serious comment, where it was just something that made us laugh. It was meant to be just a brilliant noise up. It came from the banner that was held up after Nakamura scored a screamer in a 2–1 win over Rangers at Parkhead near the end of the season in 2008. Some wee guys behind me pulled out a banner, pointing it at the Rangers fans. We just thought it was really funny and it got blown out of proportion and a few people misread it and said it was something serious or that we were making some grand statement. We weren't.'

Born in May 1976, Stuart Braithwaite grew up in Lanarkshire. He was a true music obsessive during a time when you would wait for the day of release of your favourite band's new record. Stuart's love of punk, metal, indie and alternative goes back to an almost antediluvian era when the only way to pacify less mainstream tastes was tune into John Peel or take a punt at your local independent record shop. Growing up he had little time for football in a less fragmented culture where music was an all-consuming passion: 'It wasn't something that interested me at all. My interest in football started because of my friendship with Martin (Bulloch) our drummer. He's always been obsessed with Celtic and I started checking the results just to see what kind of mood he'd be in. I knew he wouldn't be saying much if they lost because he couldn't talk. It then dawned on me that I really cared about it and that I'd been sucked in and started going. I became part of the fold. I'd be a lot more into music if it wasn't for Celtic, it takes up a lot of your time and that's something quite specific to Celtic fans, other clubs don't have the same passion and obsession as Celtic supporters. They really care. The attitude is not, "My team lost; I'm raging." It's a lot deeper and emotional, but who knows, maybe there's a Hamilton supporter having the same chat we are right now ... but I doubt it. My life would be very different, even down to what you do on a Saturday afternoon or a Wednesday night.

'Obviously there are two big teams in Glasgow. Rangers represented the establishment and traditions relating to the monarchy and unionism in Northern Ireland. These are ideas that I wouldn't fancy so Celtic were the anti-authority club. I don't think you can say that now with someone like John Reid as chairman. I emailed Celtic when there was talk of it and I said I wouldn't renew my season ticket. Of course, I completely reneged on that, but I was appalled when he came in. To me he is the worst example of a careerist politician, these people whore any ideals they once had just to get a foot up the ladder.'

For Stuart anti-authoritarian doesn't necessarily mean an Irish Republican identity, something that is almost becoming an antiquated idea for a new generation of Celtic supporters. At the same time new and valid expressions of Irishness are often widely misinterpreted: 'Part of me thinks half the reason these wee guys are singing the songs is because somebody has told them not to. Who likes to do what they're told? I think there are guys a lot younger than me that want to reconnect Celtic with that anti-establishment feeling. When we were in our twenties we got into a lot of trouble for mouthing off and having a laugh, we've toned it down a bit as we've got older. When you go to some supporters' clubs you hear some bizarre stuff. We went upstairs to this pub in Boston and I spoke to some of the guys. From their views they obviously hadn't been back to Scotland or Ireland in a very long time. The things they were saying were out of touch and they wouldn't be saying them if they lived here. I'm not from an Irish background. I don't see it as exclusive but at the same time

I'm not antagonised by it. We went to the Tokyo CSC and the fans there were just really into Celtic, they were singing "The Celtic Song", they just got what it's all about.

'In Scotland the media seem to be up in arms about anything Irish. That says more to me about their prejudice; it's never something that makes me uncomfortable. The other thing is that players come to Celtic because of the Irish connection. It's easy to be cynical about it but guys like Robbie Keane came here because of a loyalty and connection to the club. He and others would never have played in Scotland if they didn't have that feeling for Celtic.'

Significantly the band's Travels in Constants EP, part of a catalogue-only series, united collectors of Celtic memorabilia and Mogwai fans in their hunt for a rare disc that paid homage to the Lisbon Lions with two atmospheric shots of the 1967 European Cup final on the sleeve. The Lions along with Jock Stein and his relationship to Lanarkshire hold a particular resonance with the band. Says Braithwaite: 'The English don't make managers like Jock Stein. I think the Lisbon Lions are one of the most important football teams ever. The way Stein orchestrated the media was incredible, he would hold a press conference and get the papers saying exactly what he wanted on the Monday morning. I love the stories and reading about when Stein left the house to play for Celtic on Saturday morning, his dad would leave at the same time to cheer on Rangers. That must have been a strange experience. I like the fact that he had this strong connection to the fans; he liked the people that supported Celtic and wanted to win for them. I think Alex Ferguson has carried a lot of Stein's philosophy on if you look at the way he got rid of David Beckham. He wasn't up for putting up with his antics. A lot of other managers would be too afraid to sack the star player. When he sold Ronaldo that was a brave move. Stein wouldn't have had time for players that didn't respect him and Ferguson is the same.

'I think Martin O'Neill used a similar ability with the media to Stein. Through his personality he used the cameras and press to speak directly to Celtic fans. He came to a Mogwai gig once, I knew his daughter through a friend of mine and he had a beer with us after the gig. He was brand new. It was just after the Clyde game where we got beat. I was talking to him about it and he was so down to earth. He was like, "These things happen sometimes, you just don't turn up and the other team play well, but the league is the most important thing and I think it's in the bag." He was just so passionate about it, he was really into it. O'Neill is a charismatic and likable person; he's someone that you could really warm to and believe in. Apart from that he was a brilliant manager and it's important to have a guy that knows what he's doing. The other thing I liked about him was that he was proper old school. We heard a story that after Neil Lennon dyed his hair peroxide blonde, O'Neill called him into his office and asked him what he was doing. Lennon's response was: "I want to stand out." O'Neill told him: "If you want to stand out then try and score a few goals for us." What I loved about that was you could imagine the exact same scene with Stein. Neil Lennon is another likable guy in contrast to the monstrous wild bampot image that gets portrayed in the media. When you see a manager get excited, that's what you want. He's just really passionate about Celtic.'

While both Noel Gallagher and Mani have expressed a desire to see Celtic play in the English Premiership it's not something that would appeal to Stuart. 'I don't like the English league. I don't fancy travelling to Bolton on a Wednesday night. I'd rather see Celtic play Motherwell. The whole thing is greed just to make more money and tickets would go up. I think market forces have changed football and the way things are going will mean that Celtic and Scottish football will come off the big stage a bit. It wouldn't surprise me if things were to go back to their roots, maybe there will be more of a focus on local players. I'd like to see it become more about building a team with less stars. Some Celtic supporters tend to over-praise players and there's a real scapegoat mentality on the internet. People decide who is shite. Sometimes we sign a player on a free transfer from Hibs and the truth is he's just no that good and all of a sudden the player is perceived as this big superstar letting us down. If what happened in Lisbon happened now all those players would end up going to Madrid or Barca. It's a bygone era. Nothing like that will ever happen again which is quite sad.'

Perhaps not since the days of The Smiths has an authentic rock 'n' roll guitar band captured working-class life in Britain so eloquently as Glasvegas. Once again it was former Creation Records boss Alan McGee who brought the band to public attention in 2006 after witnessing another illustrious gig at King Tuts, the legendary Glasgow venue where he discovered

Oasis. McGee has suggested they could become 'the biggest band in the world' and it's not hard to see why. Forget the stumbling attempts of The Libertines and The Arctic Monkeys, Glasvegas so far have made the first great debut album of the twenty-first century featuring a string of singles that attempted to take pop music back to its roots. Rousing sing-along anthems about absentee fathers, social workers and street fighting in the East End of Glasgow were getting played on the wireless where they gloriously raged with angst and sublime melodic hooks. Pop music wrapped in a sonic soup of Jesus and Mary Chain guitars sounded like it really meant something for the first time in well over a decade. On no account should rock 'n' roll be a moderate art form and James Allan is a vital testimony to the principle. When promoting the band's second album *Euphoric Heartbreak* in the *NME* the Glaswegian referenced Ridley Scott's science fiction masterwork *Blade Runner* and was pictured with a memorable quote from the film scrawled across his chest. Another shot showed his hands clasped in prayer, his eyes staring fervently into the camera lens.

References are important to James Allan: the gothic portrayal of Glasgow on the cover of their self-titled debut was a nod to Vincent van Gogh's *The Starry Night*. Whether it's Elvis Presley or former Celtic player Andy Walker, Allan shows no discrimination in comparing their greatness; he doesn't look at brilliance through provincial blinkers. The culture of football in Glasgow has perhaps influenced the four-piece more than anything else. For Glasvegas the passion, community, identity and history of the Old Firm has energised their efforts more than cinema, art, literature, politics and, most significantly, pop culture. Growing up in the shadows of Parkhead James Allan is a particularly ardent Celtic supporter. His cousin Rab Allan, the band's guitarist, and bass player Paul Donoghue follow Rangers. Ex-professional footballer Allan plied his trade as a winger at a string of clubs in Scottish football with the hope of one day signing for Celtic. When the dream failed to materialise he poured the heartbreak and energy into Glasvegas. With such intense loyalties on either side of the Glasgow divide, derby day is undertaken with caution among family and friends in the Glasvegas camp.

Says Allan: 'We don't talk about football in the band, it's something we all feel really intense about and I wouldn't want to upset Paul or Rab. A couple of seasons ago we all watched Celtic play Rangers at Parkhead in a New York bar. It was 2–2 and Celtic got a penalty and we scored. I never said a word; I just sat there. We wouldn't slag each other about it because it means too much. I grew up in Dalmarnock near Parkhead, my dad's a Celtic fan but my granny and aunty support Rangers. The thread of how we feel about the teams is the same and without the rivalry it just wouldn't be the same. It's a beautiful and powerful thing that reflects Glasgow, which is an intense place.'

It was initially Celtic's double-winning centenary team that fired up the singer in his boyhood days following the Hoops. That season was the end of an era where the club largely fielded local heroes prior to what's largely referred to as the barren years during which Rangers held a nine-season tenure of domestic dominance. The success of the centenary team, however, has endured in the collective conscience of Celtic support. The 1987–88 season saw the Hoops hit peak form, playing thirty-one games unbeaten in the league after a 1–0 win at Easter Road in November. They remained on top of the league until the end of the season, finishing ten points clear of Hearts; losing only five out of fifty-five games including a spell in Europe. 'I take a lot of influence from that team, more than any band or musician. I can still name it: Bonner, Morris, Rogan, Aitken, McCarthy, Grant, Miller, McStay, McAvennie, Walker, Stark. That's my team!' says Allan with tangible pride. 'I'd love to have been a sub or even just trained with them, I'd still love to meet them. The players around that time were as artistic as any painter.

'I've been happy a lot of my life but I don't know if I've ever been happier than when Frank McAvennie scored the winner against Dundee United in the Scottish Cup with seconds to go, it's still one of the happiest days of my life. I remember going to Butlins on holiday the next day with my cousin, we were both in our Celtic tops. I loved the ethos of Celtic around that time, the never-say-die attitude – there's a lot going on behind that, it's says a lot about the character and heart of the team. Not only that but they played with absolute vision and flair. It was the same with the semi-final against Hearts when Andy Walker scored in the dying minutes. I see Andy Walker in the same way I see Elvis, he's still my favorite player of all time. He would just float on to a pitch and start to glide. I used to wear out videotapes just watching this guy's skill. He had great charisma. It was the small details like tucking his football top into his shorts; I was in awe of him.'

Perhaps Allan has taken on the showmanship and spirit of his early Parkhead coming-of-age experiences and translated them into the dynamics of Glasvegas: 'For me it's as if somebody has poured a bucket of magic dust all over Celtic Park and anyone who walks through the doors gets the same touch of magic. Something quite powerful happens when you see the green and white Hoops run out on the park. I remember going to matches when it was the turnstiles, walking into the Celtic end, you'd hear the rumble of the crowd and it would go right through your chest. By that point I would see the players warming up – it would all take you to another place.

'This place, that was five minutes up the road from my house in Dalmarnock, was a paradise and if something can make you feel like that, it's an amazing positive thing.' For Allan that spirit and determination remains in the Celtic team with players such as current captain Scott Brown. Although his dream of playing for Celtic never came to fruition he maintains it's still something he can dream about despite his success with Glasvegas: 'Win, lose or draw I'm a Celtic fan. I have no problem with how we win the league as long as we win. You can't play like the Dutch team of 1974 every week. The thing to remember is Celtic will rarely get beat without giving the other team a good battering. Scott Brown I think is an absolute athlete; he's a machine. I love players like him that have a look in their eyes, they totally mean it and they believe in what they are doing. You can tell they are hungry, you can see that in the ground or even on the television. You can feel how much a player like him wants to win the game for Celtic.

'I'm living the dream now, the band is touring the world, but my biggest dream beyond everything was to play for Celtic – beyond meeting Elvis, even to that degree. It's a shame in my lifetime it will never happen but I think sometimes that's the way dreams are meant to be. Maybe they are meant to be there to always dream about.'

AFTERWORD

FOR YEARS A picture of my uncle Terry, wearing his Celtic top and holding me as a newborn sat on my aunt Betty's mantelpiece. He'd run home from school each day to give me a nurse. Although it might not sound like it I always felt like I had a choice in whether I should become a Celtic fan or not. There are two sentiments expressed in this book that I must agree with now. Firstly, that deciding which team to support is a big decision, and secondly that it comes with responsibilities. There's a lot of grappling to be done, which is how anything worth holding onto in life should be.

At my primary school St Marks in Edinburgh most of the boys in my class were Celtic supporters with strong connections to the west and Ireland. The first boy to pull on the Hoops at school was Michael Conway, I remember him in both the Charlie Nicholas V-neck and the lime-green away kit. To this day they remain two of the most memorable kits Celtic have produced. We played football every day, before school, break time, playtime and after school. What the cantankerous old janitor who confiscated our main resource failed to realise was the importance of our relationship to the ball, without it there would often be a monumental lunchtime pagger and when I look back all I can remember is fighting and football in the playground and nothing much in between.

We weren't interested in lessons. We lived and breathed for a kickabout and football was on our minds morning, noon and night. About the only other thing I enjoyed were the rousing hymns at Mass such as 'Colours of Day'. They were anthems you could really chant and I often reflect on the ecclesiastical joy that these times brought. These were the experiences that marked you out as Catholic because the music tuned you into an experience that would stay with you for the rest of your life and even now when I sing a few words from 'Do Not Be Afraid' or 'Bind Us Together' I'm back in the gym hall belting it out beside Stevie, Mikey, Martin and the rest of the boys. It was no Dead Poets Society but one teacher, Mrs McNaughton, noticed my interest in language and storytelling.

My mother had looked after Maureen McNaughton as a baby in Fauldhouse, West Lothian. My grandad was also great friends with her father, Paddy Brannan, a butcher who would drop off a parcel of meat when money was tight. Although that encouragement stayed with me, ultimately my memories of primary school relate to football. Today the Nintendo DS and *Call of Duty* are like cyber heroin along with a raft of other new technological distractions; when I look back to the early 1980s I think, 'thank God for football and Celtic' because they were the only things that held our attention and a lot of life's lessons, experience and personal development came from that world.

Throughout those early stages of compulsory education in the 1980s I lived with my uncle Terry and my gran. In the morning my gran would come in with breakfast and the paper and fling open the curtains. There was forever a story involving Charlie, Mo or Frank in their respective Celtic eras, dominating the front pages with some story relating to their champagne lifestyles and the back pages scoring for Celtic. In those days my uncle was more like a big brother, my other uncles were much older and had families. As Terry got ready for work, initially as a glazier who was afraid of heights, and later a printer, he would read about some wonder goal from Charlie as one of his morning songs in the form of 'Waterfront' or 'Two Hearts Beat As One' would blast and crackle out the speakers with hymnal brush strokes. He'd often ask 'any chocolate ma' before he left for work and would give me a bit going out the door into what seemed like permanent blue sky days. In Terry's bottom drawer were all his old Celtic tops, worn out and covered in stoor. For a number of reasons they just couldn't be worn, they weren't even nylon, they were like a strange material made from my nana's message bags. My mother would regularly buy me the Scotland home kit but the time had come. For every Catholic there comes a time to question hereditary and locked-in belief systems and by the age of nine I knew what I was getting into and I wanted to pull on the Hoops.

At the start of the 1985–86 season I began to harangue my uncle to take me west to see Celtic but he had an inventory of excuses: 'Kim's coming over', 'I've got a hangover', 'I'm working', 'I've got band practice', 'They're away at Aberdeen'. I was still too young for my gran to let me off the leash, but by way of compensation my uncle reminded me my birthday was coming and bought himself a bit of time. When the day came we met his girlfriend Kim in the town. Kim Hunter was a Led Zeppelin fanatic, thankfully by this time my uncle had given up on his attempt at a Ziggy Stardust haircut and had opted for a more successful long curly Robert Plant look much to Miss Hunter's liking. We met outside St James Centre, perhaps Edinburgh's most resented building, one that more resembles a university campus than a shopping centre. Once inside we bustled through an endless corridor of shoppers to reach Inter Sport. 'Are you still wanting that Celtic top wee man?' my uncle asked. I knew what the answer was but I'd lost the power of speech. This still happens sporadically, often when I know what to say but nerves or fear of confrontation have got the better of me. My heart was pumping and my spirit raced as I tried it on. Your first Celtic top is like your First Holy Communion; it's a big commitment and the photos sit on the mantelpieces of mammies, grannies and aunts for the rest of eternity. Perhaps what made it even more memorable was the fact my hero was buying me my first kit, well the top at least and Kim was digging deep for the shorts.

My uncle explained that this was the start of becoming a man, that it was a lifelong commitment, there was no going back or changing to another team no matter what happened, even if Celtic got relegated or all my friends supported another team. I had no memory of seeing Celtic win the league. The two-horse race between Celtic and Rangers we have today didn't exist and the competition was everywhere. Aberdeen had just won the two previous league titles, Dundee United the season before that and the big contenders at the end of the 1985–86 season were Hearts. My uncle reminded me that he also was gifted a Celtic top at the same age not long before his da died. 'Your mammy can get you the socks,' he added as we left the shop.

So on Friday 18 October 1985, the same day Nintendo launched in New York City, I proudly sported the Hoops for the first time and again the day after while watching the highlights of Motherwell v Celtic on telly. The signs were good after Paul McStay scored two in a 2–1 victory and we famously won the league on the last day of the season in Michael Conway's lime-green away kit. In the years that followed my uncle began to find moderate success in a band that resembled the New York Dolls, at least on their fly posters that seemed to cover the length and breadth of Edinburgh, bringing a certain local notoriety. We never did manage to get to that Celtic game before he moved to London in the 1987–88 season but sometime in the early 1990s I decided it was time for me to pick up the torch and carry the Celtic flame for the family.

Unlike my primary years, at St Thomas Aquinas secondary school I was firmly in the minority as a Celtic supporter. Hibs were the dominant force at the big school and the casual movement was in full flow. There was a major obsession with Hibs, designer labels and organised violence that swept everyone up in its wake. Police CID made more than one visit to the school looking for leads. Some lads even appeared on the front page of the *Sun* fighting outside the ring after a boxing match. When Hibs won the Skol Cup in October 1991 it energised the entire spirit of the school. The non-Hibs teachers had formed the Morningside Celtic Supporters' Club some years before, when the Hibs boys found out they asked the teachers concerned if they carried green handbags to Parkhead. Their collective confidence had been growing since the triumph of the 'Hands off Hibs' campaign. The scalping of Rangers in the semi of the cup that year created a buzz of intense excitement among the emerald greens who were battering everyone on and off the pitch. After their cup win the streets of Edinburgh were rammed as the team returned home to mount an open-top bus. Celtic supporters were marked out with the usual clichés: 'We created you,' 'We wore the green and white first,' 'You stole our players and the shirts off our backs,' 'We wear the Irish harp on our chest; we're the more Irish team' and so it went on. For some it was just banter, for others they'd lose their heads. There was a definite bitterness that some kids never grew out of. This was after all an argument that was over a hundred years old. It only made you ask the question, what defines my support of the club today, at this point in time? This is something I and many of the people I've interviewed over the years continue to do as Celtic supporters. There was, however, a much more serious and recent reason for bad blood between Celtic and Hibs. It's worth noting that there is always going to be a disconnection among fellow supporters of a club as there is among communities of people in any society, organisation or group, Celtic fans included. Some reasons are more serious than others but one of the most talked about in living memory remains the Celtic supporters who threw the CS gas grenade into the Hibs end at Easter Road in November 1988 causing widespread panic and chaos in the ground, damaging relations between supporters of the two clubs to this day.

For me Celtic didn't present a psychology that was about hating other teams. I'm not saying we didn't have those supporters but what I really loved about Celtic was a certain blend of glamour and shabbiness. When I started to travel to watch Celtic in the early 1990s both my school and Parkhead were literally crumbling. At the end of the 1989–90 season we finished fifth in the league and in those five years in which we won nothing Celtic failed to finish in second place in the league once and came in at various spots behind the likes of Hearts, Hibs, Motherwell and Aberdeen. During those years presentation was everything to the Hibs boys and they were pristine: short back and sides, shirts tucked in and Stone Island jumpers. The Celtic fans looked more like extras in *Boys from the Blackstuff*. They exuded a different kind of confidence that wasn't gleaned from outer appearances. For a particular type of Celtic supporter growing up in the 1980s and early 1990s it was a bit more cultured. It was about referencing certain bands or movies, family and an approach to life was more important than designer labels and short haircuts. One fan in my year, Big Stu, was one such character. A tall thin placid guy who, like myself, was a student of the electric guitar. His dad looked like Paul Weller in the video for *Changing Man* and his mum was an extremely cool barefooted bohemian redhead who had an LP signed by all five original members of the Stones.

Being Edinburgh boys and the fact that most of our mates and teachers were Hibs fans, the 'Battle of the Greens' would take on extra significance. On 12 September 1992 we boarded the Celtic bus outside The Carousel bar on Ferry Road. At the time we were preoccupied with Nirvana, the Seattle trio had changed our world almost overnight; we'd discuss everything from obscure B-sides and coloured vinyl to cardigans and guitars. Kurt Cobain even said in the *NME* that if he lived anywhere apart from Seattle it would be Edinburgh. Nirvana had played some now legendary gigs in the capital and had developed fleeting friendships with a number of Scottish bands including The Vaselines, Teenage Fanclub, BMX Bandits and The Pastels, most of whom Nirvana shared a bill with at some point. Significantly Eugene Kelly of The Vaselines and later Captain America came from Parkhead and his parents were from Donegal. It was no surprise eventually to find that Cobain's roots were also Irish. There's little doubt that had his ancestors travelled across the water to Scotland instead of Canada he probably would have joined one of the above and been a Celtic supporter like Gerry Love of Teenage Fanclub and Stephen McRobbie of The Pastels. These were the kind of conversations we'd have on the Celtic bus amid the 'Boys from the Blackstuff' playing rebel songs, smoking dope and urinating out the window while the bus flew down the motorway alongside the Hibs buses travelling away for the day. It was around this time we started to sing 'The Fields of Athenry', since then I've met a lot of Irish people who think the song is a bit tawdry but to me it was about standing up for yourself, your team and your culture but doing it with grace and humility. The other thing was that it was a song that your granny would've sung, it felt communal and connected. There was something of the joys and struggles we all shared wrapped up in the singing of the song. Despite getting beat 3–2 by Hibs that day and it not being a 'Battle of the Greens' due to Hibs running out in a purple and black kit, Celtic were a delight to watch. We went home in awe of a goal from a scissor kick by the Maestro. The opener remains one of the most memorable goals I've seen scored from a free-kick by the supremely talented left back Dariusz 'Shuggie' Wdowczky. Across the motorway our reverence for the Polish international and Paul McStay was disturbed by two Hibs boys from our year, Johnny Haddow and Graham Law, flicking us the V-sign while jumping up and down on the Hibs bus gangway in celebration of a much coveted victory.

If getting the Celtic strip was like a First Holy Communion then that first game against Hibs was Confirmation and there was undoubtedly an anointing that took place. Celtic have been there since birth but I've ultimately chosen them . . . or maybe they chose me. I write these closing words in the aftermath of the League Cup final against Rangers in March 2011. Once again after seeing some of the best football being played by the Hoops in years in the second half of the 2010–11 season, hope was dashed at Hampden. Catching the train at Kings Park with the Celtic support I was able to tune into the various conversations after giving up my iPod as a Lent sacrifice. In front of me father and son discussed Neil Lennon's conduct in the previous game against Rangers. The elderly dad suggested losing your temper 'wasn't the Celtic way'. 'I'd like to see you dae it the Celtic way getting death threats, sent bullets and having you and your family under twenty-four-hour protection while trying to manage a football team,' his son responded without missing a beat. As the train rolled on the doors unexpectedly flew open at Mount Florida station. One Rangers fan jumped on and behind him a good hundred made their way towards our carriage while singing and gesturing wildly. The doors suddenly whacked shut almost clipping these big blue bears of men on the nose as we flew off to Central Station. A voice picked up again in front of me: 'Thought that was us. I'm in need of some quiet time and reflection after that' as his face shifted from bemusement to mild amusement. 'What time is it son?' croaked the old man. 'It's just after six da,' said the forty-something Celtic fan dressed completely in black. The old man shifted from side to side, as he rose up in his seat. 'It's too late,' he said unscrewing the top from a flask that had been buried deep within his inside pocket, 'That's us missed the *Songs of Praise* this week boys,' he announced to the carriage, tongue firmly in cheek as he took a fly gulp. And so there it was, even in defeat the nature of what it means to be a Celtic supporter, beautifully illustrated.